Praise for *The Only Way Through Is Out*

"In this courageous memoir, the reader feels keenly both the writer's anguish and her emerging strength as she chooses between a safe, comfortable path and a leap into the unknown. With raw honesty, Mullen is willing to make herself vulnerable on almost every page of this story of poignant loss and sustaining gain, as she stills the external voices in her world and listens to her own truth."—Mary Alice Hostetter, author of *Plain: A Memoir of Mennonite Girlhood*

"An honest and insightful delve into coming out later in life, *The Only Way Through Is Out* is filled with tears, laughter, and, above all, hope." —Lara Lillibridge, author of *Girlish: Growing Up in a Lesbian Home*

"Suzette Mullen reveals how she unearthed her true sexual identity from beneath a mountain of cultural, familial, and internalized heteronormativity. Swimming upstream, she emerges in midlife as the heroine of her own story, and as inspiration for any reader struggling to express their most authentic self."—Robin Rinaldi, author of *The Wild Oats Project: One Woman's Midlife Quest for Passion at Any Cost*

"A memoir of discovering one's sexuality and finding the courage to act, the book has a strong positive message for the many people who come out later in life—the late bloomers, as they are known in the queer community. Such stories are important, and this one is told well and fun to read."—Lori Soderlind, author of *The Change: My Great American, Postindustrial, Midlife Crisis Tour*

"An affecting coming-into-consciousness narrative that burrows into the urgencies of queer awakening and carries its reader through the agonies and ecstasies of living one's truth. Suzette Mullen masterfully conjures the battling inner voices that prolong the reconciliation of her Christian beliefs with the urgings of her body and heart. A touching, visceral story that celebrates giving into queer joy, no matter how long it takes." —Alden Jones, author of *The Wanting Was a Wilderness*

Living Out

Gay and Lesbian Autobiographies

David Bergman, Joan Larkin, and Raphael Kadushin, *Founding Editors*

The Only Way Through Is Out

A Memoir

SUZETTE MULLEN

THE UNIVERSITY OF WISCONSIN PRESS

Publication of this book has been made possible,
in part, through support from the
Anonymous Fund of the College of Letters and Science
at the University of Wisconsin–Madison.

The University of Wisconsin Press
728 State Street, Suite 443
Madison, Wisconsin 53706
uwpress.wisc.edu

Gray's Inn House, 127 Clerkenwell Road
London EC1R 5DB, United Kingdom
eurospanbookstore.com

Printed in the United States of America
This book may be available in a digital edition.

Library of Congress Cataloging-in-Publication Data

Names: Mullen, Suzette, author.
Title: The only way through is out / Suzette Mullen.
Other titles: Living out.
Description: Madison, Wisconsin : The University of Wisconsin Press, 2024. |
Series: Living out: gay and lesbian autobiographies
Identifiers: LCCN 2023015009 | ISBN 9780299345501 (hardcover)
Subjects: LCSH: Mullen, Suzette. | Lesbians—United States—Biography. |
LCGFT: Autobiographies.
Classification: LCC HQ75.4.M85 A3 2024 |
DDC 306.76/63092 [B]—dc23/eng/20230814
LC record available at https://lccn.loc.gov/2023015009

For Andrea and the LaLas.

And for every human who is longing to live out loud

but is afraid of the cost.

Contents

PART THREE

PART FOUR

Author's Note

This is a work of creative nonfiction. The events in this book are my memories and are true to the best of my recollection. Other people may have different memories. Some names and identifying details have been changed to protect the privacy of individuals. To improve narrative flow, the order of some events has been altered and some events have been compressed.

It may be helpful for some readers to know that there are scenes and mentions of suicide ideation.

PART ONE

The Path

The strangest thought flew into my mind one morning after I dropped off my young sons at school:

I have to touch her. I'm going to die if I don't.

A strange—and innocent—thought that years later threatened to blow up my life.

~

"Can you think of one friend you would trade lives with? Even one?" Evan, my ever-so-patient husband, said in our Montauk, New York, living room one fall afternoon in 2012. New empty nesters, we were having yet another "If Only Suzette Could Figure Out Her Life" conversation.

Certainly the path was out there, if only it weren't so elusive. I envied the glow on the faces of my friends who seemed to have found their way. Lisa was writing a novel inspired by her family history. Anne had successfully run for Houston City Council and later joined a Fortune 500 company. Reenie lit up like a Renaissance Madonna when she talked about her work with people in poverty. Damn, I wanted to feel that alive too.

Evan sat cross-legged in an ivory swivel chair, stroking his salt-and-pepper beard, apparently waiting for the answer to what I had assumed was a rhetorical question. I straightened the pillows on the taupe sectional opposite him and silently scrolled through my friends list. Even those glowing friends had crosses to bear and challenges to face. Teenagers who were struggling. Curmudgeonly husbands. No husbands at all. My cross was the shame I carried about a professional life that hadn't lived up to my expectations.

To my left, the Atlantic Ocean roared outside the bay window, unlike the day of my father's funeral, eighteen months ago, when the waves had rolled gently, forming perfect cylinders. That afternoon, a sea breeze had brushed my face as my sister and I walked along the shoreline, talking about the big questions you ask when a parent dies and you're faced with your own mortality. What makes up a meaningful life? What really matters?

This fall afternoon in my living room, I was still pondering those questions as well as Evan's question as I headed into the kitchen. A pot of chicken soup loaded with zucchini from our garden bubbled on the stove. I stirred it and tasted it. Added salt.

Who *would* I trade lives with?

Maybe something was fundamentally wrong with me that I couldn't be more content.

Or maybe I was just a woman with too much time on her hands having an embarrassingly ordinary midlife crisis.

Because I couldn't answer my husband. Nobody had it better than me.

~

Stories have many beginnings. This is one of mine:

"Music time!" my nursery school teacher calls out. Yay! I rush into the room with the big black piano and sit in the front to be near Mother Brian, who is in charge of music. Dee Dee and Judy, my best friends, sit down next to me.

A fun idea pops into my head when Mother Brian starts playing one of my favorites. This song has two sets of words, and when Mother Brian and the other kids sing one set, I'm going to sing the other! My special secret! I can't wait to giggle with Dee Dee and Judy afterward.

No one says anything when I sing in a whisper voice. But I want everyone to know what a smarty-pants I am, so I sing loud like the people on the radio. Mother Brian stops playing the piano and glares at me. "Suzette! That's unacceptable! Go to the back of the room."

My body gets all hot as I walk to the back. Everyone is looking at me. I want to disappear like Casper the Friendly Ghost. I hope Mother Brian won't tell Mommy. I hope Dee Dee and Judy will still be my friends. I never want to feel this way again—ever. From now on I will follow the rules.

~

Reenie, my best friend, often saved me from myself. Like the day in 2007 she called and said, "Suzette, come with me. I could use your help delivering food to a few families—you can be my translator."

It was true my Spanish was better than Reenie's, but this invitation was likely a ruse designed to shake me out of my funk. I had recently left a child advocacy organization and had no idea what to do next professionally. It was as if Reenie could see forty-six-year-old me on the other end of the receiver, lying on the couch, bingeing on *Real Housewives*, and counting the hours until Will and Patrick, my teenage sons, returned home from school.

Say yes, an inner voice nudged me, as I turned off the TV to give Reenie my full attention.

Two days later, Reenie and I carried bags loaded with milk, oranges, and blocks of cheese up the steps of a dilapidated gray shack in Houston's Fifth Ward. She tapped lightly on the screen door. "Hola? Teresa?"

I peered through the torn screen and gasped. Six twin mattresses covered with tattered blankets and stained pillows lined the living room floor. A diapered toddler sat on one of those mattresses, watching cartoons on a large TV propped up on a cardboard box.

A very pregnant Teresa with a wailing baby on her hip came to the door and led us to a small kitchen in the back. Open Styrofoam containers with refried beans and tortillas littered the peeling Formica counter to the left of a sink overflowing with dishes. The air was thick with the smell of rancid grease. I began to breathe out of my mouth instead of my nose, like I always did in public restrooms.

Noise, noise everywhere—the TV blaring from the living room, the baby still crying as she burrowed into Teresa's oversize T-shirt. I helped unpack the groceries in the kitchen and stood stiffly, purse on shoulder, sunglasses in hand, feeling like an understudy waiting in the wings while the real actors were on stage. Why was I here?

Reenie patted baby Gloria's head. Sharon, a social worker from the preschool where Reenie worked with my husband and where I had volunteered on and off for years, thumbed through a stack of papers. Teresa's toddler sprinted in from the living room and tugged on his mother's sweatpants. Teresa didn't flinch; her brown eyes were vacant.

I tried to catch Reenie's eye: *Are we going soon?*

She extended her arms toward Teresa and offered to hold Gloria. "Suzette, why don't you and Sharon talk with Teresa for a few minutes." She pointed her chin toward the kitchen table where Sharon was sitting.

I didn't want to admit to Reenie how out of place I felt, so I took the purse off my shoulder, rummaged around for a notebook and pen, and sat down at the table in a metal folding chair.

"Teresa's landlord is gouging her with rent increases," Sharon said. "She doesn't have a green card. Her husband's in jail, and when he was arrested, her food benefits ID card was in his wallet. She can't get the police to return it to her." She didn't mention the other obvious challenges—that Teresa didn't speak English, that she had five children under six with another on the way.

She didn't mention those mattresses in the next room that kept haunting me. The way they were lined up side by side like coffins at a military funeral, only draped with ratty blankets instead of American flags.

Or the stench from the dirty diaper that was wafting through the kitchen. Diapers. How many packages did Teresa go through every week? How did she pay for them? How did she get to the store with all those kids?

"Teresa needs an immigration lawyer and I don't even know what else." Sharon looked straight at me. "Can you point us to some help? You're a lawyer, right?"

Was I?

I shifted uncomfortably in the folding chair. Seventeen years ago, I had left corporate law and hadn't practiced since. Could I still call myself a lawyer?

Lean into this, the voice inside me said.

"Yes, I'm a lawyer, but I'm not practicing now," I answered Sharon, in the way I had grown accustomed to over the years. "But I can do some research, make a few calls. I'll let you know what I find out."

Reenie bounced Gloria on her hip. "Do you need more time to talk?"

"Yes," I said, surprised by how easily the word flew out of my mouth, since minutes before I had been ready to run out the door.

Ayúdame, I entreated the Spanish language gods for help, as I turned to Teresa.

"¿Dónde está su esposo?" I asked, knowing her husband was in jail but not knowing which one. Maybe it didn't matter, but I needed more information.

I jotted down the name she gave me. What else was urgent?

The lease. Was there a written one? And if there was, had Teresa read it and understood it? "¿Tiene un contracto para la casa?" I asked. Teresa shook her head. I wasn't surprised. Add to the list: see if the Houston Volunteer Lawyers Program accepted this kind of case.

The food benefits card. There had to be a way to get a new one. "¿Llama el departamento para comida?" Teresa peered at me quizzically. "No es importante," I smiled to myself. My language skills would have to improve beyond Spanish 101 if I was going to help families like Teresa's.

I leaned back in the chair, stretched my arms above my head. My watch said it had been only thirty minutes since I sat down at the table, but I felt as if I'd been there much longer. The Greeks had a word for times like these: *kairos*, a moment of significance or occasion, time that can't be measured by a clock. *Kairos*, a moment of "rightness," when doubt dissipates, when saying yes becomes imperative.

Reenie—and my inner voice—had led me here.

It wasn't the first time they steered me in the right direction, and it wouldn't be the last.

~

Ask her for coffee. Ask her, the Voice urged me when Will, my older son, was in kindergarten. At first, I shook it off. It felt totally awkward to ask Reenie, who was Will's teacher, to meet outside of school, even though she and I had developed a friendly working relationship over the past few months. We'd been meeting regularly to work on a behavior plan for Will, who had been diagnosed with ADHD earlier that fall.

The Voice nagged me for days: *Ask her, ask her.* The only way to get it to shut up was to say yes, despite the awkwardness. A few days later, I lurked at Reenie's classroom door like a nervous teenager, waiting for the right moment to pop the question. Finally I choked out the invitation.

"Yes," she said with no hesitation.

The night of our coffee, my hands trembled as I freshened my lip gloss and smoothed my pixie cut. I had added a silver-and-blue stone necklace to my usual pearl studs, Gap khakis, white T-shirt, and jean jacket. Didn't want to look like I was trying too hard.

But every cell in my body was screaming: *Something Big is about to happen*. The pull toward Reenie was so strong, so scary—so *foreign*.

Stop. Being. Ridiculous.

"I don't know why, but I'm really nervous about tonight," I said to Evan, who was perched on the edge of our whirlpool tub, still in his Brooks Brothers suit.

Like I'm going on a first date, I didn't add. With a woman twelve years older than me. With a *grandmother*.

As I stared at myself in the mirror, Evan lifted himself off the edge of the tub and wrapped his arms around me. "You're shaking, sweetie."

"I know, it's nuts." I leaned my head against the spot on his chest that felt made just for me.

Why was I making such a big deal out of it? I was just having coffee with my son's kindergarten teacher.

Reenie and I sipped our coffees in the corner of the cafe. "I often meet people here," she said.

This isn't weird. She does this all the time. My legs shaking under the table, I took another sip of coffee, wondering what to say to her.

"How's the Beanie Baby hunt going?" she asked. Will had chosen these wildly popular, hard-to-find, small stuffed animals for his weekly in-school good behavior reward. Every time he raised his hand, kept his hands and feet to himself, or used an "inside voice," he earned a marble to put in a jar in his kindergarten classroom.

"I'm getting tired of driving all over town trying to score them," I said.

We both laughed. It was easier to laugh than share what I really thought about Beanie Babies. That after all the hours I spent hunting for them, Will would chew on them and toss them in a corner. That hearing a tip from another mother about the latest Beanie Baby source was often the highlight of my day. That I couldn't believe my life had come to this, and I didn't see any way to change direction. But I didn't say any of that to Reenie.

"I can't thank you enough for all you've done for Will," I said instead.

Say more, say more, the Voice whispered.

Across the table from Reenie, I was under a spell—a wonderful, magical spell where time was suspended. This woman was an enigma, but somehow, I felt I could tell her anything. "I don't know why, but I was really scared to ask you to coffee," I said after a few moments of silence. "But it felt like something I had to do."

She smiled, reached across the table, and took my hand. "A number of women have told me they feel drawn to talk with me."

Thank god I'm not the only one who feels this way.

"Let's make sure we do this again," Reenie said as we got up to leave.

"Yes," I said breathlessly. "Let's."

~

Montauk, more than Houston or any other place I'd lived, was home. I first visited this beach town as a child in the late 1960s when it was a haven for middle-class families like mine, not the Hamptons playground for the rich and famous it later became. My family camped at the state park in a pop-up tent trailer, and later my parents—both public school teachers—built a modest house in the hamlet, where they would eventually retire.

Evan and I lived three blocks from my parents' in a house we'd originally bought as a vacation home. We moved there full time from Houston in 2012 after our younger son graduated from high school.

Inside that beautiful home, my midlife malaise would finally lift.

And inside that same beautiful home, a bombshell would explode that my husband and I could never have predicted.

The Unspeakable

In May 2012, Evan squeezed my hand as our New York–bound plane lifted off from the Houston runway. "And *we're* off on our adventure!"

I smiled and returned the squeeze, wondering if he could sense the stress beneath the smile. I wished I, too, could view our empty-nest chapter as an adventure, but at fifty-one, it felt more like life or death, a last chance to figure out my path. Maybe I was being overly dramatic, but the thought of going to my grave without doing the work I was put on this earth to do or living the life I was meant to live felt unbearable.

Nine months into our move to Montauk, I still didn't have clarity about how I wanted to spend my next chapter. Evan wasn't making much progress either, but that didn't seem to bother him one bit. "Maybe the reason I haven't figured out my next steps yet is because it's your turn to go first," he said to me one afternoon.

My turn. I loved him so much in that moment, for his generosity, for seeing what I couldn't see myself. I had been waiting for him to put *his* stake in the ground, and then I would fit *my* life around *his* choices. Which I was starting to realize had been my MO for most of our marriage. It felt safer to let Evan make the first move. If things didn't work out, it wouldn't be my fault. I hated making mistakes.

~

Thanksgiving 1993, the first time I'd ever roasted a turkey or hosted the holiday. Evan's siblings and their families would be joining us, plus his mom.

Evan's older sister marveled (laughed?) at the ten-page, single-spaced, timed-to-the-minute to-do list I had written up to guide me through the day.

With a two-year-old and another baby on the way, I couldn't leave anything to chance. But who was I kidding? This wasn't just about being an exhausted young mother—I'd been making lists my entire life. If you followed your plan, everything would work out.

~

Ten months after we moved to Montauk, the Voice resurfaced when I was journaling: *You're a writer*, it whispered. *Stop fighting it.*

I almost burst out laughing. Of course. Loose-leaf binders overflowing with book ideas and outlines. Armloads of journals moved from house to house. A box full of letters I'd written and received in high school when I was an exchange student in England, including one where my father wrote: *Everyone is asking: Is she going to be a writer? Have you considered this?*

It was well past time to claim my call as a writer—and it did feel like a calling, not another detour or false start. Exactly the path I was intended to walk. Exactly the person I was intended to be.

I decided to write a memoir about how I had struggled to find my professional path and how I had finally found my way.

My spirits lifted. My days felt purposeful.

~

Once Reenie and I no longer lived in the same city, we had a standing call each week, usually a video one.

"How's your writing going?" she would ask nearly every time.

"Great," I would say. Which was the truth until it wasn't.

~

One day in March of 2015, I opened my laptop to work on my memoir but what I wrote instead was this:

I have to touch her. The thought wouldn't leave my mind all day.

A chill went through me as I lifted my fingers off the keyboard. I hadn't thought about that moment for almost two decades and WTF? It didn't have anything to do with the story I wanted to write.

Seventeen years ago, a perplexing thought had flashed through my mind after I dropped Will off at his kindergarten classroom: I had to touch Reenie. I was going to die if I didn't.

I tried to forget it as I went through my day, but when Reenie opened the classroom door a few hours later at pickup time, every inch of my body was vibrating. I had to touch her. There was no other choice.

"Hi there," I said softly as I reached for her through the crowd of moms and kindergartners.

When my fingertips grazed her forearm, an electric charge went through my entire body.

Bam!

I touched my arm, felt heat radiating off it.

What was this?

My body felt warm and tingly for hours. What the hell was THIS?

I closed my laptop and looked at the ocean outside my window. The sea was as calm as a lake, unlike the waves of panic crashing over me. The words I'd written felt like a stick of dynamite—words that no one else should ever get close to.

But wasn't that exactly what writers were supposed to do? Write the Real. The Hard. The Dangerous. Once I'd heard an author say he felt called to write "the Unspeakable," the stuff everyone thinks about but would never say out loud. "Chances are," he said, "if I've thought about it, someone else has too."

That day at the author talk, I hadn't needed to ask myself whether I had an unspeakable. Damn right I had one. My hand shook as I wrote *RS* in faint print in the upper lefthand corner of my notebook.

RS. Reenie's initials.

~

Our move to Montauk weeks away, I was in major decluttering mode when I pulled out a stack of journals that had been jammed inside the top drawer of the massive mahogany file cabinet in our living room.

A faded purple spiral notebook was marked #1: January–March 1998, the winter Will was in kindergarten, the year Reenie was his teacher. Evan was rapidly climbing the ladder at his money management firm, and I was a stay-at-home mom of two young boys. I smiled as I flipped through the first few pages, but soon all I saw was Reenie this and Reenie that—Reenie all over the pages. I sounded like a lovesick puppy. The next few journals were more of the same. If those entries had been written by anyone else, I might have doubled over in laughter at the over-the-top language or felt compassion for the poor writer. But this wasn't funny. It was pathetic. Humiliating.

No one could ever see these cringeworthy pages. What if I got hit by a bus and Evan or the boys came across them while sorting through my belongings?

That was not going to happen. I sat on the floor and methodically went through every notebook. Tore out every offending page. Grabbed a large trash bag from the garage and shredded the pages by hand. Dumped the kitchen garbage on top of the shredded paper. Put the bag out by the curb for the next day's trash pickup.

Thank goodness those pages—and feelings—were gone.

~

My phone buzzed as I sat with the unspeakable words I'd just typed. It was my sister.

"What are you doing?" Beth said, her usual greeting.

"Working on my memoir." Part of me wanted to talk to her about what I'd written. We were close, each other's only sibling, and we spoke most days. But once the words were out of my mouth, I couldn't take them back. I trusted my younger sister with my heart and I didn't. "I've gotten into some pretty vulnerable stuff," I said, at once wanting to say more and not.

"Do you want to talk about it?"

"Guess," I said. Maybe talking about it would reduce the panic rising inside me. I could simply tell her I'd been writing about a crush I'd had on Reenie a long time ago. A silly crush that Beth and I could chuckle about together.

"Is it that lezzie stuff with Reenie?" she said.

Oh shit. She knew. Oh shit. Who else knew? I laughed awkwardly. "No comment."

"I always wondered what was going on with you and her. You were always saying 'Reenie this' and 'Reenie that.' I just thought it was all very weird and strange."

Weird and strange. Did everyone think that about my relationship with Reenie?

I didn't want to talk about this anymore. "How are Rob and Claire?" I said. My nephew and niece—much safer topics of conversation.

~

You have to tell Lila about Reenie, the Voice whispered, when I woke up on the second day of a weeklong spiritual retreat in October 1999. That afternoon I had a meeting scheduled with Lila, one of the retreat leaders.

I can't do that, I shushed the Voice. In the two years I'd known Reenie, I hadn't told a single soul how consumed I was with her.

After lunch, Lila and I sat on the lawn overlooking a lake. An insistent beat pounded inside me:

I have to do this.

I can't do this.

I'm going to die.

To my right, a raft of ducks glided on the lake. Serene to the naked eye, under the surface they were likely paddling furiously. Could Lila tell how furiously I was paddling too?

I waited for a sign. A cardinal. A sudden wind. I glanced at my watch. What was the worst thing that could happen? After this week, I never had to see this Lila person again.

I took a deep breath. "I have a friend who's become too important to me," I said. "All I do is think about her. All I want is to be with her." I lowered my eyes to the ground. "It's killing me. I've tried to get rid of these thoughts, but I can't."

A few seconds passed. "How would you feel about being homosexual?" Lila finally said softly.

I paddled faster and faster. Was that what this sounded like? No! No! No! I wasn't *homosexual*!

My eyes returned to the ducks. They were easier to look at than this person who thought I might be *homosexual*. I wasn't! I had been intimate with only four people in my entire life, all men.

"I don't think that's it," I said, my voice quavering. "But I'm terrified. I've never felt this way before."

Lila put her arm around me. "You seem to be really fighting your feelings. Would you consider seeing someone professionally?"

The idea hadn't occurred to me. I'd never been in therapy. But yes. I'd do anything. Anything to fix THIS. Heal THIS. Get rid of THIS.

We sat side by side in silence, with me thinking about how I could convince Lila I wasn't homosexual. "Reenie's touch is the most important thing to me," I said. "I have an overwhelming need to be held by her. That's the image I replay over and over in my head."

"That sounds like mother love," Lila said.

Mother love? The idea filled me with relief. It was still weird and confusing, but not as scary as being homosexual.

That evening while watching a movie with the rest of the group, I felt a pull toward Lila, which surprised me. I imagined hugging her and holding her hand, even lightly touching her breasts.

What is THIS*?* I wrote in my journal that night. *I want to be with Lila. I feel it in my loins.*

~

I owed ten pages to Kerry, the book coach I had hired to help me with my memoir, but allowing her—or anyone—to read my unspeakable felt impossible. Maybe I'd delete the scene, send her nine pages instead of ten.

"What do I do?" I whispered to myself.

You know what to do, the Voice answered.

I did know.

I had finally found the work I was meant to do.

I was a writer, and real writers didn't play it safe.

They wrote the whole big messy story, not a sanitized version of the truth.

Trembling, I hit Send and the pages flew into cyberspace.

But as soon as my finger lifted off the keyboard, I wanted to scream, *Come back!*

What had I done?

Evan was puttering two floors down in his basement study, blissfully unaware of what I'd sent out into the world. Will was crunching numbers on Wall Street and Patrick was studying economics in college, both likely thinking this was an ordinary day. And Reenie? I was probably the furthest thing from her mind as she put out fires at the preschool.

I closed my laptop and hugged myself, trying to stop shaking.

But I couldn't ignore what my body was telling me.

Something Big had been unleashed.

And one thing I was about to learn: the body doesn't lie.

~

Two days later, an email from Kerry arrived.

I wiped my palms on my jeans and inhaled as I scanned her feedback. Minutes later, I leaned back in my chair and exhaled. Positive comment after positive comment. Kerry thought these were the best and most authentic pages I'd shared with her. Damn, I'd done it! Real writers took risks—and this risk had paid off.

Then I read these eight words: *This sounds exactly like someone falling in love.*

A comment about the "I had to touch her" scene.

WTF? Someone falling *in* love? Not someone who just loves another person?

I read the comment again.

In love with Reenie? In all the years I'd known her, I'd never used those words to describe how I felt about her. I loved her, of course, but that was a different kind of love. I knew what it felt like to be *in* love. I'd been *in* love twice—with Alan, my first boyfriend, and with Evan.

When you were *in* love, you thought about the person all the time. You longed for their touch. Your body felt warm and tingly when you did touch them.

Fuck.

I felt sick to my stomach and incredible clarity all at once. This couldn't be happening. Evan and I had barely started our life as empty nesters. I had just found my professional calling. We were—I was—finally settled. Finally where I wanted to be after all those years of searching and wandering.

But the truth was staring me in the face: Kerry was right. Seventeen years ago I had fallen in love with Reenie, which was terrifying to admit.

But what my body was telling me in this moment was even more terrifying.

I was still in love with her.

The Man I Love

Row after row of red velvet seats rocked with volunteers, homeowners, church members, Black, White, Latinx, men, women, young, and old as a praise band played. All of Houston, it seemed, had come together to celebrate the completion of the Habitat for Humanity 1998 Jimmy Carter Work Project.

"Where is she?" I asked Evan as I scoured the massive First Baptist sanctuary for Reenie. She had promised to meet us here. "Where is she?"

"You're here for me, remember." The edge in his voice surprised me.

My heart leaped when I spotted her. "Congratulations," I said when she made her way into our row. I buried my face in her curls. Felt the heat radiating off her arms browned from the week in the sun. Evan greeted her too and moved back to his seat.

Reenie to my left, Evan to my right—my heart so full I felt it might burst. I would have died if anyone had known what was going on inside me. The hours I spent daydreaming about her. The number of times I walked by her classroom, hoping to catch a glimpse of her. That the only place I wanted to be was in her arms, in Reenie-land.

THIS was deeply scary territory. THIS was totally out of control. Filled up when I was with her and emptied as soon as she left.

The audience stood as a choir took the stage and began to sing "Joy to the World." Reenie swayed her arms in the air like a gull soaring over the ocean. Evan had a similar faraway look in his eyes as he clapped and sang along. I was on my feet too, watching an enchanted world from the other side of a window, seeing but unable to touch.

I wished I could be like Evan and Reenie. I wished I could clap and dance and wave my arms in the air and not care what anyone thought. I wished I could beam with joy like the singers on the stage. I wished I could let go and fly. But I couldn't—and I didn't understand why.

Reenie's arm brushed against mine as we sat down after the choir exited the stage. I couldn't hold in my feelings any longer. I squeezed her hand. She squeezed back.

I turned to her. "I love you," I mouthed.

"I love you too," she mouthed back.

Did Evan notice I was holding her hand? Just in case, I took his hand too. Gave it a squeeze. Whispered, "I love you."

Which was true. I loved them both in different ways. Evan was my husband, and Reenie was my what? I had no language for what she was for me.

After the celebration ended, the three of us walked to the parking lot. When we reached Reenie's car, I hugged her goodbye, not wanting to let go. Since school was out for the summer, the spontaneous visits to her classroom door at drop-off and pickup wouldn't be happening. Soon I'd be vacationing in Montauk with Evan and the boys. Without her.

As Evan navigated Houston's busy freeways, my thoughts shifted to dinner and the plans the boys and I had the following week.

"You really hurt me tonight," Evan said when traffic came to a standstill.

"What?" I had no idea what he was talking about.

"When you took Reenie's hand before you took mine. You were supposed to be there to celebrate *my* week. *I'm* your husband, not her, Suzette. Be present for *me*." The soft green specks in his hazel eyes had disappeared, swallowed up by a hard yellow light warning me: *caution, caution, caution.*

"I'm sorry," I said, scrambling to think how to diffuse the situation. "I took your hand too," but as soon as the words left my mouth, Evan's face tensed more. I was ready for him to say, "Stop acting like a lawyer," which was his usual response when I told him why he shouldn't be feeling the way he felt. My typical MO with Evan was offense first and retreat if he got really angry. But this time he didn't say anything, which frightened me more.

A few minutes later, he pulled our minivan into our garage and turned off the ignition. As I reached for the door handle, he put his hand on my left thigh.

"Suzette, I need to say something."

I stared out the car window, wondering how long this scolding would take.

"Look at me," he said.

When I turned to face him, his eyes were ablaze.

"I'm starting to feel like there's a third person in our marriage."

I shook my head, but a chill went through me. Why had he said that?

Before this day, he hadn't said anything negative about my friendship with Reenie—at least nothing I can remember now. I'd thought I'd kept these scary and out-of-control feelings a secret from him—and from her.

He felt like there was a third person in our marriage? I wanted to know why—and I didn't have the courage to ask.

Evan's comment lingered in the air as we walked into the house. I paid the babysitter. Opened the fridge to contemplate dinner. I had responsibilities, things to do. This was my real life. Reenie was the life I lived only in my head.

~

Christmas week 1990, I tucked a home pregnancy test in my suitcase, hoping I'd have a chance to use it while Evan and I were visiting my parents. I should have bought stock in EPT, this company that held out hope of life-changing news for $12.95 a shot. In the early months when I thought I'd get pregnant easily, I bought twin packs and gave myself permission to test early, knowing there would be a backup in case I jumped the gun, which I often did. Month after month, the sticks produced the same disappointing empty space in the result window.

We joined an infertility support group where we heard about couples who had tried to get pregnant for years without success and other couples whose marriages hadn't survived the stress. If anything, infertility had brought Evan and me closer. He held me each time I cried when my period came or when an invitation to yet another friend's baby shower arrived in the mail. He didn't act squeamish when he injected me with Lupron, part of the regimen to shrink the endometriosis that was the likely cause of our infertility. He said everything would be okay, somehow, some way. His steadiness grounded me. Helped me from spiraling into despair.

I wanted to be pregnant. Buy maternity clothes. Have a baby shower held in my honor. Rock my baby in my arms. Be a mother, like all my other friends.

On December 26, I woke up before sunrise in my childhood bedroom. A double bed had replaced the twin bed that used to be there, but not much else had changed. The light blue shag carpet, the matching white-and-blue desk and bureau purchased at a garage sale, the small closet, once plastered with Partridge Family and Farrah Fawcett posters, remained.

How strange to be back in the bedroom where I had holed up writing English papers and watching baseball on my small black-and-white TV instead of partying with friends. The bedroom I retreated to after my first boyfriend dumped me. The bedroom where I would sit at the window watching the neighborhood kids play dodgeball in the street, at once wanting to be part of the group and knowing I wasn't.

I eyed the EPT box I'd left on the bureau the night before. This was the day I had circled on my calendar to take a pregnancy test if my period hadn't started. All week I had held my breath every time I went to the bathroom, praying I wouldn't see menstrual blood. Praying the outcome would be different this time with my endometriosis surgically removed and the boost provided by Clomid, a medication that stimulated ovulation.

I couldn't wait any longer. Besides, I had to pee, which was convenient since my urine contained the answer. I gave Evan's hand a squeeze, grabbed the EPT box, and headed to the bathroom.

A couple of minutes later, I returned with the stick. "Can you set your watch?"

Evan nodded. "Five minutes, right?"

I climbed into bed and let Evan spoon me. The warmth of his body helped me believe I'd be able to handle the result no matter what.

After the longest five minutes ever, Evan's alarm went off. "I can't look," I said. "You do it."

Please. Please. Please.

"Come over here," he said.

There it was. A no-doubt-about-it pink line.

~

Eighteen years into our marriage, the argument was likely about sex or rather about the lack of sex Evan and I were having, or why I didn't care enough about him to initiate sex or why I didn't care enough about him to care about the things that mattered to him, sex being one of those things. The other possibility: how he felt I never paid attention to him, that he wasn't even a top-ten priority.

"I can't take this anymore," he said, disappearing into the walk-in closet in our bedroom. Minutes later, he emerged, a suitcase in hand. He'd threatened to leave before, but I'd always been able to talk him down. I'd promise just about anything in those moments. Agree to couples counseling, although we never went. Vow to initiate sex occasionally, which I would do until I forgot again.

But he'd never packed a suitcase before.

My dad had packed a suitcase and more two or three times, but always came back. One summer he set up our tent trailer at Hither Hills State Park in Montauk and made sure Mom knew how to use the hibachi and propane lantern before he left. He'd return at the end of the week to pack us up.

Late one morning, Dad appeared, days before he was supposed to. As soon as Beth and I saw him walking down the sandy path with a big smile on his face, we ran to him. "Daddy!" we screamed. He was back. Until he left again.

But Evan wouldn't leave. I called his bluff. "Where are you going?"

"Don't know yet. A hotel somewhere. I'll call when I get there." His voice was flat. Resigned. No longer angry.

"What are you going to tell the boys?" He'd never go through with it. He'd never leave them. They were still young: Will thirteen, Patrick ten.

"Boys," he called into the hallway.

Shit. He was doing this. He was doing this.

The boys lay between us on our queen-size bed. Evan told them we'd been having problems and that he was going away for a few days. Patrick sobbed and Will stomped off to his room.

My family was falling apart. This couldn't be happening.

I looked at Evan. "Don't do this."

He rubbed Patrick's back to calm him down. Minutes later, he put the suitcase back in the closet.

He didn't leave.

He would never leave.

~

The night after I received Kerry's comments, I climbed into bed next to the man I loved and the man who loved me.

"Cuddle?" he said, his usual bedtime request.

"Sure." I felt like a jerk as I lay my head on his chest and wrapped my left arm around him. I'd never lied to my husband about anything big, except, of course, these unspeakable feelings, which I'd been lying about to myself and him—and Reenie—for seventeen years.

You have to tell him, that goddamn inner voice whispered.

But really, what was the point of telling him, and what was there even to tell? It wasn't as if I'd had an affair. And it wasn't as if I was going to run to Reenie and tell her I loved her "that way." Kerry was the only one who had read those unspeakable pages, and those eight words she had written that had upended my world? Maybe she'd dashed them off without thinking, or maybe it had all seemed so obvious that she assumed it must have been obvious to me too.

But as much as I wished it were otherwise, the Voice was right. Evan was my husband and I owed him the truth, especially since I was starting to understand it myself. Besides, I knew this secret would eat me up if I kept it from him. Maybe it would be enough to take a baby step: read him those Reenie pages and massage the truth a little. Maybe he would think it was no big deal that a long time ago I had fallen for my best friend. Maybe a little confession would allow me to put this behind us so we could carry on with our very nice life.

~

The kitchen table was littered with circulars from the Sunday papers, empty coffee mugs, and a white paper bag from the Hot Bagel Shop, the best bagels in Houston in 1990. I skimmed through the *New York Times*, throwing section after section on the floor. Evan's left arm dangled by his side as he penned in answers to the crossword puzzle with his right. He looked as if he didn't have a care in the world.

I wished I could feel that way too, even for an hour, even for a minute. Maybe my heightened stress was a side effect from the drugs I was taking in anticipation of my endometriosis surgery. I'd made a bargain with myself to stick it out at the law firm until I had a baby, but after what happened over Memorial Day weekend with a partner at the firm, I'd revised the bargain to "you can quit when you get pregnant."

Marion, a newly minted partner, had sentenced me to the library to research an arcane legal question over the holiday weekend. After two days that turned up nothing relevant, I handed her the best case I could find. She didn't look up or say a word as she skimmed through the pages. "This isn't what I was looking for," she finally said, barely raising her eyes from the page to meet mine.

"It isn't what I was looking for either, Marion. But I've looked everywhere. There's nothing more helpful." I crossed my arms, trying to hold myself together.

But then she literally threw the case at me, the pages floating in the air like giant snowflakes. "Go back to the library and see if you can find anything else."

My reaction wasn't my finest moment, although it would become legendary among my fellow overworked and underappreciated junior associates. "Why are you such a fucking bitch?" I screamed and ran out of her office.

Two months until surgery. Four months after that to start trying to conceive. At least six more months at the law firm. I didn't think I could do it another day.

I refilled my coffee cup. "Maybe I should quit now," I said to Evan.

He looked up from his crossword. "What are you talking about?"

I brought him up to speed on the lengthy conversation I'd been having with myself.

"You can quit whenever you want," Evan said slowly. "You know I'm making enough that we don't need your salary. But it's your decision. I'm not going to tell you what to do."

You can quit whenever you want. A get-out-of-jail-free card. A gift from the man I loved.

~

I lingered in front of the open refrigerator, as I often did in those early years of stay-at-home motherhood, searching for inspiration.

What the hell was I going to throw together for dinner?

As I stared into the refrigerator, the theme song from *Barney & Friends* drifted in from the family room where three-year-old Will was bopping along with TV's favorite purple dinosaur. Two-month-old Patrick was asleep in his bouncy seat atop our kitchen's butcher-block island. To my left, Evan had loosened his tie and was parked on a barstool with a nearly completed crossword in his hands.

I closed the refrigerator, let out a sigh, and plopped myself down on the barstool next to Evan. "I don't know what to make for dinner."

He inked in another answer, put down the paper, and turned to face me. "Suzette, I still don't understand why you're so resistant to planning menus." Ever since I left the law firm, Evan had been urging me to plan menus, like his mother had when he was growing up. She had a rotation: spaghetti with meat sauce and green beans, pork chops with black-eyed peas, chicken tetrazzini, and roast beef with rice and gravy. It made life easier, he said.

He spoke to me in the same measured tone he used when he was trying to reason with Will, who had a hard time keeping his hands to himself. "Don't talk to me like I'm your child," I would have barked back if I could have summoned the energy. But that night, I couldn't. Besides, it didn't take my Harvard Law degree to know I had a losing case. Planning menus made sense. My refusal to do so was perplexing since I loved to plan practically everything else in my life. But every time Evan asked me to plan menus, I bristled. It made me feel like the 1950s housewife his mom had been, which was absolutely not the vibe I was going for.

~

The morning after Kerry's comments landed in my inbox, I brought Evan his coffee and the newspaper, as I did every morning. The secret, which was no longer a secret to me, burned inside me. If it had been about anything else, I would have run to Reenie and unburdened myself. But obviously, that was not an option. I didn't think I'd ever be able to tell her how I felt.

I walked over to my desk and picked up the pages that contained the unspeakable. Evan was lying supine on the couch, tackling the crossword. There was never going to be an easy way to tell him what was going on inside me, but sharing those pages with him felt like my best option. "I want to read you something," I said, trying to keep my hands and voice from shaking. "It's about Reenie."

"Okay." He dropped the newspaper to the floor. He looked so relaxed, so completely unaware of the bombshell I was about to throw into our marriage. He didn't deserve this, but I couldn't keep lying. I just couldn't.

Shit. I swallowed and began reading, glancing occasionally at him. His face was expressionless.

"When my fingertips grazed her forearm," I continued, "an electric charge went through my entire body."

I stopped there, forcing myself to meet his eyes.

"Okay," Evan said, then he was silent, as if waiting for me to . . . what?

"I didn't realize it then," I stammered, "but I'm coming to understand that I was in love with her."

Past tense only. That was as truthful as I could get.

He sat up, his face red. "You betrayed me. You betrayed our marriage."

No, it wasn't like that, I wanted to say. But I stood silently, arms crossed, eyes to the side. There was nothing I could say to make this better.

"I knew," he said, his voice softening.

He knew?

"Remember the Habitat celebration?"

Of course I remembered, but I was astonished he'd been holding that moment inside him all this time. We'd never spoken about it since that day, seventeen years ago, and here I was reopening that wound, an asshole move if there ever was one. I put the pages on the coffee table and sat next to him on the couch. Kissed his forehead. "Sorry, my love. I didn't understand what was going on."

"I know," he said, more gently.

I leaned into his body. *This* was safe and solid. *This* was where I belonged. Sure, we'd had rough patches, but what marriage didn't?

There was so much to look forward to in this empty-nest chapter. Travel. Family weddings. Grandchildren.

Maybe we could forget those pages.

Listen and Lean In

When I struggled with a big question, Reenie would say, "Just listen for the next thing and lean in—it's as simple as that."

Listening and leaning in seemed simple for Reenie. For her, it translated to talking with God, and some days it seemed as if she had God on speed dial. She'd say, "God told me this," with a certainty that unnerved me. At least some of the time, the voice inside Reenie's head seemed to be God's voice. Was that true for everyone? Was that true for me?

If only I could ask Reenie what to do about the truth bomb I'd thrown into my marriage. If she knew what was going on inside my beautiful house and my beautiful life, would she still advise me to "listen and lean in"?

Or would she never speak to me again?

~

To discern means to discriminate—to make a distinction between two morally good options, choosing the one that aligns more closely with God's call for your life.

The instructor's lecture rolled through my mind as I lay in the sun outside the retreat center in the fall of 1999. Our assignment: choose an issue for discernment and frame it as a yes-or-no question. "Don't overthink it," the instructor said. "It's just an exercise."

Don't overthink it. Ha! Overthinking was what mothers like me did. You had to think ahead to get things done and prevent meltdowns. Evan would have never remembered how the boys liked their bagels in the morning (Patrick, plain or poppy, toasted with cream cheese; Will, plain, whole, DO NOT CUT IN HALF!), so I'd written those instructions on the lengthy list I'd prepared before leaving for this retreat.

Okay, I'd try not to overthink it.

I closed my eyes as I attempted to come up with an issue to discern. The warmth of the sun enveloped me, just like Reenie did when we hugged. Shit, I couldn't escape her. I was supposed to be learning about how to choose between morally good options, and what I was doing was the opposite of morally good: daydreaming about someone who was not my husband. There was no yes-or-no question here, nothing to overthink. THIS had to stop. It simply had to.

~

After I met Reenie, my inner voice woke up.

Two months into Will's kindergarten year, I left a psychologist's office with a twenty-page report about Will in my hand, feeling as if I was swirling under the sea—not knowing which way was up or where to go. Later, Will's ADHD diagnosis would seem self-evident and not earth-shattering. But in 1997, ADHD was largely in the shadows. It felt scary—and shameful.

Ritalin. Therapy. Behavior plans.

I didn't know anyone whose kid had ADHD. There was no one to talk to. Evan had gone back to his office after the appointment. I had no way to reach my mom or sister—no cell phone yet, and even if I'd had one, I didn't know if they'd understand how afraid I felt. About Will's future. About my ability to parent him. About everything.

With his wispy brown hair, chubby cheeks, and dancing hazel eyes, Will was the miracle baby I'd been waiting for during those years of infertility. He was a miracle—and a challenge. By age three, he was reading, composing songs on our piano, and scribbling roman numeral equations with his crayons. But he also regularly left me wishing I could dig a hole and bury myself when he had a public meltdown. "Will, not William," he screamed at an end-of-season soccer party, when he smashed his "incorrectly" engraved trophy on the ground. I wanted to die when the team mom hurried over to help me pick up the shards of gold-and-green metal.

A couple of weeks into his kindergarten year, Reenie had called Evan and me in for a conference without telling us why. As soon as I saw the sober-looking faces crowded around the child-sized table, I knew it wasn't good news. This wasn't a parent-teacher conference—it was an ambush.

Evan squeezed my right hand. I squeezed back and, with my left, tried to stop my legs from shaking. Reenie fingered the gold cross around her neck. They were "concerned" about Will's behavior. They recommended that we have him "evaluated."

Silence descended upon the classroom. It was as if everyone other than Evan and me knew exactly what was going on with Will but wouldn't clue us in.

"What do you think they suspect?" I said to Evan, attempting to steady my voice as we walked to the parking lot.

"I have no idea." Evan's face looked paler than normal. He usually said everything would be okay, and the fact that he didn't sent a chill through me.

The ADHD diagnosis came six weeks later.

I glanced again at the envelope containing the psychologist's report and turned the key in the ignition. Drove to Will's school, even though it was an hour before pickup time. I didn't know where else to go. "I don't know what to do. I don't know what to do," I whispered.

Go into the school, the Voice said in a tone so forceful that it propelled me out of the driver's seat. Seconds later, it carried me onto an empty hallway where shiny black-and-white linoleum tiles stretched before me. I stepped lightly on them, as if afraid I'd be caught in the school with no explanation, an hour before dismissal. The door to the kindergarten classroom, like all the others, was shut. Was Will having a good day? How would I break the news to him? To Reenie?

At the end of the hall, I took a sip at a water fountain and another, even though I wasn't thirsty. I was stalling, waiting for something to happen.

I have to talk to someone. Have to or I'm going to explode.

But the hallway remained empty. I turned the handle on the fountain again, watched the water bubble up, bent over to take another sip.

A teacher rounded the corner. Asked how I was doing. In a shaky voice, I told her about Will's diagnosis. She hugged me and told me her sons, who were students at this same school, had ADHD too. "Everything will be okay," she said. Her boys were doing well. It was hard at first, finding the right medication, coming up with effective behavior plans. "But don't worry. The school will work with you."

I didn't know whether to cry or laugh. What were the odds that the only other person in the hallway at that moment was the exact person I needed to lift me out of the darkness, to give me hope?

"That's a God thing," Reenie said, when I told her about the encounter at the water fountain.

I nodded although I'd never used language like that and had never expected to.

Later I would label that moment at the water fountain the start of my spiritual journey—or my "faith journey," as I would refer to it in those years. The Voice knew something my logical self didn't. Something mystical was operating in the world—call it God, the universe, a higher power, an inner knowing. Whatever its name, it had my back.

"I'm done with church," I'd declared to my parents after my First Communion, and my burned-out Catholic parents had been more than happy to oblige. But living in Houston, Texas, I was firmly planted in the Bible Belt; my boys attended a church-affiliated school; and Evan had grown up in a churchgoing family and wanted to continue that tradition. Christianity was my context, and it's what I used to make sense of the mysteries behind the Voice.

And besides, that was Reenie's context too.

~

In 2004, six years into our friendship, Reenie and I had one of those magical "listen and lean in" moments when everything in the universe feels aligned.

After the executive director of the inner-city preschool where Reenie now worked had unexpectedly resigned, the thought that Evan would be the perfect person for the job had swirled around my head. But I hadn't said anything to anyone. That idea could be the best thing ever for the preschool and for Reenie and for me—or it could be a total disaster.

"I'm going to miss you so much," I had said when Reenie shared the news that she was leaving Will and Patrick's school to become the program director of this inner-city preschool. "I'm happy for you but sad for me." Gone would be the daily conversations and hugs at her classroom door.

"Come with me," she had said. "Come and get your hands dirty."

I had said yes, even though I knew nothing about preschoolers except my own and had never worked with people in poverty. Yes meant more time with her.

Reenie found endless tasks for me at the preschool: shadowing challenging students, helping her pick lice off a child's scalp ("Now *this* is getting our hands dirty," we laughed), and various administrative projects. Later, I became a board member.

Leave me alone, I told the Voice or whoever or whatever had planted the thought in my head about Evan applying for the executive director position. Our lives were settled. Evan had recently left his money management career to focus on social justice and was serving as the interim executive director of Houston Habitat for Humanity. I had found my place at the preschool as a board member and volunteer. How would it work if my husband became my best friend's boss?

But the Voice kept nagging me, much as it had when it urged me to ask Reenie to meet for coffee.

This time, Reenie and I were sipping sauvignon blanc instead of coffee. "I've been thinking about something for a while," I said slowly, setting my wine glass on the table.

She turned to me, giving me her full attention like she always did.

"I'm terrified that once I say it to you, I won't be able to take it back."

She nodded in that encouraging way I loved.

"I've been thinking that Evan would be the perfect person for the ED position. But I'm scared about what that would mean for all of us."

I'm scared about what that would mean for you and me.

Her eyes filled up. "I told God I wasn't going to say anything to you about this unless I was given an opening," she said, taking my hand. "God told me the same thing about Evan two weeks ago."

Together, we called Evan and told him our idea. He said he'd think about it. A month later, he became Reenie's boss.

They would work together for the next eight years. Until Evan gave notice and we moved to Montauk.

~

It wasn't as if the Voice had never spoken to me before I met Reenie; it was more that I tended to ignore it.

One morning in the fall of 1987, when I was twenty-six, I fluffed up the floppy polka-dotted bow tie around my neck before my first official day of work at the law firm. *Not this, not this*, the Voice had whispered.

I shook it off. It was too late to change course. I'd had three years of law school to choose a different path than the lockstep corporate-law one the vast majority of my classmates were on, but for some reason, I'd chosen the very path that wasn't right for me. A lack of imagination? Student loans to pay off? No wise mentor to encourage me to listen and lean in? A lifelong aversion to taking risks? Likely, all of the above and more. The safe—and ultimately unsatisfying—choices we make don't happen in a vacuum.

Two years later, when that dissatisfied partner threw my research across her desk and into my face, I had confirmation. The Voice had been right.

I should have listened to it.

~

The week after Reenie and I met for coffee the first time, I stepped onto my neighborhood tennis court like I had most weekday mornings for the past three years. Practice for the Houston Ladies Tennis Association doubles league.

The women in this tennis league were serious and so was I. What had started out as a distraction from diapers, grocery shopping, and playdates had turned into a commitment that sometimes felt more like a full-time job.

Some days when I pulled on my tennis skirt, I felt a pit in my stomach. Not that there was anything inherently wrong with playing tennis, but the person staring back at me in the mirror in tennis whites was someone I swore I would never become.

"I hate to see you give this up already," the senior partner had said to me the day I gave my notice at the law firm. "Although, you know my daughter has an MBA from Wharton, but she seems content playing tennis and being a member of the Junior League." He raised his eyebrows.

I raised mine too. I imagined Ladies Who Lunched playing tennis and volunteering when they weren't lunching or hitting balls on the court. That wasn't me. That would never be me. I would be working somewhere, doing something *productive*.

I came from a long line of hard workers. Immigrant grandparents who ran a delicatessen. A dad who supplemented his teaching salary working weekends at that deli. A mom who worked full-time and went to grad school at night. I picked up a paper route at age twelve, added a second one a few months later. Took out hefty student loans to pay my way through law school—to earn a degree that was gathering dust.

As I tossed the ball in the air that morning on the neighborhood court, the Voice whispered: *Pack away your tennis skirts. Pack them away.* My racket swiped my thigh as I caught the ball with my other hand. I couldn't stop shaking as I returned to the service line. WTF?

All those mornings I had stared at myself in the mirror, wondering how I had become a person I didn't recognize. The days I'd felt a pit in my stomach. I'd finally gotten the message.

The next day, I packed away my tennis skirts for good.

My tennis hours became reading hours. When the boys were at school, I pored over theological texts Reenie lent me and emailed her my thoughts afterward. When she and I would meet for coffee, we'd inevitably end up talking about God and God's call on our lives. She taught me about the concept of *kairos*, that moment of rightness when doubt disappears and saying yes becomes imperative.

I was convinced that someday the Voice would finally whisper: *This. Yes. This.*

~

Wake up. Wake up, my body seemed to be telling me as I ran my fingers over the rough spackled walls and inhaled the smell of fresh paint in the bungalow Evan had helped build during the 1998 Jimmy Carter Work Project. My head was in a jumble. The main room in this house, which contained the kitchen and dining and living areas, was about the same size as our bedroom. Somehow I hadn't realized that Habitat's mission of "simple, decent, and affordable" translated into linoleum floors, vinyl siding, no garage, and not an inch of wasted space.

"Ready to go?" Evan asked.

"Give me a second."

Wake up to what? Maybe this was a message about conspicuous consumption. Eight years ago, Evan had been right when he said we didn't need my corporate law salary. In the years that followed, we'd bought a big house and spent thousands decorating it—Oriental rugs, antiques, custom bedding. We'd donated a lot of money to charitable causes too but maybe that wasn't enough. I had never known wealth like this, and it was delightful not having to worry about money. But some days I felt as if I was playing a part, the lady-to-the-manor-born.

I reached for the front door and the Voice stopped me:

Sell your house and move someplace simpler.

A sick feeling swelled up inside me. That couldn't be right. We were in our forever dream house. Will and Patrick were only six and four. Their best friends lived across the street. The basketball hoop in our driveway was a magnet for the neighborhood kids.

But what I was hearing was nothing compared to what Millard and Linda Fuller, the founders of Habitat for Humanity, had been called to do after a crisis in their marriage. Millard said that as he prayed about their future, he had felt a sensation of light coming over him: a call to give away everything they had—millions of dollars—and start over. When he told Linda, she had agreed that was what they needed to do.

I'd once heard a theologian speak about people's reluctance to pray about their future. He said they were afraid they'd be called to do something radical, like move to Burundi. He laughed: "Don't worry. Most people don't get called to Burundi."

Selling our house wasn't as scary as being called to Burundi, but it was scary enough. I wanted to think I'd be willing to do it if that was what I was being called to do, but I didn't know if I could trust what I was hearing inside myself. What if I told Evan about the Voice and set this whole thing in motion, and it turned out to be a giant mistake?

Eventually I told Evan what I'd heard in the Habitat house—and I told Reenie too. Likely she advised me to listen and lean in, which I did on and off for *six years*. Even after Evan and I had done the math and discovered we could fund ten Habitat houses if we sold our house and bought one that cost half as much, I kept weighing pros and cons. The cost of being wrong and being responsible for potentially hurting my children felt terribly high.

My head and my heart were at war. My head was telling me not to "downsize" when we were in our early forties and our kids were young, especially when most of our friends were "upsizing." But eventually my heart won out. The decision to sell our dream house simply felt right. We bought a patio home. Will and Patrick played wall ball when the homeowners association banned basketball hoops in our common driveway. They weren't scarred for life. What had felt like a big deal didn't turn out to be one. I had listened and leaned in, and everything had worked out.

~

When I was forty-one, I made a pilgrimage to Iona, a tiny isle off the southwest coast of Scotland.

A missionary named Columba had left Ireland in 563 for Scotland as "an act of self-imposed penance for a bloody mess he had caused at home," according to the Historic UK website. On this windswept sliver of land the Celts called "a thin place," Columba founded a community and built a new life.

I was attracted to mystics and adventurers like Columba. To the idea that life wasn't just a random series of events and that intentional listening would lead me somewhere meaningful, hopefully closer to myself.

And the Christians who turned a blind eye to clergy sexual abuse, didn't believe in a woman's right to choose, or thought homosexuality was an abomination?

They weren't my people.

And as far as I knew, they weren't Reenie's either.

As I hiked around Iona with the other pilgrims, Joan, our leader, stopped us at an intersection. "Look around," she said. "This is the only crossroads on the island."

My eyes scanned the landscape. One truck in the distance. More sheep than people. Space to hear God's voice and to listen.

"Think about the crossroads you've faced," Joan said. "How was God with you there? Then pray for guidance for the crossroads you'll face in the future."

I can't remember now if I followed her admonition to pray for guidance.

But if I'd had any idea of the crossroads I'd be facing after writing the unspeakable, I surely would have dropped to my knees.

~

After telling Evan about the unspeakable, I tried to listen and lean in for the next right thing to do—I really did—but all I heard was silence. No direction from the Voice. No "Talk to Reenie." No "Don't talk to her."

Could Reenie sense what I was hiding during our Sunday afternoon calls? So often in our relationship, I'd felt as if she could see straight into my soul. That she knew things about me I didn't even know myself.

I was at a crossroads, and the one person who could help me most was smack in the middle of it.

Zone of Privacy

The Voice was MIA; Beth already thought my relationship with Reenie was weird and strange; and Evan and Reenie—my normal go-tos when it came to problem-solving—were out of the question. The only other person who could help me navigate this crossroads was Alice, my former therapist, who was seventeen hundred miles away in Houston. I had started seeing Alice sixteen years ago when I came to her with "concerns" about my friendship with Reenie. I reached out and scheduled a video appointment.

"I don't know what to do with these feelings," I said, after I told her about writing the unspeakable and the ensuing revelation about being in love with Reenie. "Should I tell Reenie? It feels dishonest to keep this from her."

"You don't have to share every thought you have. It's not dishonest to keep a zone of privacy," Alice said.

I'd never thought about a zone of privacy, but wasn't that exactly what I'd been maintaining all these years, living one life in my head and the other out in the world? "But what if I'm actually gay? What am I supposed to do then?"

"So what if you are gay?" Alice said. "You don't *have* to do anything about it. You've made a choice to live a certain lifestyle, and if you're happy with it, you don't have to change." She told me how one of her clients with a "same-sex attraction" had stayed in his marriage and incorporated his "friend" into his family.

I closed my eyes and smiled. It didn't matter whether I was gay or not. I didn't have to do anything about it. Nothing had to change.

~

I didn't tell Alice what had been happening in my bedroom.

That I'd been locking the door as soon as Evan went down to his office in the basement.

That those damn pages had unleashed a fire inside me I couldn't extinguish. That I kept touching myself, hoping the madness would stop.

This must have been what it felt like to be a teenager with raging hormones. It was ridiculous. Me, a fifty-four-year-old woman ready to jump on top of anything that moved. And as soon as Evan got into bed, I did just that.

"I don't know what's going on," Evan said, as I kissed him all over, "but I'm not complaining."

Every night for two weeks, I initiated sex, probably more times than I had in our entire marriage. Evan kept smiling, never asking what was going on. I wondered if he made the connection between my appetite and the pages I'd shared with him and decided he wanted the sex anyway.

Did other women cheat on their husbands like this? Was this even cheating? I didn't talk to Alice about that either. Google was the only safe place to find answers, safe unless Evan happened to see my browsing history, that is. I made a mental note to clear it after I searched:

Is it just her? Woman falls in love with best friend. Sexual fluidity. How do you know if you are gay?

Damn Google. Thousands of search results came up, including some books that looked interesting—like *Dear John, I Love Jane: Women Write about Leaving Men for Women* and *Living Two Lives: Married to a Man and in Love with a Woman*—none of which I could order since I shared an Amazon account with Evan. But there wasn't a single reliable test to determine whether I was gay or not. I did learn one thing: I wasn't the only married woman who had fallen in love with a female friend.

Evan was on cloud nine after our lovemaking. Reenie was in the dark about my feelings. I was lying to the two people I loved the most.

But maybe the right thing to do was to keep pretending so everyone else could be happy.

~

My mother hadn't used the term *zone of privacy*, but she'd asked my sister and me to keep a big secret.

"Where's your dad?" a friend had asked at my fourteenth birthday party.

I mumbled something about him helping my grandmother, which was a lie. My parents were separated again—for the second or third time. Mom worried what people would think if they knew.

~

"Do you feel like you just want to consume every inch of Reenie?" Alice had asked in one of our early therapy sessions.

"Yes." That was *exactly* how I felt.

"Do you think about Reenie sexually?"

I averted my eyes. "Sometimes."

I DID NOT WANT TO TALK ABOUT THIS.

"Do you just think about her breasts—touching or kissing them?" Alice continued. "It's not uncommon for women to have that desire, especially women who weren't breastfed."

I did not want to talk about breasts or anything related to sex. But maybe Alice was offering me a reasonable explanation for the thrill I used to feel when the latest *National Geographic* featured topless African women. Or why I had asked several babysitters if I could touch their boobs, or why I felt like I hit pay dirt in college when I found issues of *Playboy* stashed away at the homes where I was babysitting.

I was bottle fed, like many babies born in the sixties. Maybe that's why I liked boobs so much. I hadn't heard this theory before, but there could be something to it.

But I didn't think about just Reenie's breasts.

I looked down at my lap. "I think about pretty much everything." Which was all I was willing to discuss about my sexual fantasies. Maybe lots of women thought about being with women, but who knew? I had never talked to anyone about any of this.

"The desire is so strong," I said wistfully. "It makes me sad to think I'm never going to find out what it's like to be with her." I wouldn't have an affair, even if Reenie was a willing participant, which I knew she wouldn't be. She wouldn't break up someone else's marriage, like the woman who had played a role in breaking up hers. Besides, Reenie had a beau. And leaving Evan? Impossible. I'd never do it.

Part of me wanted Alice to bring up sex again, but she never did.

And neither did I.

~

There was no zone of privacy with respect to finances in my marriage. After nearly twenty-nine years, I didn't have a single credit card or bank account in my own name. Since I paid Alice for the video appointment with a check from our joint account, I had to tell Evan about meeting with her or he'd find out on his own.

There had to be a way to tell him without making it a big deal. Alice said I didn't have to share every thought. I'd center the conversation on the unspeakable pages, a tactic that had worked before.

"I spoke to Alice yesterday," I said after I brought up our coffee and we were both fully caffeinated.

"Houston therapist Alice?"

I nodded.

"What about?"

"The feelings about Reenie that came up in those pages I read to you."

"Okay."

I couldn't read the expression on his face, although knowing him, I couldn't imagine this was the end of the conversation.

"We talked about whether I might be gay." There I said it, and the world hadn't ended.

"What did Alice say?" I couldn't tell if that was anger in his voice or panic.

"She said, 'So what if you are gay? You're happy with your life with Evan. You don't have to change anything.'"

I took his hand. "You know I love you, don't you?"

"Yes, and I love you too. And I agree with Alice. So what if you're gay?"

My heart burst. My husband loved me, even if I was gay, which I probably wasn't.

"But I have to say, I don't think you're gay. I think this whole thing with Reenie has always been about mommy issues. She's been the nurturing figure you've been longing for all your life."

I nodded, but on the inside, I was shaking my head. I'd been willing to believe the mommy theory years ago when Lila and Alice suggested it, but I knew it couldn't be the whole truth. Did straight women lie awake at night fantasizing about making love to their mother figures?

But maybe it didn't matter why I loved Reenie. What mattered was that Evan and I still loved each other.

Alice had shown me the way forward. Maintain the zone of privacy with respect to my feelings for Reenie. Stay the course with Evan.

Nothing had to change.

~

Shortly after the video appointment with Alice, Evan and I vacationed in Italy. Bought leather jackets in Florence. Had massages on the Amalfi Coast. Ate poached shrimp overlooking an infinity pool.

Nobody has it better than me.

We made a visit to Houston, where Patrick was working that summer, and celebrated his twenty-first birthday watching the Astros at Minute Maid Park. A middle-aged woman in the row in front of us put her arm around another woman.

Were they a couple? I couldn't take my eyes off them. Gentle touches to the thigh, an arm being patted. A brush of the lips. They *were* a couple. My body ached.

I wanted to sit with my arm around Reenie at a baseball game. I wanted to kiss her lips. I wanted to touch her thigh.

That was never going to happen. Not now. Not ever.

I have a good life. I love my husband. I don't have to change anything.

Evan and I sipped mojitos on the beach with our summer friends. Saw *Hamilton* the first month it opened on Broadway. Cheered the Astros at Yankee Stadium with Will and Patrick. Attended a charity dinner for a conservation group. "You always look so together," the host said, touching the sleeve of my new leather jacket.

We picnicked on cheese and bread from Zabar's and sipped North Fork sauvignon blanc in Central Park. Evan snapped a photo of me, supine on the lawn, plastic cup in hand, the sun hitting me just so.

Perfect summer night, I posted on Facebook.

My perfect life received lots and lots of likes.

After the picnic, we made our way to the band shell area, already packed with people, mostly younger than us, and settled into a spot close to the stage, behind a metal barrier. But the stage wasn't where my eyes spent most of the night. They kept returning to two young couples on the other side of the fence. Women in sundresses rubbing each other's backs, playfully kissing each other, swaying to the music. Did Evan notice them too? Did he know Ingrid Michaelson had a huge lesbian following, a fact I discovered when I Googled her after we returned home?

What I would have given to sway freely on that side of the fence, to have my whole life ahead of me, to satisfy this longing that wasn't going away. But I was with my husband, a kind, loyal, smart, and handsome man who loved me. Where the world said I should be and where I had chosen to be.

"Isn't this great," Evan said, putting his arm around me.

I put my arm around him. *Stop this*, I silently scolded myself.

We went to see the Broadway musical *Fun Home*. The show had many poignant moments—a young girl singing about her attraction to a woman with short hair and a ring of keys on her dungarees. A thirtysomething sitting at her desk, drawing cartoons to make sense of her life. A college freshman, her hand on the doorknob, staring at a sign about a gay and lesbian support group.

"Please, God, don't let me be a lesbian," she pleaded.

I wiped a tear from my cheek, hoping Evan didn't notice. I didn't want to be a lesbian either. Because if that's what I was, how could I stay in my marriage? And how could I possibly leave? It was much easier to keep acting as if nothing had to change.

~

My sister aspired to be on stage—I was never much of an actor—but neither one of us was a big fan of dressing up. Especially not for Halloween.

Maybe our distaste for the holiday had something to do with the fact that Mom always made us wear the costumes from our ballet recitals: Sailor. Storybook character. Angel. Bluebird. Goldfish.

If Mom's desire was to create picture-perfect daughters for Halloween, she succeeded. Our ballet costumes were fancy—much higher quality than the store-bought ones my friends wore.

But I didn't want fancy.

I wanted to be able to choose who I wanted to be.

~

I rarely read a book more than once, but once I hit fifty, I couldn't stop reading Richard Rohr's *Falling Upward: A Spirituality for the Two Halves of Life*.

On page 85 I starred this passage: "Your false self is your role, title, and personal image that is largely a creation of your own mind and attachments. *It will and must die in exact correlation to how much you want to find the Real*. 'How much false self are you willing to shed to find your True Self?' is the lasting question."

I had shed my identity as a corporate lawyer, as a tennis-playing stay-at-home mom, as someone more focused on the trappings of wealth than social justice. And finally, claiming my call as a writer had made me feel more Real than ever. But Rohr made it clear that finding the Real was a journey, not a destination—a continual dying to self to find one's true self.

I wanted to believe I'd be willing to keep shedding false selves.

I wanted to believe it.

But Alice had offered me another option: to keep a zone of privacy by boxing up my feelings instead of admitting them and acting on them.

How much did I really want to find the Real?

The Real

In October 2015, seven months after I wrote the unspeakable, the executive director of the preschool who succeeded Evan called. The school wanted to honor us at their annual gala in April.

"What do you think?" Evan said.

"What do I think? Absolutely yes!" I smiled. How good it would feel to be recognized alongside Evan for my work there. While he had been at the helm of the preschool for eight years, I'd served in multiple capacities for over a decade: board member, grant writer, website designer, special education advocate, and as a "buddy" to several preschoolers, loser of more games of Candy Land than I could count.

We'd buy a table for the event and invite our Houston friends. Reenie, of course, would be at the top of the list.

I smiled again, imagining what it would feel like to bask in the limelight, sitting between my husband and my best friend.

The same place I had been seventeen years ago at the Habitat celebration. Sitting between the man I was married to and the woman I loved.

Fuck.

I stared at the ocean through the living room window, and a different picture came into my mind: an empty seat between Evan and Reenie at the table we'd bought. My name crossed off the honoree list.

Someone—somehow—had found out my secret.

The real Suzette—the one who wouldn't be getting accolades for selflessness—had been unmasked.

~

One morning before dawn during spring break 1998, I tiptoed into the closet of a San Diego hotel room with a Bible and my journal. The boys and Evan were still asleep. I had planned to read scripture and pray, a daily practice Reenie had introduced me to, but every inch of my body was focused elsewhere, fifteen hundred miles to the east, in Houston, on her. *I can't stop thinking about her*, I wrote in my journal. *The longing is so strong, the ache so deep.*

Something was terribly wrong with me. A normal thirty-seven-year-old woman didn't spend all day dreaming about being in the arms of her son's forty-nine-year-old kindergarten teacher.

~

We called Dr. Febo, my junior high math teacher, Dr. Gaybo.

Mr. Maggini, our high school biology teacher, Mag the Fag.

Our junior high social studies teachers who team taught and definitely rocked a lesbian vibe, whether or not they were actually lesbians, were known as Pit and Pat, aka Frick and Frack, lesbian style.

I joined in the naming-calling with practically everyone else.

~

Beth flipped through *Seventeen* magazine as I doodled *KAG, KAG, KAG* all over the cover of my spiral notebook, both of us sprawled on our beds in the bedroom we shared in Montauk.

KAG were the initials of Mrs. G., my tenth-grade history teacher, who was glamorous and ahead of her time. Chic bob, oversize glasses, flowy pants when most of my female teachers in the midseventies were wearing skirts or dresses—and the softest-ever cowl-necked sweaters. She always smelled powder fresh: a slight hint of perfume, but never overpowering. I'd walk by her classroom multiple times a day, hoping to catch a glimpse of her. If Mrs. G. was sitting at her desk between class periods, I'd pop in to say hi.

Her handwriting was cool—lowercase *a*'s and *g*'s that looked like typewriter characters. I had started writing that way too.

If only I could get those a*'s exactly the way she wrote them.*

"What are you doing?" Beth said, peering over my shoulder.

I shoved the notebook under my pillow, but not before Beth saw the *KAG*'s all over it.

"You are so gay," she said. My face burned. Later, I hid the notebook in my bureau. I wouldn't let Beth—or anyone—catch me doing that embarrassing thing again.

~

"What is that?" Evan said on Election Night 2004 as he peeked at my laptop screen.

"Nothing," I said, my face burning as I shut the laptop.

"It's not nothing," he said. "How long have you been doing this?"

"This is the first time," I said. "I promise I'll never do it again." I was sure he knew I was lying about never having watched lesbian porn before, and whether I'd be able to stop myself from doing it again was anyone's guess.

He didn't say why he was angry, but I had a good idea. I rarely seemed interested in having sex with *him*. He had tried pretty much everything—even suggesting we watch girl-on-girl porn together.

I didn't really want to watch lesbian porn, with or without him. It was sleazy and exploitative. What I wanted was something I couldn't have.

~

There she was, Memorial Day weekend 1999, waiting for me on a bench outside our church. Silky ivory sleeveless blouse. Tanned arms. I sat down next to her and hugged her tightly. Felt her breasts press against mine. Neither of us spoke a word for what felt like forever. I wished it could be forever.

~

In 1998, the Lambeth Conference, a worldwide meeting of 750 Anglican bishops, voted overwhelmingly in favor of a resolution describing "homosexuality as incompatible with Scripture" and forbidding the ordination of noncelibate homosexuals or the blessing of same-sex unions.

The leadership of the large Episcopal church Evan and I belonged to supported the resolution, which rubbed my liberal sensibilities the wrong way.

Soon, we transferred our membership to Reenie's church, which wasn't actively discussing the issue. I hadn't felt a need to actively discuss it either.

~

Seconds until 1978!

"Ten, nine, eight . . ." we shouted in unison in Mike's basement as Dick Clark counted down from Times Square.

Happy New Year!!

A dance began that all my high school classmates knew the steps to. George grabbed Margaret, Kevin grabbed Anne-Marie, and so on. They were all making out—*really* making out.

I'd heard rumors about Anne-Marie sleeping with Kevin, but that wasn't too bad because they'd been going out since ninth grade. But were they really having sex? And Tricia? She'd make out with anyone.

I walked over to the keg and refilled my Solo cup, even though the beer was warm and nasty. It felt better to look busy, to look as if I didn't care.

Thank goodness Jimmy wasn't at the party, although he probably would have ignored me if he had been there.

"Sure," I'd said last spring, when Jimmy asked if I wanted to go see *Beatlemania* on Broadway. It was supposed to be almost as good as the real Beatles. Four of us took the train into the city and had burgers and cheesecake at Junior's. I was having so much fun until the middle of the first act, when Jimmy reached over for my left hand. *And kept hold of it until intermission.*

I stared straight ahead, keeping my eyes fixed on the faux Beatles crooning on stage. As soon as the first act curtain dropped, I let go of Jimmy's sweaty palm and raced to the restroom, returning with a plan.

I sat on my hand for the entire second act.

That had been seven months ago, and Jimmy and I had never spoken about what had happened. I felt like a shit about the whole thing. But thank god he didn't try to kiss me. And thank god he never asked me out again.

I did want a boyfriend someday. Just someone more my type.

~

While Evan was in his basement study, I was Googling on my laptop in our bedroom, two floors away. The books about coming out later in life that I hadn't been able to order on Amazon popped up. So did a "Modern Love" essay by Maria Bello about coming out as a modern family and a blog called "A Late Life Lesbian Story," which rang truer than I wanted to believe. Because while I might be sexually fluid or a little bit gay, I certainly wasn't a full-on lesbian.

~

Ian Dury and the Blockheads' 1978 smash "Hit Me with Your Rhythm Stick" blared from the eight-track player in the semidetached house in the center of the quaint British town of Knutsford. Teenagers downed Shandies—beer and lemonade—at a rapid rate. I was bored, ready to leave this party my host sister had dragged me to. Nick, one of her friends, staggered over to me. "You look like you need a kiss." He planted a slobbery one on my lips.

I pushed him away. Wiped my mouth with my sleeve.

At seventeen, my first kiss. *Ewww.*

Journal entry the next day: *I wonder what will happen with Nick. And I really don't care. That's why I'm rather worried about my sexual preferences.*

I had no memory of writing that entry or having those worries when I was in high school. But there it was. Three sentences inside a tiny spiral notebook. In pale blue ink. In my handwriting. Incontrovertible evidence that THIS hadn't just started with Reenie.

~

"God's telling me the time isn't right for a visit," Reenie said during one of our Sunday afternoon calls a few months after I wrote the unspeakable. I'd invited her to come to Montauk when Evan would be in Houston for a board meeting. "I don't know why yet," she added. "I'm trusting the reason will be revealed eventually."

I felt a weird mixture of disappointment and relief. I didn't tell her I suspected that I knew the reason. That her God might be on to me. That Something Bigger Than Me might be trying to protect my marriage and my relationship with her. Because three or four days with the two of us alone in this house would have been playing with fire.

~

When I woke up one morning in late November, eight months after writing the unspeakable, nothing appeared terribly different. Like most recent mornings, my jaw ached and my head felt fuzzy from tossing and turning.

But somehow everything *was* different.

I didn't know why. I still don't. People tend to change when the pain of not changing outweighs the pain of the change, but it was impossible to recognize that in the moment. Apparently, seventeen-plus years of being in love and in denial was my tipping point—the moment I couldn't live with this secret inside me for *one second longer*.

I had to get THIS off my chest and out of my system. Now. Maybe if I told Reenie the truth and she closed the door to a more intimate relationship with me, as I expected she would, I could put the genie back in the bottle, accept my very nice life with Evan, and stop dreaming about a future with her.

Screw Alice and her zone of privacy. It was time to get real and talk to Reenie.

~

"Your father used to lift the baby carriage over the curb so you wouldn't feel the bumps," Mom told me after my father died. He wanted to protect me from pain, from the very start. How sweet. How impossible.

PART TWO

Open Doors

The universe, higher power, inner voice, God, or whatever, was fucking smart—and fucking devious.

The way it orchestrated "coincidences" and opened doors in such perfect ways.

A teacher showing up at a water fountain exactly when I needed her.

Lesbians popping up at baseball games and concerts—seemingly everywhere—when I was trying to stay the course.

And the doors that opened—and closed—after I decided to get real with Reenie.

~

Diane, my new therapist, led me into her office. "What brings you here?" she asked.

I gave her the Cliff Notes version of my story. "Every time I talk to Reenie, I feel like I'm lying. I can't bear it any longer."

"What do you hope would happen if you told her your feelings?"

"I don't know." What I didn't say was that I hoped THIS would be over once I talked to Reenie. The lying. The wondering whether I was a lesbian or bisexual or sexually fluid or some other label. The living one life in my head and another in my reality. THIS had been going on for eighteen years. THIS had to end.

"What's your curative fantasy?" Diane asked.

"What do you mean by that?" Alice, my first therapist, had never used psychological terms with me.

"Curative fantasy," Diane said, "is what you hope will really happen. What you believe will relieve your suffering."

What would relieve my *suffering*? No one, not even me, had ever labeled what I was experiencing "suffering." Suffering was reserved for people with real problems, like poverty, abuse, or serious illness, not for women like me with problems of their own making. But whatever its name or whatever its source, I was in hell and Diane was suggesting there was a way out.

"I don't know," I said again. "Part of me would be thrilled if Reenie said she loved me too, but then I might have to do something about it, which feels impossible. I'm ninety-nine percent sure she'll say she doesn't feel the same way, but what if she does?"

How could I even think about leaving Evan? The truth, which I couldn't admit to Diane because I couldn't admit it to myself, was that I thought about it a lot. Reenie and I could move into a little cottage in the country, far away from everyone we knew. We wouldn't need much as long as we had each other.

For the past eighteen years, it had just been the two of us in our own little bubble, at least in my mind. A 24/7 version of the afternoon when I'd sat in the shade next to Reenie, far from the other moms in the sun, at Will's kindergarten end-of-the-school-year pool party. Reenie and her towel inches away from mine. Me feeling her next to me, imagining our bare thighs touching.

"I don't know if you're gay," Diane said. "You could be or you could be sexually fluid. But I see that you love her. I see that you do."

I see that you love her. Warmth rushed through me. Six simple words no one had ever said to me before. Diane believed me. She wasn't going to try to talk me out of my feelings or call me weird and strange. She wasn't going to suggest I had mommy issues or that I should maintain a zone of privacy.

In her eyes, I was simply a human who had fallen in love. Wow. What a different way to think about all that had happened.

"Part of me," I said, "wants Reenie to say she doesn't love me 'that way' because then I can get back to my life and not have this weighing on me."

I might not have been able to own my curative fantasy, but I did know there was only one way out of this hell. Telling Reenie how I felt. Even if that meant losing her. Which I couldn't. But I also couldn't keep lying.

As soon as I left Diane's office, I opened the calendar on my phone. In three weeks, Evan and I were heading to Costa Rica for a vacation with Will and Patrick, then he and I would be in Houston for a few weeks. Evan had a day trip planned to San Antonio to discuss family business with his siblings. If Reenie could get off work that day, she and I could have hours of uninterrupted time together.

That would be the day I would tell her how I felt. That would be the day I might lose her or I might get back to my life or I might be given the chance to start a whole new one.

Five more weeks and this living hell could be over.

~

Costa Rica, Day 4: While mountain biking with the boys, Evan flew over his handlebars and badly broke his collarbone when his front tire skidded on a big rock. The local surgeon said surgery could wait until we were back in Houston, the following week.

"You all go to the beach," Evan said the day after the accident, insisting he'd be fine alone.

The boys and I ordered lunch at a beachside cafe. "How's your book going?" Will asked while we waited for our food.

My book? I was surprised he was interested. That he even remembered. I hadn't talked to either of the boys about it in a long time.

"I've finished the first draft and I'm revising now." How much I would need to revise remained to be seen, with everything that had gone down this year.

"When's it going to be published?" Will said.

I laughed. "I'm a long way from that."

"So, what do you still have to do?"

"Tons! First, I have to finish editing, then I need to find an agent or a publisher."

"How long's that going to take?"

Damn that kid, grilling me about everything like he was an investigative reporter. But maybe Will was right. Maybe it was time to give myself some deadlines.

"I don't know, Will, maybe a year? Then another year to get it published."

"So, we're talking January 2018, two years from now," he said.

It sounded like a reasonable goal. If only I had known.

Patrick smiled. "Is there anything in your book that will surprise us?"

I laughed. But shit, if the unspeakable ended up in the book, the boys would eventually find out about it. If Evan had been with us that day, I would never have considered talking about Reenie, but here we were. It was as if a higher power had conspired to orchestrate this moment with the three of us. I didn't think the universe had placed a boulder in front of Evan's bike causing him to crash, but still. *Brava, Universe. Door open.*

"Actually, there is something." My voice shook. I wasn't about to tell them I still had feelings for Reenie, but I could use the same approach I'd used with Evan nearly a year ago. The book. My go-to explanation for all of THIS.

"This is hard to talk about," I said. "But a long time ago I had feelings for Reenie that I didn't understand. That's part of what I'm writing about."

Patrick looked at me wide-eyed. "What do you mean?"

Don't make me spell this out.

"It's called sexual fluidity," I sputtered. "It's pretty common. I've been doing a lot of research on it."

No shit. Self-help books I couldn't order. Essays about "modern families." Blogs about late-in-life lesbians.

Sexual fluidity was a real thing—and it felt like a safe place to land. But despite all my internet research, I still wasn't sure what THIS was, and Diane, my new therapist, wasn't sure either.

"How did it go?" Evan had asked after my first appointment.

"Good. I told Diane the basic story, and she said it could be sexual fluidity or I could be gay. It's still too early to tell, but I think she's going to be helpful."

"If you're sexually fluid, isn't it possible you could flow back?" Evan smiled and returned to stir the chicken curry on the stove. He probably didn't see me shaking my head. Maybe it was *possible*, but I'd call it unlikely.

I wasn't going to get into that level of detail with the boys. My goal: normalize THIS so they wouldn't freak out.

"One study found that over sixty percent of *heterosexual* women have had sexual feelings for other women," I said.

Both boys' mouths were agape. Maybe they were as surprised as I had been to learn how common these feelings were. Or simply astonished their mother had been attracted to someone other than their father—and not just someone, but a *woman* who had been in their lives since they were little. Or maybe they were surprised I was sharing this information with them at all.

"Does Dad know?" Patrick asked.

"Yes," I said.

Both boys' faces relaxed. THIS wasn't a secret from their father. THIS wasn't a big deal. Their mom was still the same mom they'd always known.

"And what about Reenie?" Will asked.

"Not yet, but I'm going to talk to her about it when we're in Houston." I had let Evan know I planned to talk with Reenie when he would be in San Antonio with his siblings.

"Okay," he had said, but the tightness in his voice suggested he didn't want to hear more.

"I don't want Reenie to be shocked by this when she reads my book," I said to the boys. I hadn't figured out what I was going to do about everyone else in my life. My mother, my sister, all my friends. How damned embarrassing. If my book ever got published, I might need to go into witness protection.

"Are you worried this will put a strain on your relationship with Reenie?" Patrick asked. Perhaps an unusual question for a twenty-one-year-old, but one that didn't surprise me. Patrick had emerged from the womb with a heavy dose of empathy.

"Yes," I said, "but it's a risk I have to take."

"I think she'll be fine with it," Will piped in. Will had an opinion on how Reenie might feel? Usually, he was more in his head than his heart. If he thought Reenie would be fine with it, maybe that meant he was too.

The church Will attended was part of a denomination that believed "homosexual practice was sin"—the old, tired "love the sinner, but not the sin," or "it's okay to be gay, just don't act on it." It bothered me that my son belonged to a church that espoused those beliefs, but I hadn't said anything to him. I had left one church because of its stance on LGBTQ+ rights, but because I had so few queer people in my life, the issue didn't yet feel personal for me—and my relationship with Will was. This wasn't a battle I felt I needed to fight then.

"Will, I hope you're right."

Twelve more days until I'd know whether Reenie would "be fine with it." That is, unless the timing of Evan's surgery closed the door on that conversation.

~

Hours after his surgery at Houston Methodist, Evan was asleep in his cousin's guest room. Claudia and her husband had graciously invited us to stay with them as long as we wanted—so much nicer for Evan to recuperate in a home than a hotel room.

I set an alarm on my phone—four hours until his next round of pain meds—and crept back into the adjoining bedroom where I'd be sleeping. I propped myself up on the bed and typed *sexual* on my laptop and Google magically filled in the rest. There, near the top of the search results, was A Late Life Lesbian Story, the blog I'd been reading on and off for months.

My pulse quickened when I read an entry posted just days ago:

> Join us in the new Facebook group! It's a secret group for women questioning their sexuality or coming out later in life, so if you want to join, you need to send me an email. Tell me why you want to join the group so that I can make sure you'll be a good fit.

Was I a "good fit"? I didn't want to be a good fit.

Just write the email, the Voice said. *Just do it.*

Before I could talk myself out of it, I typed: *I'm 54, married for 29 years, two young-adult sons. Fell for an older (hetero) woman when I was 36. We're very close friends but nothing sexual has ever happened. I thought it was just her (and maybe it is), but now I'm questioning everything. My husband knows (sort of), but not the extent. I am totally confused, have no idea what to do, and need all the support I can get.*

And before I lost my nerve, I pressed Send.

An hour later, the blogger responded with instructions on how to join her Facebook group.

They called themselves the LaLas.

It was a "secret" group, but to be on the safe side, I set up an alter ego profile: "Suzie Kew," a play on the Suzy Q nickname I'd occasionally been called as a child. Every time Evan fell asleep in one guest room, "Suzie Kew" retreated to the other and scrutinized the LaLa page. Every time Evan woke up, Suzette played dutiful wife and nursemaid.

There were at least fifty other women in the world who had asked themselves, "What is THIS?" as they struggled with a relationship with a female friend. What a relief to know I wasn't alone.

I have cut my husband's heart deeply by telling him that I'm queer, one of the more religious LaLas posted in the Facebook group. *I so want to be authen-*

tic and not bear false witness about who I am, but sometimes I think that death would be easier. Then, I think about my daughters and I can't leave like that. So I pray and tell God I am open. Sometimes I pray for God to help me love my husband again. Sometimes I pray for an escape.

I had been having some of those thoughts too.

The LaLas increased my vocabulary. An *LLL* was a "lifelong lesbian" and a *C* was a "catalyst," the person who first caused you to realize you had feelings for women. Not all LaLas had catalysts, but a lot of them did. And while some of the LaLas still had intact relationships with their catalysts, it appeared that most of those relationships had led to heartache.

In seven days, I'd find out whether mine would end in heartache too. Evan had been cleared to travel to San Antonio.

The universe had opened the door for me to tell Reenie my truth.

The Talk

"See you tonight," Evan said as he exited the two-bedroom hotel suite we'd moved into after we left his cousin's. I poured myself coffee. I needed it. I'd been up much of the night, stressing about this day that could change the trajectory of my life—and of Evan's and Reenie's lives too.

Three hours until she arrived. A run would pass the time and clear my head. I laced up my sneakers and headed toward the neighborhood where Evan and I had bought our first house. The little gray bungalow where I made the decision to leave the law firm, where I beat infertility, and where Evan and I sponge-painted Will's nursery was long gone, replaced by a redbrick two-story house. Who knew what was going on behind those closed doors. Maybe the couple inside would grow old together or maybe one of them would wake up one day and question everything they thought they knew about themselves.

Back at the hotel, I showered, put on skinny jeans and a black top, made more coffee, and arranged pineapple slices on a plate. Nothing left to do but wait. How was I going to choke out the words "I am in love with you"? What if she never wanted to see me again after I said those words? What would I do if she said she loved me "that way" too?

My hands shook as I reached for my laptop.

In an hour, I'm meeting with my catalyst to tell her how I feel, I wrote on the LaLa page. *I'm terrified.*

They popped in one by one:

You can do this.

We are with you.

You are a woman who can do hard things.

"We can do hard things" was one of the favorite LaLa mantras, originating from author Glennon Doyle, a darling of many in the group.

Yet from the moment my dad lifted my baby carriage over the curb so I wouldn't feel the bumps, I'd been raised to believe that hard things were to be avoided at all costs. Mom had directed Beth and me to take circuitous routes to avoid highways when we were new drivers. When things got tough at the law firm, I had quit. The privilege of wealth and an accommodating spouse had allowed me to delegate hard things or avoid them all together.

But there was no one to delegate this task to and there was no avoiding it. *You must do this thing, no matter the consequences*, the Voice was insisting.

A few minutes after ten, my phone buzzed.

Reenie was here.

~

Two months into Will's kindergarten year, I crushed a 5 mg tablet of Ritalin into some applesauce, like my mother used to do with Bayer's after I outgrew St. Joseph's baby aspirin. I'd been reluctant to medicate Will for his ADHD but felt less conflicted after meeting with a neuropsychiatrist.

Still, I worried. Will's stomach might hurt. He might develop insomnia. His personality might change. As challenging as this kid could be, I couldn't bear for him to lose his sparkle.

I tucked a jar of applesauce and the Ritalin bottle into a brown paper bag. Will would need a second dose at lunchtime. I also put in a six-pack of Ensure, a nutritional supplement, in case he didn't feel like eating lunch. *Ensure.* It broke my heart. That was for old people or the infirm, like my dad with early onset Parkinson's, not rambunctious kindergartners like Will.

That morning at the classroom door, I discreetly handed Reenie the paper bag. We'd already gone over everything—the timing of the medication, the applesauce, the Ensure.

She patted my arm. "Don't worry. I'll be watching him all day."

Hours later, I stood outside the kindergarten classroom, arms crossed, foot tapping, waiting with the other moms and nannies who were early too.

The moms were bantering about tennis and playdates and spring soccer versus T-ball. Did they really care about those things, or did we all keep it light because it was too hard to talk about the real stuff? Like how it felt to have a child who didn't fit in. Or how it felt to be a mom who didn't fit in either.

When the classroom door finally opened, Reenie headed straight to me through the crowd of mothers and hugged me. "Will was like a different child today," she whispered in my ear.

"Thank god," I whispered back.

"You have to see this." She took my arm and led me into the classroom. Will was sitting on the carpet, calmly playing cards with two boys. "He couldn't have done this before today."

I could have stood there forever, her arm around me, watching Will. Everything would be okay. She and I were on the same team.

Maybe that was the moment I fell in love.

~

I hugged Reenie in the hotel lobby, wondering if this would be the last time we'd ever touch or the beginning of something I'd only fantasized about but never truly believed could happen.

"Coffee?" I said, once we were in the suite, hoping she didn't notice the trembling in my voice. I placed the pineapple on the coffee table. Reenie sat on the couch. I sat in an armchair to her right. The whole day ahead of us. Or not.

In her late sixties, she was still beautiful. The first moment I remember noticing her looks was the one and only time she and her beau came over for dinner, about a year after that first coffee date. I'd grown used to her schoolmarm vibe—slightly dowdy clothing, gold cross, little or no makeup. But that night at my house, her skin was more luminous than usual and her makeup made her green eyes pop. Plus she was wearing the black cashmere sweater set I'd given her for Christmas. "It was on sale," I said when she protested a little.

I had bought the same sweater set for myself. Still owned it. It had lasted a lot longer than Reenie's relationship with her beau. A few years after that dinner, he was out of her life, which was a relief to me. I hadn't liked the way he treated her.

She put a slice of pineapple on her plate. "How's Evan feeling?"

"The surgery was rougher than we expected," I said.

"Poor guy."

"Yeah." The poor guy should have made it to San Antonio by now. A good wife would have checked on him. "Let me make sure he's there." I reached for my phone.

"And the boys?" Reenie asked a few minutes later. As I filled her in on the latest with Will and Patrick, I checked the time on my phone. We'd been talking for an hour—about everything but the one thing I needed to say.

"How's work going?" I asked, doing my best to keep my voice steady. I still had a long list of topics I could raise—her daughter, her grandkids, her church. This was agonizing, like inching my way into icy waters instead of diving in.

"How's your writing going?" she asked after we exhausted the work topic.

My writing. I figured she would ask about that eventually. The writing that had led me to this moment that felt both impossible and inevitable.

My goddamn writing.

Three months ago I had written the last lines of the first draft of my memoir:

> I was still afraid of making the wrong decision, but I was not going to stay stuck this time. I wasn't going to straddle the path, live halfway anymore. I had to be willing to risk making mistakes. I had to commit. I had to trust my inner voice to lead me where I needed to go.

It was a great ending, but it was bullshit. I wished I'd said "fuck you" to the Voice that had urged me to write the unspeakable. I wished I could turn back the clock and go back to the happy-enough life I used to have. The life where I didn't worry about maybe being gay or about losing the two most important people in my life. The life where I wasn't about to say the most vulnerable words a human could say to another human.

"It's taken some interesting twists and turns," I said slowly.

Breathe, just breathe.

"Tell me."

"There *is* something I need to tell you."

She nodded, looking straight into my eyes, like she always did. I was thirty-six again, back at our first coffee, being drawn in by those eyes, being drawn in by a mystery bigger than me, bigger than her.

I sat down on the couch and put my arms around her. Buried my face in her thick hair. "I need to tell you something," I said, "but I'm so afraid of losing you."

"You can't say anything that would change how I feel about you," she said.

"Anything?"

"Anything. You could tell me you had murdered someone, and I would still love you."

I laughed a little, but this wasn't funny. I moved back to my chair, put my head in my hands. "I know I have to do this, but I don't know if I can."

"Maybe you're not ready," she said.

I was never going to be ready, but I couldn't keep this secret any longer. "No, I have to tell you."

She nodded again.

I moved back to the couch and hugged her again. I couldn't believe what I was about to do. I had thought I would go to my grave with this secret.

"I was writing about the early years with you," I whispered, "and after I read some of the scenes I'd written, I realized I had been in love with you."

"Awww," she said, as if she were talking to a child.

I can't stop now. I have to tell her the rest.

"And I think I still am."

The world stopped in that moment. Was I breathing? Was she? I had to know if she was in love with me too, afraid like me to say the words aloud. I took her hands in mine, wishing I had the courage to look her in the eye, but instead I stared off in the distance. "I'm guessing you don't feel the same way?"

Tell me you feel the same way. Tell me you don't. Tell me you do.

But she didn't say anything. Seconds later, she simply shook her head.

Okay. She didn't love me "that way," which was what I'd expected she'd say whether it was true or not. This wasn't wonderful news, but it also wasn't terrible. She was still in the room with me.

"I can't lose you," I repeated.

She squeezed my hands. "You aren't going to lose me," she said firmly. "Nothing is going to change between us."

My shoulders relaxed. Nothing was going to change.

We walked to a Mexican restaurant for lunch. Ate fish tacos. Chatted about church and her family.

We can do this. We are going to be okay.

"Can we talk about THIS a little more?" I said, after we returned to the hotel. Because a couple of sentences from me and a shake of the head from her wasn't enough for me to put the unspeakable to bed.

"Yes," she said.

"Did you know I felt this way about you?"

~

The day after we met for coffee the first time, I wrote this letter and gave it to Reenie:

February 1, 1998

Dear Reenie:

I had a wonderful time the other night.

Beforehand, when I was praying about our time together, something strange happened. I got this unbelievably warm feeling in my chest—right where my heart is. It was a REAL physical sensation. I thought—this is bizarre. Then a couple of days later I prayed again and the word LOVE—the actual letters—flashed through my head. Now God had my attention—I thought, yes, I do love Reenie. But I certainly can't tell her that. I'll have to find a way to dance around it. I prayed about it again, and a clear image came into my head. I saw myself giving you a hug and saying, "I love you, Reenie."

I didn't have the courage to say "I love you" the other night. However, it has been nagging at me ever since. I hope I can say those words someday and it won't make you too uncomfortable. I know in theory it shouldn't, because isn't love supposed to be what life is all about? It's just that we don't often express love, even if we feel it, in such naked terms.

Thank you, Reenie, for being so supportive. God is doing amazing work through you.

I hope we can continue to build on our friendship,

Suzette

I have no memory of how or whether Reenie ever responded.

~

"No, I didn't know how you felt," Reenie said at the hotel, "but I knew you were very attached to me and sometimes that made me uncomfortable."

~

One evening, the summer after I met Reenie, I followed her into a classroom at her church. We were the only ones in the building. As soon as she closed the door, I wrapped my arms around her. Breathed her in. Didn't want to let go.

"I love you," I whispered in her ear. "I missed you so much." I'd just returned from a month in Montauk with Evan and the boys.

"I missed you too."

She lifted two chairs from a stack in the corner of the room and placed them on the carpet, facing each other. We sat down, knee to knee, Jesus Loves You posters behind us. I reached for her hands—or did she reach for mine?

Then I put my head in her lap.

In her lap.

What the hell was happening to me?

I expected her to say something like "it's okay" or do something like pat my head.

But she didn't say or do anything. We both stayed there frozen like blocks of ice.

I finally raised my head but kept my eyes on the floor. "I'm so embarrassed. I don't know why I did that."

"I don't know why either." There was an edge in her voice I hadn't heard before. Was she angry?

"Do you think I'm crazy?" Because I was starting to think I was.

"No," she said, "but I don't understand *this*."

I didn't understand THIS either. THIS defied definition. There was no language for THIS.

I looked her in the eye. "Do you still love me?"

She nodded as her eyes welled up. "Yes, but I'm afraid my love is blocking you from God's love."

My eyes welled up too. Couldn't I have her love and God's love too?

~

"Uncomfortable"? Was that what I'd heard in her tone that night in the Sunday school classroom? I didn't ask.

Did she feel "uncomfortable" when she visited me in Montauk the first time, a year after I put my head in her lap?

The first full day of that visit had been a success. Evan had been a doll, tending to Will and Patrick while Reenie and I walked on the beach and visited my favorite spots around town.

"I'm heading up," Evan said after he put the boys to bed.

"I'll be up soon." I owed him some attention, but Reenie and I were still cleaning up from dinner.

She dried a pot and handed it to me. I put it away, wiped my hands on a dish towel.

"I should let you go," she said.

You should, but I don't want you to.

A scripture passage flashed through my mind. "Greet each other with a holy kiss," Paul had written to the church at Rome. A *holy* kiss. Holy, meaning sacred, set apart, of God.

A holy kiss. If it was okay to greet someone with one, it must be okay to say good night with one as well.

It was okay to kiss her. People in the Bible did it all the time.

I moved toward her, intending to kiss her cheek, but she turned her head at the last minute. My lips brushed her neck instead. I pulled back, felt my face flush. Why had she moved like that? Did she think I was trying to kiss her "that way"? No, I wanted to say, that was a *holy* kiss.

But there was no way I was going to try to explain that messed-up kiss. I wasn't going to jeopardize our friendship—our relationship—our whatever the hell *this* was. "Good night," I said, giving her a quick hug, and hurried upstairs to Evan. That night, I lay in his arms, but my mind and body were on her alone.

All these years later, I could still feel the brush of my lips on her neck. My head in her lap too. Uncomfortable. Yes. For both of us.

"What does Evan know about *this*?" she said.

"He knows I've been struggling. He also knows I'm talking to you today."

"And Will and Patrick?"

"They know too."

"Does anyone else know?"

Why was she cross-examining me? "Only my therapist," I said. "I probably don't need to say this to you," I continued, "but I'd appreciate if you'd keep this confidential. Please don't even tell Liza," I said, referring to a mutual friend.

"Don't worry," she said. "There's no way I would tell her."

"I'm so relieved we've talked." And I was. I could be real with her again, and maybe she could help me find a way out of THIS. "I was so afraid you might run out of the room, and I'd never see you again."

"You aren't going to lose me," she repeated.

I wasn't going to lose her, which had been my biggest fear before telling her my feelings. But now something even scarier was staring me square in the face.

I'd been engaged in magical thinking, hoping that somehow THIS was just about Reenie—and I was pretty sure she would say she didn't feel the same way—and then I would be done with THIS.

But the relief I'd expected to feel had been replaced by a deep knowing I couldn't ignore any longer. THIS wasn't just about her. THIS was a desire for a woman's touch. And THIS wasn't going away.

Sacred Vows

It rained on August 23, 1986, our wedding day, which was supposed to be good luck. I cried because I wanted everything to be perfect. We'd already had a big scare when Evan came down with a bad case of the chicken pox the week before.

My father, four years away from a Parkinson's diagnosis, walked me down the aisle of the Wellesley College Chapel. I wore my mother's simple and elegant Priscilla of Boston wedding gown; my bridesmaids donned Laura Ashley pink floral dresses with puffy sleeves. Evan and his groomsmen were in classic black tuxedos, Evan looking a little peaked, but we made it through.

The photographer retouched the photos where Evan's chicken pox scabs were visible. No sign in our wedding album that anything was—or would be—other than perfect.

~

You might have to leave Evan, the Voice whispered as I put on my running shoes the morning after Reenie and I talked.

No! I didn't want to leave Evan—I just wanted to end the lying and the secret-keeping. The Voice was a motherfucker that couldn't be trusted. It had led me to Reenie, which had led me to unspeakable feelings, which had led me to this shit show.

But this motherfucker had also led me to good things, like claiming my call as a writer, selling our big house, and focusing on social justice. The problem was that it was impossible to know when the Voice was leading me to something good or leading me into deeper shit. And this "you might have to leave Evan" BS? It was one thing to fantasize about running away with Reenie, but it was another to take action. Besides, Reenie had closed that door.

"Going for a run," I said to Evan, key card in hand.

"Wait," he said. "I want to hear about your time with Reenie."

"There's not much to tell. We cleared the air."

"That's not fair." He reached for my arm. "Talk to me. You're shutting me out."

"Okay." He was right. It wasn't fair.

I sat on the couch in the same spot where Reenie had been less than twenty-four hours earlier. "I told her how I felt about her and asked if she felt the same way. She said no."

"So your love is unrequited?"

"No, it's not like that."

His face flushed. "What would you have done if she said she felt the same way?"

"I don't know," I said, just as I had told my therapist. But I did know. If Reenie had said she was in love with me, I would have dropped everything. I would have followed her to the ends of the earth.

"There is something else I need to tell you," I said, "I'm realizing THIS isn't just about Reenie. My attraction to women is real."

Evan's face grew redder. "I am not interested in an open marriage." His words sounded formal, hard.

"Who said anything about an open marriage? I'm not interested in that either."

"There's no middle ground for me," he said. "We're either fully married or we're getting divorced."

"Nobody's talking about divorce," I said, ignoring the fact that this was exactly what the Voice had been talking about. "I just want you to know THIS is real for me. But I don't know what to do with it."

I put my head in my hands. When I looked up, Evan's face was as hard as his words had sounded.

"I'm sorry," I mouthed and went into my bedroom and closed the door.

I texted Reenie: *Things are moving at breakneck speed here & I'm terrified.*

She responded immediately, asking why I was terrified.

Because I have a decision to make. A huge one that could impact many lives. I'm terrified I might leave my marriage.

I couldn't believe I was thinking this way. I wasn't from a family who followed through with divorce.

~

"Girls, this is Sandra," Dad said, smiling, as Beth and I sat on the brown corduroy pullout couch in his apartment, where we stayed every other weekend. This was Separation #1. Or #2? Or #3?

With Dad's arm around her, Sandra was smiling too. Her teeth were gleaming white, her shoulder-length hair the color of a Kraft caramel. She seemed nice enough, but it sucked. I didn't want my parents to get divorced. My only friend with divorced parents was Jessica, who spent a lot of time at bowling alleys with her dad, which was fun but must have gotten tiresome after a while. If I didn't do something soon, Dad might get serious with this Sandra person and it might be too late.

"Mom!" I yelled as I walked in the door after Dad brought Beth and me home. "Dad has a *girlfriend*!"

She looked surprised. I told her everything I knew, which wasn't much.

"If you want to get him back, you better get on it," I said.

A couple of weeks later, Dad moved back home, bringing the brown pullout couch with him and never mentioning Sandra's name again, at least not to Beth or me.

Soon, a lime-green slipcover was draped over the brown couch, matching the new lime-green wall-to-wall carpet in our house. Occasionally, the brown corduroy would peek out and one of us would silently adjust the slipcover. We became experts at smoothing things over, ignoring what was beneath the surface.

I didn't know much then about what had caused my parents' separations or their eventual reconciliation, but years after my father's death, Aunt Carol—his sister—told me Dad came back because he couldn't bear to be away from Beth and me.

There were no young children or teenagers keeping me in my marriage. Will was twenty-four and Patrick was twenty-one. But still. No one, except Evan and that motherfucking Voice, was talking about divorce.

~

Three years earlier, about eight months after we moved to Montauk, Evan lay on the couch, penning his way through the crossword as he did every morning. How could he be so relaxed? Didn't he realize we had things to figure out? We'd agreed to engage in an intentional discernment process for our empty-nest chapter—we weren't going to just float along and live by default.

"We need to get going on this discernment thing," I said, hands on hips. My notes from the discernment course I'd taken years ago were on the coffee table.

"Okay." He put the crossword down.

"The first thing we have to do is pick a discernment question," I said. "Best if it's a yes-or-no one, but we can start with where we want to live long-term or what work we want to do."

"All right," he said, waving his hand toward the ocean on the other side of the sliding glass door. "I want to believe I'd be open to anything, but the hardest thing for me would be giving up this house."

I didn't tell Evan the thoughts that flew into my head.

I could give this house up.

I could give this all up.

~

The instructor at the discernment course had said that the best a person could do was "relative certitude," to say that they had listened to the best of their ability, that they were as clear as they could be. The idea of relative certitude had surprised and disquieted me. Maybe relative certitude worked for small decisions, but shouldn't you know for sure before you took action on something big?

~

I went for my run, and when I returned, I texted Reenie again: *Can I c u before I leave?*

Evan and I were flying back to New York in three days. I had to process what was swirling around my head with Reenie. Get confirmation that I was listening correctly. That there wasn't something I was missing in this equation. She and Evan were my gut checks. The people I trusted more than I trusted myself.

Reenie had a certainty about the way the universe worked that was both comforting and perplexing, given that I'd been taught "relative certitude" was the best anyone could do.

One time in the early years, we were outside when a dark cloud loomed in the distance. A thunderstorm? Oh no! Reenie's car! It was a fifteen-year-old sedan with unreliable brakes and a moonroof that leaked so badly she had duct-taped a garbage bag on the inside.

"Have you been able to get your car fixed?" I asked, willing the cloud to disappear.

"Not yet," she said. "God will make a way in God's time." She told me a story about not having enough money to pay her electric bill after her divorce. The day the bill was due, a check for the exact amount had slipped through her mail slot.

A chill went through me. "How does God do stuff like that?" I said. Surely, God must have planted the idea in someone's head to help with her electric bill.

Was God sending me a message to pay for her car repair?

Yes, this must be God speaking to me. I had been wanting to do something for Reenie. She had done so much for me.

"Would you let me help you?" I asked. "You can't drive around with bad brakes."

She shook her head. "That's not the way God works," she said firmly, in a way that left no room for argument.

I didn't challenge her, but later I wondered how she could be so certain about the way the universe worked for me.

Reenie responded to my text. She could meet for an early-morning coffee the day I was flying back to New York.

I wiped away a tear and smiled. Nothing had changed.

~

That Friday, we carried our coffees to a table outside a Galleria-area Starbucks. The view wasn't pretty—a shopping-center parking lot—but it was a glorious sunny day in the high sixties. Ahhh, Houston in February.

"So, what's going on?" Reenie said. Was that an edge in her voice? We were both wearing sunglasses so I couldn't see her eyes.

"I think I'm being called to do something I couldn't imagine a week ago." I expected her to nod in that encouraging way I was used to, but her head didn't move. Maybe she was just listening intently.

"Remember, I felt the same way about selling our house?" Of course she remembered. We'd spent hours—years—discussing it.

"At first I couldn't imagine selling it, but when I eventually trusted what I was hearing inside myself, everything worked out." She would get this. She was the one who had always counseled me to listen and lean in for the next right step.

"Leaving Evan is completely different from selling your house," she said. There was no mistaking the edge in her voice this time. The only other time I'd heard this tone was after I put my head in her lap in the Sunday school classroom.

"No one got hurt when you sold your house," she continued. "You are going to hurt so many people if you leave your marriage—you've already hurt me."

Her words knocked me over. What had happened to "nothing is going to change"?

"I thought you were okay with what I told you. Help me understand how I've hurt you."

"You've already told Will and Patrick about this. Maybe I'll never see them again, but I don't know how we're ever going to have a relationship after this. And Evan, he was my friend too. How can I ever face him again?"

She was worried about her relationship with my kids and my husband? I'd never thought those relationships mattered much to her. True, she and Evan had worked together at the preschool for eight years, and she had been Will's teacher. But in my mind, it had always been about the two of us.

"Evan doesn't hold you responsible," I said. "He's not mad at you. You are not responsible for THIS."

"Okay," she said, her voice a bit softer.

We sipped our coffee in silence. This was not the meeting I'd expected. I glanced at my phone. Fifteen more minutes until she had to leave for work.

"When my husband was contemplating leaving me for Janet," she said, breaking the silence, "he used to say to me all the time, 'Don't you want me to be happy?'"

She was comparing me to her ex-husband, who'd had an affair? It was as if the Reenie I'd known for eighteen years had been snatched away and a hard-hearted twin had taken her place.

"Suzette, you have to decide whether you are going to choose your own happiness or honor your vows."

The light hug she gave me after we picked up our empty coffee cups and headed to the parking lot made it obvious to me which choice she thought I should make.

That afternoon, I stuffed the in-flight magazine in the seat pocket in front of me and looked over at my sleeping husband, his right arm in a sling. Several weeks until his collarbone would be fully healed. I lightly placed my right hand on top of his left, touched the gold wedding band he'd never taken off since the day we exchanged our vows, almost thirty years ago.

For better or for worse. In sickness and in health. 'Til death do us part.

The LaLas were all over the place about marriage—some already divorced, some in open marriages, some trying to make it work with husbands. None of these options seemed right for me. I'd once privately dismissed a friend who had left her marriage because she "wasn't happy." In my world, it was okay to get divorced if your husband was a cheater, an abuser, or a freeloader, or maybe even if he was just an asshole. But Evan was none of these. Not even close.

Reenie's words echoed in my ears: "You have to decide whether you are going to choose your own happiness or honor your vows." But she had also said: "You just need to listen for the next thing and lean in. It's as simple as that."

There was nothing simple about the mixed messages she was sending me or the ambiguous ones I was hearing from the Voice.

That son of a bitch had said, "You *might* have to leave Evan," not "You *have* to leave Evan."

Maybe there was still a way out of this pain.

LaLa Land

Good morning, LaLas. I'm living in a pressure cooker. H had surgery 3 weeks ago—can't do much on his own right now—no driving, needs help drying off after shower, getting dressed, tying shoes. I know he will heal (soon, please!), but with his situation on top of our marital issues, I'm about to explode from stress. Have a great therapist, thank goodness. My prayer for myself and any LaLas who are struggling: Help me do today. Help me trust the way will become clear. Help me believe that in the end, all will be well, even though right now I feel like I am tumbling in the ocean, unable to see the light.

~

Out of shower, Evan texted. *Can u come up?*

I'd been sleeping downstairs in the guest room since we returned to Montauk two weeks ago. It would be easier for Evan to recuperate if he had the whole bed to himself, we'd decided.

I loved the guest room. No snoring husband. No worry about being pestered for sex, although with Evan's broken collarbone, I was safe in that regard for the time being.

When I arrived upstairs, Evan was standing on the bath mat soaking wet, looking nearly as helpless as my father had at the end of his life. Twenty-plus years of Parkinson's disease had ravaged Dad's body, necessitating round-the-clock care, which my mother had managed.

For years, I thought my parents' reconciling after all those separations had been a mistake. Settling and making peace with their situation had only led to more unhappiness. But settling had led to good as well, including the life they had created in Montauk, some of their best years together.

Settling had also meant that my dad had someone to take care of him when he was diagnosed with Parkinson's. Evan's situation was different, of course—short-term versus long-term—but what would happen if one of us got seriously ill and that person didn't have anyone to take care of them?

"Thanks," Evan said, handing me a towel. I patted his back, extra gently near the collarbone, hoping he realized how much I cared about him. I dabbed the spot on his chest that always had felt made just for me. The spot I leaned into when I considered quitting the law firm, the spot I shed tears on when I couldn't get pregnant.

I bent down and dried between his legs. No visible response from his body and none from mine.

I helped him put on his fluffy white terrycloth robe, the one that reminded me of the robes we wore after our couple's massage on the Amalfi Coast last summer. He gingerly lowered himself onto the couch, started on the crossword. I looked at the whitecaps the late February wind had stirred up on the ocean.

That couple's massage felt like a lifetime ago.

How did you know when your marriage was over?

~

Country music floated through Evan's Upper West Side apartment on a Saturday night in December 1983. Partiers devoured chips and queso from a cowboy-hat-shaped platter and downed bottles of Shiner Bock and margaritas in red Solo cups.

"Let's dance," Evan said after I downed a healthy-sized margarita. He took my arm and twirled me around the living room.

We had met briefly two months earlier, but that night I had been too drunk from the sangria I'd downed on an empty stomach to remember much about him. This night in Evan's apartment, I was only slightly buzzed when he took my arm. I liked that he took charge. He was tall and handsome too.

We danced our way into his bedroom and soon my back was against the wall. He kissed me hard and pressed against my gold corduroy pants. His hands moved up and down my striped cotton sweater. I leaned into him, ran my fingers through his dark brown hair.

"Let's make love in 1984," he whispered in my ear.

He likes me. He wants me.

"Why wait that long?" I whispered back.

~

Is it possible to live, really live, without expressing your sexuality? I asked the LaLas.

Annie wrote: *How does one express one's sexuality anyway? By living it? Or is knowing it within yourself enough? I don't know. For me, I could not live fully without fully loving another person. And that was/is only possible for me when that other person is a woman. It is not the whole of who I am, but it is an essential component of me being fully myself.*

Sandy wrote: *Seems a bit like asking if you can really live without expressing your individual creativity. Without writing another book. Without leaving the safety of your hometown. Without _____ (you fill in the blank). Sure. I believe we create our own happiness. But that's not the question. You asked if you can really live without expressing your sexuality. I suppose you can if you're a monk. Are you a monk?*

Nope, I wasn't a monk. At least that's what my body was telling me as I scrutinized every inch of Sandy's profile picture.

Tan, long blonde hair, perfect white teeth. Thirteen years younger than me. Lived in Seattle with two young children and a husband. Was in an open marriage.

I love your profile photo, Sandy messaged. *The delicate way your hand is on your hip. You look so hot.*

She thought I was hot?

The woman didn't sleep. If I woke up in the middle of the night and checked Facebook, she messaged me. When I got up in the morning, she was there as well.

Sandy was wildly inappropriate for me. Too young. Thousands of miles away. Two little kids. A husband. Nothing could ever happen with us, I said to her over and over again, at least not while I was still married.

My head told me it could never work with her, but the rest of my body?

What are you doing in there?" Evan asked a few days into my online dalliance with Sandy.

"Just checking Facebook," I said. A sick feeling coursed through me as I shut the cover of my laptop. Flirting with Sandy was exhilarating, but I felt dirty, even though my therapist had said it was great that I was "exploring." If I wouldn't tell Evan or Reenie what I was doing in the guest room, it was probably wrong. I should probably stop.

What's your fantasy? Sandy messaged one night.

OMG. This was really happening, but I didn't know how to play this game. From what Sandy had told me, she had some experience with women, at least more than I did.

What's yours? I responded.

Asked you first, she replied, with a smiley face emoji.

I didn't hesitate as I typed. A gorgeous tan woman with big boobs would take off her bikini top at the beach and ask me to rub sunscreen all over her. Later, I'd wash *every inch* of her in the shower. We'd end up in bed—right here in the guest room.

Sometimes I skipped the beach and the shower and just landed in bed with the mystery woman, but whichever version I went with always aroused me. And the version with the beach and shower had a new face and a name—Sandy.

Your turn, I messaged.

Apparently, Sandy had been thinking about this too. She'd be waiting for me in a hotel room, throw me on the bed, rip off my shirt, and take off the rest of my clothes.

I'd lick you down there slowly, just like an ice cream cone, she wrote.

OMG. It felt so good to be desired by this beautiful young woman. Maybe I wouldn't end up alone if I left Evan, although fifty-five was terribly late to start a new life.

~

The northeast LaLas were getting together! In Manhattan! Amy from Providence. Nancy from Philly. Nicole, Alexis, and Gina from New York. . . . And Sandy from Seattle? WTF?

You're coming to NY? I messaged when I saw her added to the group chat.

Got a cheap flight and thought, why not?

Nothing can happen with us. Nothing. Not even a kiss.

I wouldn't get in a position where I could be tempted. I wouldn't drink too much. And although I was staying at a hotel that night, I would *not* be in that hotel room alone with Sandy.

Don't worry. I'll behave, Sandy wrote.

But I was worried. As worried about her as I was about myself.

~

I wiped my palms on my jeans as I climbed the stairs to the restaurant's second floor, nearly as nervous as I had been when I met Reenie for that first coffee.

Time to meet the LaLas.

When I told Evan about the Facebook group, he'd been gracious. "I'm glad you have that kind of support." Of course he didn't know the kind of support I'd been receiving from Sandy.

On our LaLa group chat, we'd been messaging each other for days, half-jokingly, half-seriously: What are you wearing? What *do* lesbians wear?

The last time I had knowingly been in the same space with lesbians had been over thirty years ago, in the early 1980s, when I was a Wellesley College student who favored pearls and Fair Isle sweaters. The lesbians I knew who were out at Wellesley had skewed masculine—short hair, unshaved legs, no makeup—likely one of many reasons it hadn't even occurred to me that I could be one of them.

No one would call me butch. Just a few years ago, I'd been called a Creamsicle by author Mary Karr as she took in my white jeans, white T-shirt, and pale-orange cashmere cardigan during a break at a writers conference. It made for a good story, but something deep inside me had screamed, "This is not me."

I still owned that Creamsicle cardigan. Would wear it again in a few months to Patrick's college graduation. A graduation where no one but my sister, Evan, and me would have a clue that we were anything but a happy family gathered to celebrate a big step in a young man's life.

To meet the LaLas, I had made my best attempt to look like something other than a Creamsicle or a fifty-something woman from suburbia. Dark jeans, black leather jacket, black platform sneakers, and black sweater and scarf—in Manhattan (lesbian or not) it was hard to go wrong with black.

Six LaLas were already sitting at a long table when I reached the top of the stairs. I smiled as I surveyed the group. Nothing obvious to signal the turmoil or the "differentness" buried inside each of us. We looked like a bunch of middle-aged soccer moms trying to look hip.

I said hello and kept my eyes on the stairs. Where was Sandy? Maybe she wasn't going to show. Or maybe she wanted to make a grand entrance.

A few minutes later, a blonde headed toward our table.

That's her.

"Sandy?" I stood up to give her a hug.

"Yes," she said, meeting my eyes and squeezing me tightly. She smelled fresh, like she had just gotten out of the shower, the way Reenie always smelled.

As we ate, I kept stealing glances at Sandy. She was damned cute, in her baseball cap and cargo pants. In another life, we could have had fun together. Maybe not in a long-term relationship but the occasional "I want to lick you just like an ice cream cone" moment? I could deal with that.

After dinner, six of us made our way to my hotel room. Safety in numbers. Soon, Sandy excused herself to use the bathroom—"To freshen up," she said. The rest of us kicked off our shoes and took dozens of selfies, posting them to the LaLa page. Snuggled together on the king-size bed, we screamed with laughter as the comments rolled in. It was like a giant slumber party!

"Who's still married?" Gina asked.

Nicole and I raised our hands.

"Are you still having sex with your husbands?" Nothing like getting right down to it.

"No," Nicole said.

"Yes," I said, sheepishly. There hadn't been a lot of sex between the broken collarbone and the tension in the house, but there had been a time or two. It felt wrong to say no, given everything I was putting Evan through.

"You'll never leave," Gina said with a certainty that startled me. Was the fact that I wasn't repulsed by sleeping with a man an indication I'd stick it out? I'd never been repulsed. I'd been neutral, tolerant of sex. It was something I could do occasionally to keep the peace.

But in a different life, I wouldn't ever be neutral about having sex with Sandy. And what the hell was she doing in the bathroom?

Gina knocked on the bathroom door. "What's going on?"

"I'll be out soon," Sandy yelled.

Thirty minutes later she emerged, makeup on, hair curled, tight jeans hugging her rear. She lay on the end of the bed, in just the perfect position for me to see her curves. I wanted to kiss her and would have if no one else had been there. I would have done more than kiss her.

Fuck. I was a lesbian.

Two hours later, the party broke up. Sandy *had* behaved. She hadn't tried to make a pass at me. But she did give me an extra-tight and long hug when she said goodbye.

Sandy wasn't right for me—we were at radically different stages of life, plus I wasn't going to cheat on Evan. If our marriage came to an end, I could at least hold my head high on that account. But meeting Sandy in person had served its purpose. My attraction to women had been tested in real time. I wanted to be with a woman. I wanted it so badly.

~

The morning after the LaLa gathering, I boarded a train for New Jersey to visit my sister. Beth lived only an hour away from Manhattan, and I wasn't in a rush to return to the Montauk pressure cooker. Evan was finally healthy enough to be on his own.

I'd been intentionally vague with Beth about my New York trip. "Just meeting some friends." We hadn't talked about Reenie since she called our friendship "weird and strange" just over a year ago, and I wasn't planning to raise the subject again.

Shortly after I arrived, Beth and I headed out for a walk with Sophie, her elderly Shih Tzu. We made a loop around the block and another as Sophie sniffed tree trunks, in no hurry to do her business.

"Hey, who are these friends you were with in New York?" Beth said.

Fuck.

The universe had opened doors before to hard conversations, and maybe that's what was happening again. Was I going to keep lying to my sister—and my entire family—forever? There was never going to be a good time to talk about this. I took a deep breath. "They're from a new Facebook group I've joined," I said. "I've been wanting to talk to you about it, but . . ."

"What group?"

"It's for women questioning their sexuality."

"What?"

My lips trembled. "I think I'm gay."

Beth didn't say anything more and neither did I. As we walked back to her house, I wished she would hug me, or tell me it would be okay, or say she understood or even that she didn't understand but still loved me. But even with her cold reaction, I felt a little lighter. My secret was out—and my sister hadn't called me weird or strange. Maybe I could tell her more.

I carried my suitcase up to my nephew Rob's room where I'd be sleeping the next two nights. Scott, my brother-in-law, was in the kitchen, prepping dinner.

Beth came into Rob's room and sat down on the bed.

"Tell me more about this group," she said.

I told her we called ourselves the LaLas, "for later in life." That these women felt like "my people," the community I'd never had before. I told her about my feelings for Reenie and how good it felt to finally feel less alone.

"As crazy as it sounds, I'm beginning to think I might leave Evan," I said.

"*What are you doing, Suzette?*" she said. "*This is crazy.* You know how obsessed you get with things—this is just like how you used to be with tennis."

My sexuality was like tennis? Are you fucking kidding me?

Yes, I did get obsessed with things. That was just the way I was. But suggesting I was obsessed with the idea of being gay? That was insulting. This wasn't a phase or a midlife crisis, although, of course, I also hadn't wanted to believe I was gay. A fact I didn't remember in the heat of this moment.

I crossed my arms. "You don't get this."

"You're right," Beth said, her lips a straight line.

"Can't you see how much I'm struggling? You couldn't even give me a hug earlier when I shared this unbelievably hard stuff with you. You just kept walking."

She didn't say anything. I probably should have stopped there. But I didn't. "Maybe I was expecting too much from you," I said. "Maybe you're incapable of empathy."

The screaming started. It seemed as if every hurt or slight Beth had felt over the past twenty-some years came pouring out.

Could Scott hear us down in the kitchen?

"Wow," I said.

"Wow is right," she said. "You drop this bombshell on me and expect me to *understand*? This is what you do—what you've *always* done. You don't tell me anything until it's a fait accompli, and then you expect me to jump on board with you."

It wasn't until much later that I realized she wasn't being completely unreasonable. I wasn't the only one on a journey. The other people in my life needed time to process this too. I'd been hiding THIS from myself so well, for so long, that of course I'd also completely hidden it from others, even from my sister, who knew about "the lezzie stuff."

But in my nephew's bedroom, I wasn't thinking that way. I was just thinking about how alone and hurt I felt—and if my sister had reacted like this, how would my mother react? How would my boys?

Beth and I got through dinner, but I was still shaken up. I headed up to Rob's room and went straight to the LaLa page.

My sister compared my "obsession" with thinking I'm gay to how I used to feel about tennis, I wrote.

The LaLas weighed in immediately:

Yeah, because everyone's dying to be gay, right?

You are kidding me. People act like this is a choice.

Why would anyone choose this?

Why indeed? Why would anyone blow up their nobody-has-it-better-than-me life unless they felt they had no other choice?

~

Annie wrote, *Suze, I am on a take-no-prisoners truth-telling roll tonight. You are a lesbian. The only question is: what now? Your only options are stay in your marriage and enjoy all that has to offer, joyfully and wholeheartedly. Or leave your marriage and venture into the unknown life that awaits you, with the opportunity to discover an inner peace, authenticity, and deep, fulfilling love like no other. That's it. And you don't have to decide today, or tomorrow or next week or next month. But decide you must.*

Future Stories

I nestled into the white slipper chair in the corner of my bedroom, ready for my weekly call with Reenie. Since that awful meeting at Starbucks, we'd talked nearly every Sunday but had avoided the topic of my feelings for her. I certainly hadn't told her about the LaLas, let alone Sandy. I felt like a shit lying again—at least by omission—but I didn't know what else to do.

The preschool gala where Evan and I would be honored, where Reenie would sit at our table, was less than a month away. The excitement I'd originally felt about the event had been replaced with dread. How were the three of us going to get through that evening with everything that was going on?

Forget the gala. How were Evan and I going to get through this day, and the one after that, and the one after that?

With no offices to escape to, no in-real-life friends to talk to, no outdoor activities to distract us—Montauk in March was a ghost town—the pressure in the house kept building, but neither Evan nor I seemed willing or able to make a move.

Every day was both the same as it had been before I told Reenie about my feelings for her and completely different. I made coffee and took it upstairs to Evan. We checked in about our days—mostly in monosyllables. He did the crossword. We met for lunch and dinner. Ate mostly in silence. I drank a lot of wine. We went to bed. Rinse and repeat. In the hours in between, we went to separate corners of the house, me often online with the LaLas, and Evan doing who knows what.

When we did talk, it didn't go well.

Like the day I discovered the journal entry I had written in high school about being "rather worried about my sexual preferences" and read it to Evan.

"See, this is real," I said, trying, I guess, to prove to him that THIS wasn't about mommy issues or some one-off attraction to Reenie.

"I don't know why you felt like you needed to read me that," Evan said. "Are you trying to rub this in my face?"

"No, I'm trying to make you believe me."

"Suzette, I fully understand how real your attraction for women is. You don't need to convince me you're gay. It's not up to me. You are equipped to discern this."

He was right, of course. It was up to me. And I knew I was gay—at least I knew I was attracted to women. Although I still hadn't kissed one. Although I still had some doubt about how central physical intimacy was to life. Although I still had some hope I could find my way out of this mess without hurting anyone further and without making a mistake.

Outside my bedroom window as I waited to call Reenie, the sky and sea met precisely at the horizon. It was the kind of day that caused my father, even once he couldn't tie his own shoes or bathe himself, to stretch out his arms and exclaim, "It doesn't get any better than this."

I wished I could be more like him. Grateful for what I had. Able to make peace with my life. It would be so much easier for everyone. It would be so much easier for me.

"Hi," I said softly to Reenie when we connected over FaceTime. I moved my laptop camera to show her the view from the window. "Look how beautiful this is," I said. "How can I give this up?"

I couldn't see then how unfair it was to keep bringing her into my drama and expecting her to help me solve it. But we'd played the same roles for eighteen years—the Talker and the Listener—and neither one of us seemed able to break that pattern.

Reenie's eyes welled up, as they often did when she listened to me. Thank god the Reenie from Starbucks with the hard eyes and the hard voice was gone. The Reenie I knew and loved was back. The Reenie I wanted to melt into.

"What are you hearing inside yourself?" she said.

"If I only knew," I said. "One moment I'm certain I should stay and the next I'm certain I have to leave."

The Voice was sending mixed messages. A few days ago, when I ran along the Old Montauk Highway, the view of the ocean from the top of the hill a half mile from our house took my breath away, as it always did in that spot. *You belong here*, the Voice seemed to be saying. But the next day when I looked out the kitchen window into our backyard, I thought, *I can't keep doing this.*

Reenie nodded. "It might be helpful to imagine what your life could look like in either scenario. Remember those future stories we wrote for church? You could write one for each possibility and see what they tell you."

"That's a good idea," I said. The church visioning exercise had been eye-opening and had spurred the congregation to be more creative about utilizing the church property to better serve marginalized communities.

But when I got off the call with Reenie, I was less certain.

Writing might bring me answers, but when I had written the unspeakable, it had also brought me pain.

~

I started imagining a future story without Evan. I'd have to find a place to live because I'd be the one moving out if we separated or divorced. I was the one who threw the bomb, after all.

As I scrolled through property listings in the area, one caught my eye—a tiny cottage ten minutes from our house, affordable by Hamptons' standards—it looked like the perfect writer's retreat.

A few years ago, when my biggest problem was finding time to write, I had floated the idea to Evan of a "room of my own," a place away from the Montauk house to write in solitude. Maybe I could present this cottage to Evan that way, and it could be an insurance policy too. Somewhere to live if I left Evan.

"I've been looking at real estate," I said sheepishly one morning. "Just to see what's out there." Was it obvious I was planning an exit strategy? "There's an adorable cottage that isn't too expensive. Maybe we just need to give each other some space." I doubted THIS was going to be resolved by space but it definitely wasn't getting resolved by us roaming around the same house 24/7.

"Send the listing to me," he said. "But given where we are, I think it'd be ridiculous for us to buy more real estate."

"Can we just look at it?"

"Sure. Set something up."

~

Another morning answering Evan's questions about my day in monosyllables. Did he want me to open up to him or not? I didn't know how to talk to him anymore. He pulled his bathrobe around him. "I feel like you're slipping away from me," he said, his lips trembling.

It was hard to see my husband cry—to see the pain I was causing—and to know he was right. I was slipping away. To where, I didn't yet know.

My lips trembled too. "I don't know what to do. All I know is THIS is real and it's not going away."

Tears rolled down his cheeks. "I can't tell you what to do, and if you decide you have to be with a woman, it will be very painful for me. But I will accept it and hopefully let you go with grace."

Tears rolled down my cheeks too. "There's no good option here."

Only pain in every direction.

"You want a choice that doesn't involve pain," he said, as if reading my mind. "That choice doesn't exist."

~

Another beginning to my story:

"Let me in!" I screamed as I stood on the front stoop of my best friend's house. Inside, Meg leaned against the locked storm door.

We were laughing, weren't we?

Most weekends when we were in third grade, I'd ride my bike over to Meg's and plop down on the cracked brown leather couch next to her, a giant sack of red pistachios from her dad's restaurant between us. We'd watch shows like *The Munsters* and *The Addams Family* that my mom didn't allow at home and gorge ourselves on pistachios until we were nearly sick, our fingertips deep-pink, our mouths ringed in fuchsia like clowns. I was desperate to be inside a house where TVs blared, newspapers piled up, and cupboards were filled with treats. My house was spotless. Sterile. Silent.

"Let me in!" I screamed again, pressing my body against the glass door, Meg pushing back with both hands.

Suddenly, shards of glass, red everywhere. Meg's arm through the door. Blood everywhere. Meg's screams everywhere. When you push too hard to get what you want, people get hurt.

~

The March wind howled as Evan drove us down a deserted street toward the cottage that was for sale. To our north was Napeague Bay, a popular spot for windsurfing, kayaking, and boating. That day, though, the bay was as empty as the boarded-up houses on Shore Road.

The real estate agent met us in the driveway and led us inside the cottage, which was both adorable and tiny. Adorable, that is, except for the dead baby mouse that greeted us in the entryway, which the agent inexplicably had chosen to leave there. The small bedroom's north-facing window had a sliver of a water view. The backyard patio opened onto a nature preserve.

The cottage looked like a sanctuary. A place to bathe my soul. A way out of this limbo. Space to figure what I really wanted. Too bad it was for sale, not for rent.

Evan opened the door to the shed. "We could keep our paddleboard and kayak here."

I hadn't told him about the future story idea—and maybe I would soon—but it was clear what he wanted our future story to look like. Staying together. Paddleboarding and kayaking. Even if I was gay. And part of me still wanted that too. "I know, it could be perfect," I said.

I pictured myself holing up in the cozy living room with my laptop and a cup of coffee. Finishing my memoir. Starting a new book project. Making peace with my life, like my father had made with his.

Or starting over at fifty-five.

Two very different future stories with the cottage at the center.

~

More days of going through the motions. More silent meals. The cottage wasn't mentioned again, nor was paddleboarding or kayaking.

"Suzette, I can't take this much longer," Evan said after another silent lunch.

"Neither can I." The two of us in this house together constantly. Something had to give.

"What would you think about a trial separation?" I said tentatively. "I think we both need space to figure things out." To me, a trial separation meant exactly that—you weren't sure where you would end up, so you separated to find out what you wanted. Trial separations had worked for my parents—and many LaLas were in them too.

"I'd be open to that," Evan said without hesitation. Apparently I hadn't been the only one considering that.

"Six months, maybe? We could date other people and see where we are."

His face flushed. "*I'm* not interested in dating. And I'm definitely not interested in waiting around for you while you see if there's a better deal out there."

Did he not get this at all? I wasn't looking for "a better deal." This wasn't a game I was playing. I didn't want to blow up his life—or mine. A trial separation was the only way to keep our options open instead of ending things prematurely or staying stuck in this pressure cooker indefinitely. How could he not see that? *I'm your wife of nearly thirty years*, I wanted to say to him, *not a random stranger trying to trick you.*

"That's not what this is about," I said. "I need to figure out how important this longing is inside me, but how can I know if I don't have a chance to find out?"

Because maybe, just maybe, if I slept with a woman—or even kissed one—in real life, I would find out that it wasn't that big of a deal and that would be that.

"You want a free pass, and I'm not willing to give that to you," he said, his voice rising. "You know what my biggest fear is for you? You'll blow up everything we have because you think the grass is greener over there, and then you'll be just as unhappy as you are now. You may get to live out your sexual needs, but you'll be giving up many other things."

Part of me wanted to scream at him and part of me wondered if he was right. Maybe I was one of those people who was destined to be unhappy no matter what. If I was going to be unhappy in either situation, it would be a helluva lot easier staying in the unhappy I knew.

I couldn't see it then, but Evan was right. I did want a free pass. I did want to see if the grass was greener on the other side before I walked away from the life I knew.

And I was determined to find a way to convince Evan to give me that pass.

~

One night when things felt a little less charged between us, I broached the subject of writing future stories, reminding Evan of the ones from the church visioning project. While Reenie hadn't mentioned Evan writing future stories too, maybe if we both did, we could move forward—one way or the other.

"What if we each wrote one about staying together and another about splitting up?" I couldn't say the *D* word yet. Splitting up sounded less permanent, less harsh.

"I like that idea," he said. "How about four scenarios? Good marriage, bad marriage, good divorce, bad divorce."

I nodded. Evan didn't seem to have a problem with the *D* word.

We went off to separate corners to write.

~

My stories flowed easily:

Good marriage

We stay in our house and also buy a writer's cottage. I disappear and work in the cottage when I want to and need to, sometimes days at a time. Evan and I reconnect for dates and sometimes we live under the same roof. I finish my memoir and publish it. I work on new book projects.

Evan and I find a way to be affectionate and loving, which may or may not include sex. We figure that out and also figure out how to meet our sexual needs without going outside the marriage. I occasionally travel by myself and develop new interests and new friendships independent of Evan, and he does the same.

I no longer look for his approval or the approval of others. I learn to trust myself and learn to say what I need and what I want. I'm able to do that without feeling selfish or being worried about being called selfish.

Good divorce

I buy a small house in or near Montauk, close enough to retain relationships I've built here—beach friends, writers group, etc. I date and may or may not end up with another long-term relationship, but I'm happy with myself. I learn to be okay being alone. I write my memoir and publish it. I earn a living as a freelance editor. I'm frugal with my spending, but I find I don't need much. I love my work. I can get lost in it for days, but I have community too—old and new. I practice yoga, exercise, and find ways to stay healthy.

I keep up with Houston friendships—Reenie especially—and go there as often as I can.

My relationship with my family—Will, Patrick, Beth—is different but healthy. They understand and accept me. My mother won't really understand, but we find a way to stay connected. Evan remains part of my life—we develop a deep friendship without the romantic element. We still do things together as a family at times, accepting and embracing any new partners. Evan finds a new partner and is happy, and I am happy for him and them. Sometimes I'm lonely and I wonder what I've done. But for the most part, I feel like me. I can be alone and be happy. I can be with a female partner and be happy. I can live joyfully, like my father did. I am no longer afraid to take risks.

Bad marriage

We stay in the house and may or may not have a writer's cottage. It doesn't matter because the problems are deeper than "needing space." I'm resentful and unhappy and preoccupied by my longing to be with a woman. It takes most of my energy, and I'm not present to Evan or to my life. I spend hours on Facebook and the internet, and I feel empty. I don't finish my memoir. Evan and I go through the motions—vacations, Broadway shows, dinners out—and on the outside, it looks the same—people think we're happy. But I'm not living—I'm pretending all the time.

Bad divorce

I move out and can't cope with the day-to-day, like what do I do when the smoke alarm goes off in the middle of the night? I'm lonely, terribly lonely. I drink and eat excessively.

I watch Evan build a new life with a new woman, and he's happy and I think, *What the hell have I done?*

The boys side with him, and while I have a relationship with them, they spend more time with him. I suspect they blame me for the breakup.

The mutual friends disappear or become his. I still have a few friends and make new ones, but I feel ill at ease in this new life. I wonder if I am really gay or if I totally misread my feelings. I go on some awkward dates and fear I will be alone forever.

My work suffers because I am depressed.

My relationships suffer because I am depressed.

Eventually, even the people who love me and have stood by me tire of me. I want to die.

Finished, I texted Evan.

Printing mine out, he replied. We swapped pages in the living room and went back to our separate corners to read.

~

My heart pounded as I read Evan's stories—especially the good divorce scenario. Since he was "curious by nature," he wrote, he had "enjoyed dating" and had fallen in love again. What made the divorce successful in his mind was that he "almost never compared the old with the new." He "lived in the moment joyfully with gratitude for the past." My heart hurt but I also felt relieved. Maybe I didn't have to feel guilty if this was where we were heading.

But the good marriage story broke me open. Evan would give me space. We'd both develop more independent interests. We'd go to couples counseling and recommit to our marriage. To honor that recommitment, we'd have a private ceremony on the beach on our thirtieth wedding anniversary, which was this August. It would not only be a "good marriage"; it would be a "new marriage."

I wiped a tear from my cheek. A new marriage, a new start. The two of us standing on the beach holding hands, facing each other, trusting we could find a way to love each other with this new understanding of who we were.

Evan believed it was possible to save our marriage with the help of a counselor. Part of me wanted to believe that too.

But the only way I could see our marriage surviving was for me to first find out what it was like to live as a gay woman, which meant having the ability to date. My vision of a trial separation, not his.

Someone had to help us break this impasse.

"Let's find a couples counselor to help us navigate this," I said at dinner the night we shared our future stories. In the past, Evan had been the one suggesting counseling, and I'd always put him off.

He said yes.

I emailed Diane, my therapist, for recommendations. She sent me the names of two counselors, both men, which I wasn't crazy about but those were our options. I scheduled initial consultations; we'd meet with each of them after our trip to Houston for the gala.

Could either of these men help convince Evan to do a trial separation my way? Could we work on our marriage and save it? Did I even want to save it? I didn't know, but having those appointments on the other side of the gala felt like a lifeline.

~

"I couldn't see the way back to my room that night," Reenie said years ago when she told me about a retreat she attended. "Then I noticed there were low lights along the pathway, each one giving just enough light to see the next step. I kept walking, and step by step I made it back."

Heart Friends

During one of her visits to Montauk, Reenie and I walked along the shoreline, hand in hand. She stopped to photograph a flock of piping plovers. Took a closeup of their footprints in the sand. Occasionally, she stooped down to pick up pieces of sea glass and various unusual stones. When she spotted a small heart-shaped stone, she handed it to me. "Here you go, heart friend."

"Heart friends" were friends for life, no matter the circumstances, as opposed to "friends of the road," friendships based on shared experiences that had a more limited life. Reenie and I had learned about these types of friendships from Stan Ott, an instructor in one of our spirituality courses.

Heart friends were precious. You didn't get many in a lifetime. I squeezed Reenie's hand and put the stone in my pocket. I planned to keep it forever.

~

Sunday at noon, four days before the preschool gala, Jenni's Noodle House was practically empty when Reenie and I arrived. We ordered shrimp and vermicelli salads and found a table outside where we could sit undisturbed for hours.

We might need every one of those hours to get through everything I wanted to talk to her about. The LaLas. The future stories Evan and I had written. The feelings for women that weren't going away.

"You would love these women," I said when I told her about the LaLas. "I wish there was some way you could get to know them." I lightly touched her arm, the way she and I used to do all the time. "Are you *sure* you aren't gay?" I said, in retrospect a poor attempt to be playful.

She shook her head. "Suzette, you need to make a choice," she said in that same hard tone she'd used at Starbucks. "You are kidding yourself if you think you can work on your marriage and be involved in this group."

Who did she think she was? She didn't know the whole story. Evan and I would be meeting with *two* couples counselors after we returned to Montauk. If that wasn't working on my marriage, what was?

"Evan's fine with me being in this group." If he was okay with it, why couldn't she be?

"Then Evan's kidding himself too. You need to get very clear on what your goal is: do you want to live out your sexuality or honor your commitments?"

There it was again, a slightly different version of the question she'd posed at Starbucks: would I honor my vows or choose my happiness? Her ex-husband had chosen happiness, which apparently was not the right thing to do.

"That's why this feels impossible," I said. "I want to do the right thing, but I don't know what that is."

"It sounds to me like you've already made your choice. I hear all kinds of energy in your voice when you are talking about this *group*."

She acted like she knew me better than I knew myself. Maybe that was true.

"Anything else you want to tell me?" she said.

I hadn't planned to say anything about Sandy because there wasn't anything to say. I'd cut off contact with her shortly after the New York LaLa trip, not willing to risk Evan finding out or risk further temptation. But as the Talker, I often felt as if I was in a confessional when I was with Reenie, needing to get everything off my chest.

"There is one more thing," I said. "This younger woman in the group and I flirted for a while, but nothing happened. It's over now."

"Suzette, you've already gone outside your marriage," Reenie said, her voice even harder. "You need to own your choices."

"This is hell," I said. Why didn't she understand how hard this was? In the past, her eyes would fill up as she listened to me. But this day her eyes were dry. What did she want me to do? I'd broken off things with Sandy, and I was going to counseling with Evan.

"*You* are keeping yourself *and* Evan in hell by not making a choice."

Maybe she was right, but this was the biggest decision of my life and I wasn't about to rush it. Shit, it had taken me *six years* to decide whether to sell my *house*. Wasn't thirty years of marriage worth spending more time to listen and reflect? Diane, my therapist, had encouraged me to slow down and explore my options.

"Diane said I shouldn't rush," I said.

"Don't pay attention to what I'm saying," Reenie said. "I'm just your *friend*. Pay attention to what Diane is telling you. She's the *professional*. You're paying *her*."

Wow. I'd never heard that kind of talk from her. What was going on?

I tossed and turned Sunday night. I needed more time with Reenie to talk through things. The gala was Thursday. We'd be flying back to New York Friday.

I feel a little greedy asking you this, I texted her, *but do you have ANY more time this week before I leave? Even just an hour?*

Reenie responded. She didn't have another *second* this week.

If a text could talk, I imagined it was using that same hard voice I was becoming all too accustomed to.

What had happened to my heart friend?

~

The night of the gala, Evan and I stepped up to the podium at the country club.

I had gone for Badass rather than Lady Who Lunches with my wardrobe: Navy-blue leather dress, metal belt, stilettos. But as I squinted through the bright lights toward a sea of half-empty wine glasses and the two hundred people—business colleagues, close friends, Evan's cousins, and his siblings who had flown in for the occasion—all who had paid good money to celebrate the school and fete us, I felt like a hypocrite, not a badass. One more night to pretend to the world that Evan and I were the perfect couple.

I cleared my throat and stepped up to the mic. So many people to disappoint—and one person to win back.

"I want to talk about the power of a single invitation and the power of a single yes," I said, looking straight at Reenie.

She had arrived near the end of the cocktail hour with her plus-one, our mutual friend Liza. We'd said hello but that was it. I'd saved a place for Reenie next to me at the table, but Liza had sat there instead. This speech, brief as it was—Evan and I had each been given five minutes—was my chance to publicly declare how much Reenie had changed my life and the lives of the families the preschool served. Maybe in some small way my speech could make up for the fact that Evan and I were the ones being honored—and not her—because no one deserved to be recognized more than Reenie.

Her "come with me and get your hands dirty" invitation and my yes to that invitation had paid dividends we couldn't have imagined then: A special education advocacy group that I initiated. Evan coming on board to provide strong and stable leadership for eight years. The opening of a second preschool, more than tripling the capacity of students, a massive project during Evan's tenure.

"Thank you, Reenie, for that invitation." I tried to meet her eyes, but she wasn't looking at me. "I'm so glad I said yes," I continued. "The power of a single invitation. The power of a single yes. I want to encourage each of you to invite others into this important work. Who knows what will happen if they say yes?"

I could have written a dissertation on saying yes instead of this five-minute speech, and maybe someday I would. Saying yes to the Voice nudging me to ask Reenie to coffee. To selling my house. To bringing groceries to Teresa. But saying yes to the Voice urging me to write the unspeakable? To joining the LaLas? To telling Reenie about my feelings? Apparently those yeses didn't sit right with Reenie.

The audience clapped loudly as I stepped aside for Evan. I tried to catch Reenie's eye again but couldn't. I hated how out of sync we were. Something was going on. Was it jealousy about Evan and me being honored instead of her? Anger about my flirtation with Sandy? Or maybe she was just tired. I had no idea.

~

The Sunday after the gala, I was back in Montauk, curled up in the white slipper chair, a darkening sky behind me. Time for the weekly call with Reenie.

She'd been so cold at the event. The opposite of what I'd expected. I'd thought she'd be proud of me. Pleased about the shoutout in my speech. Hell, it had been a love letter to her, giving her credit for my and Evan's involvement at the preschool.

Something had shifted in our relationship and I didn't like it. Maybe this was what it felt like to have someone you love slip away. But heart friends didn't slip away.

"Hey there," I said when she appeared on my screen.

"Hey," Reenie said.

Thank goodness she was smiling. Seeing her face made me long to run my fingers through her hair. Touch her cheeks. Her lips. Kiss her. Kiss her. Kiss her.

Maybe someday, somehow I would really kiss her.

I'd come close ten years ago when she made another visit to Montauk, this time with our friend Liza. Evan was in Houston that week handling business at the preschool, and the boys were at camp. Dinner that night had been lobster, which had been a hit, as had the prosecco we'd washed it down with. When Liza went upstairs to call her husband, Reenie and I were in the kitchen, cleaning up after dinner. As I laid a salad bowl on the counter, I felt an urge to kiss her, much as I had years earlier when I planted that awkward holy kiss.

The impulse startled me. It had been years since I spent most of my waking hours fantasizing about her. Maybe it was just the prosecco talking.

But there I was in my kitchen, dying to kiss my best friend; instead, I kept doing dishes. Later, I wondered if I would have had the nerve to act on my feelings if Liza hadn't been in the house with us. Probably not.

No, I'd never kiss Reenie unless she signaled she was open to it. I'd learned my lesson from the holy-kiss and head-in-lap incidents. I'd had the opportunity when she visited me in Montauk for several days shortly after my father died; I hadn't even thought about kissing her then. Maybe grief had swallowed up my desire for her. Or maybe I hadn't been willing to risk losing her.

Because I could not bear to lose her.

Like old times, this Sunday we talked for nearly two hours, her voice as soft as her eyes. What a relief to be back in sync.

"Next Sunday, same time?" I said.

"It's a date."

~

We'd had that special in-sync feeling from the start.

January 6, 1999

To: Reenie

From: Suzette

Subject: Does it get any easier?

> Reenie, I feel such a sense of emptiness and disconnection with the moms at school. It's like I'm speaking a language they don't understand. Do you know what I mean? I feel so despairing.

My body filled with warmth when I read her response. Most of the time she felt the same way. She got me. She was the only one who did.

Over the years, our special bond grew. Those magic moments, such as our having the same idea about Evan becoming the executive director of the preschool. We had felt called to undertake projects together: fundraising to rehab a house for the disabled husband of one of Reenie's colleagues, advocating for economically at-risk families in special education, envisioning a preschool on the grounds of our church. Ours was a friendship of depth and commitment unlike any I'd ever known.

We didn't go to the movies or go shopping together or hang out at each other's houses, other than her occasional visits to Montauk. In eighteen years, I'd been invited inside her home only two or three times. And I knew very little about her private life. Because I was the Talker and she was the Listener.

But what mattered was that we were heart friends.

Heart friends who were, thank god, back in sync.

~

After my FaceTime call with Reenie, Evan and I ate dinner together. I drank two glasses of wine. He retired to the couch with the newspaper. I poured another glass of wine and headed upstairs to our bedroom. Stared out the window at the black sky.

There was still so much unresolved with Reenie. The "I was in love with you and I still am" and the shake of her head when I asked if she felt the same way was only the start of a conversation. We had to talk more about *us*. I needed to tell her how I *really* felt about her. I needed to know how she *really* felt about me.

The Voice was urging me to reach out to her—or was it the wine? I typed on my laptop:

> Reenie, I am so grateful to have you in my life. I love you and value what you have to say—and I give your opinions a lot of weight. I

> know ultimately I have to be the one to sort out what is true and right for me. No one—not you, not Diane, not Evan, not the LaLas—can do that for me.
>
> We haven't talked much about you and me—because that's super awkward and uncomfortable. I hope we can get to a place where we can do that. I want to tell you how I really felt and how I really feel now. I want to hear how you felt and how you feel now. I want us to be real with each other.
>
> You've been one of the greatest gifts of my life. I love you.

I hit Send. Based on past experience, it was unlikely she would respond, or she might say there was too much to express in an email. But at least she knew I wanted to talk more about the two of us. And someday, hopefully soon, we would.

~

Monday and Tuesday, no response from her. Wednesday, a huge rainstorm hit Houston. Flooding everywhere, including Reenie's neighborhood.

R u ok, I texted. Nothing. Maybe her power was out? I texted Liza, *R u ok? Have you heard from Reenie?*

Liza texted back. She was fine and Reenie was too.

Something was wrong. I could feel it. I texted Reenie again: *I'm worried about you. Let me know if you are okay.*

She finally responded. Her house was dry as a bone.

One terse line after a deluge from me. Maybe she was just busy. I'd ask Sunday afternoon during our call.

Sunday morning, I carried two mugs of coffee upstairs and sat down at my desk to read my email before Evan and I checked in about our day.

He and I were still going through the motions with everything, trying to hang on until our counseling appointments the following week where hopefully we'd find someone to help us "work on our marriage" (Evan's idea) or break the impasse on what a trial separation could look like (my idea).

I opened my inbox: junk mail, junk mail, junk mail.

Then I saw Reenie's email address. My heart raced. A reply to my email from a week ago. At 10:24 p.m. Houston time. She wasn't usually up that late.

This couldn't be good. She had ignored me all week. We were talking this afternoon. What did she have to say that couldn't wait?

My hand shook as I opened the email. "Suzette," it started. Not "Dear Suzette," but "Suzette." She had made a decision: she needed to pull away from this relationship.

Pull away? WTF did that mean? Take a break for a few days? A month? Or was this the end?

NOOOOOOOOOOO.

She was canceling our FaceTime call scheduled for this afternoon. She had heard how I felt and told me how she felt, and she had nothing more to say on the subject. She hoped I would find the voice I needed to listen to. She'd pray for me to find the path to my true happiness. Which apparently wouldn't be with her. She signed off with her name. No "love." No "best wishes." No "until next time."

If it was possible to cycle through the stages of grief—shock and denial, pain and guilt, anger and bargaining, depression—in a single moment, I did. I read the email one more time and shut my laptop. Because if I couldn't see her words, maybe I could pretend this was a bad dream.

An eight-sentence email ending an eighteen-year friendship.

The signs that she was pulling away had been there for months, ever since our meeting at Starbucks, but I'd ignored them, instead clinging to her promise that nothing would change between us. That I would never lose her. That I was her heart friend, her friend for life.

But in that moment, I had no perspective. All I had was shock. Devastation. Disbelief.

"You ready to talk?" Evan called from the bedroom.

The last thing I felt like doing was chitchatting with him. I wanted to crawl back into bed and never get up. Start the day over and have it be a day I didn't receive a breakup email from the woman I loved. But it wasn't as if I could tell him I wanted to abandon our morning routine because Reenie dumped me.

"Sure," I said. I could go through the motions for another day.

After we talked about our plans, I stood up, ready to head to the shower.

"You talking to Reenie this afternoon?" Evan asked.

"No." My eyes filled up. I hadn't planned on saying anything to him—I didn't want to hurt him further—but I wasn't going to flat-out lie either.

"We were supposed to FaceTime at four, but this morning I got a really disorienting email from her."

I walked over to my laptop and read the email to him, leaving out the more incriminating parts, not wanting to pour more salt on his wounds.

"I'm sorry," he said.

"Thanks." There wasn't much more to say. I couldn't tell him my heart had a gaping hole in it. He didn't need me to tell him what it felt like to have a broken heart. He knew that feeling all too well.

By lunchtime, I'd memorized her email.

That afternoon I sat at my laptop and scrutinized every word. Wondered how many times she'd rewritten it. Wondered if she'd been struggling with it all week. Wondered if she'd slept at all after sending it.

The more I looked at her message, the more it seemed like each sentence was a topic sentence with the rest of the paragraph missing. I was less clear about her feelings than I had been before. The only clear part was that she didn't want to have anything to do with me. And what was with the "Suzette" and the "Reenie" without any "Dear" or "Love"? So curt. So cold.

This makes me terribly sad. I emailed her shortly before we were supposed to have talked. *And, if it's what you need to do, I will respect that.*

I was an adult, not a lovesick puppy anymore.

The day dragged on. What was she doing with the two hours we would have been talking? How would I spend Sunday afternoons from now on? Would I ever talk to her again?

"I'm not going anywhere," she said to me years ago during an early crisis in our friendship. "I'll be at the boys' graduations, their weddings. We're heart friends, remember?"

I woke up Monday with a heaviness I hadn't felt since my dad died five years earlier. Tuesday the heaviness was still there. I texted her: *Can we talk? Will you at least give me the courtesy to tell me what's going on?*

The silence on the other end annihilated me.

~

Valentine's Day 1981. Alan gave me a dozen red roses and a card expressing his undying love. A week later he broke up with me. No specific reason, just that he knew it wasn't right. If there were signs along the way, I missed them, just as I missed them with Reenie. That day in 1981, I learned what it felt like to have a broken heart.

This day, thirty-five years later, was at least as devastating.

Sticky Wicket

The first couples counselor Evan and I interviewed in late April, two weeks after the gala, didn't think our situation was complicated. "It's simple," he said, looking straight at me. "You want to date. Evan won't agree to it. You have to decide what's more important."

Neither one of us appreciated his quick dismissal of our situation, so we moved on to Steve, Counselor #2.

"Suzette professed her love to Reenie," Evan said at our first appointment with Steve, "and it was unrequited."

I winced. Why did he insist on such formal language to describe what had gone on between Reenie and me? But it didn't matter. Reenie was gone. Gone.

We told Steve about our impasse with respect to dating and a trial separation. "Your situation is a sticky wicket, for sure," Steve said as he wrapped up the session. "But in all the years I've been doing this, the two of you are among the best communicators I've met. If anyone can find a way out of this, it's you two."

After I got home, I Googled "sticky wicket." Merriam-Webster defined it as "a difficult or delicate problem or situation." The metaphor came from cricket, referring to soft or muddy ground around a wicket that made it difficult for a batsman because the bounce of the ball was hard to predict.

A fucking sticky wicket: whether to risk everything for a life I'd been living only in my head.

~

With Steve's help, Evan and I decided we would stick it out through the summer and separate in September. That was the only way to keep our separation on the down-low, which was a priority for me because what if this gay thing turned out to be a big nothing and Evan and I got back together? We couldn't "unring the bell" of everyone knowing I had questioned my sexuality and speculating about what went on in our bedroom.

With the summer plans we already had in place, a quiet separation any earlier would have been impossible. My niece's high school graduation and Patrick's college graduation were in June. July and August were prime time on the beach with friends. Besides, it would have been difficult for me to find a place to move into during the high tourist season in Montauk. I called the real estate agent about the cottage Evan and I had seen in March. It hadn't sold yet, and it was available for an offseason rental, September–June. Evan and I signed the lease. We'd tell anyone who asked that it was a writer's retreat.

All we had to do was pretend all was well for the next three months and figure out how and when we would eventually break the news that we had separated.

If Beth's reaction was any indication, this was not going to be easy. I filled her in on the plan: "We're not telling people, not even the boys," I said. When she made a quick visit to Montauk early in the summer, I offered to drive her by the cottage. "No, I don't want to see the cottage," she said. "I hate this. I don't want to talk about this."

~

"I've applied to volunteer at Iona," Evan said one night over dinner. "They need help starting in September."

This wasn't completely random. Evan had been wanting to visit the Scottish isle ever since my pilgrimage there fourteen years ago.

The Iona Community relied on volunteers to operate programs and provide hospitality to guests. Before THIS started, Evan had floated the idea of the two of us volunteering there together. How long had he been thinking about going? He certainly hadn't mentioned it to me. Our new normal—considering futures that didn't include the other.

"That's great." My mind started spinning. It was better than great. It was the perfect cover story for a low-risk, short-term separation and a possible way out of this sticky wicket. I imagined telling people about Evan's great Scottish adventure. And while he still wouldn't agree to a trial separation with dating, seven weeks could be enough time for me to see if I really wanted to live alone. If I really wanted to leave him permanently.

A few weeks later, Iona offered Evan a spot. He'd start right after Labor Day and return in late October.

Seven weeks apart, without anyone having to know why. The perfect gift from the universe.

~

"Good thing Evan's going to be across the ocean," Steve said, smiling at me as we hammered out the terms of a short-term separation agreement, "because whatever can break probably will, and you won't be tempted to run and ask him to fix it." I laughed, but shit, was I going to be able to do this? The separation agreement also covered dating—or more accurately, no dating. I could "explore" but nothing more. Which would have to be enough for seven weeks.

The boys said "wow" and "cool" when we told them about Evan's adventure. When they came out to Montauk for a weekend, I drove them by the cottage—"It's a writer's retreat!"—and deflected the few questions they had.

A couple of friends asked me if I was going to fly over to Scotland and visit Evan.

I smiled. "No way! I'm looking forward to him being gone." We all laughed. Funny, wasn't it?

Beth said, "Good, this will give you some breathing room."

She sounded softer. Maybe she was starting to get it.

My mother said, "Oh?" but didn't ask questions.

And Reenie? She'd have to find out about Evan's adventure from Facebook. Maybe she'd read between the lines and figure out what was going on, or maybe she wouldn't care.

~

"Want to go for a walk?" I asked Mom in August after we'd been on the beach for about an hour. I couldn't take another second of sitting next to her with her arms crossed and lips pursed.

"Sure," she said.

After we walked in silence for a few minutes, she peppered me with questions: When was Evan leaving for Iona? How was he going to get to the airport? When was he coming back? Transactional talk, the main kind of talking she and I did.

"He's coming back in late October," I said.

"You're going to miss him, aren't you?" she said.

It would be easy to say yes and keep up the pretense.

I'd learned to be careful with what I shared with her. Years ago, when I emailed to say I was applying to a spirituality program that would require me to be out of town three weeks a year, she had responded: *I can't believe you'd leave your young children that long.*

I'd filed that hurt away. Kept things light whenever possible.

But maybe this was an opening to begin sharing my truth, drip by drip.

"We actually need some space from each other," I said. "We've been having a few problems." Drip. Drip.

"Problems? Evan's such a great guy."

"Yes, he is." I told her about the cottage and that I'd be staying there part of the fall.

She didn't say a word.

"It's going to be okay," I said.

"Do Will and Patrick know?"

"They know about the cottage but not about the problems."

I was looking at the ocean and not her, but I imagined she was shaking her head and thinking, *How could my daughter have screwed up her life with this perfect man?*

~

Another beginning to my story:

As I walked to Chester Heights, a small shopping area near my childhood home, I fingered the wad of dollar bills stuffed in the front pocket of my navy pea coat. Money to buy the milk Mom asked me to pick up and treat myself to candy.

I had taken my usual detour around the grimy tunnel where the newspapers for my paper routes were dropped off and now stood on the edge of a small stream. I loved dancing across the rocks that separated one side from the other. Some days that crossing was easy—the rocks were dry. Other days they were slippery or underwater.

"I don't want you crossing that stream," Mom had said to Beth and me. "It's too dangerous." It was one of her many rules. No gum. No bikes with banana seats. Yes to *Mr. Ed* and *Leave It to Beaver*, no to *Green Acres* and *Gilligan's Island*.

But the stream was so much fun to cross, and how would Mom ever know I'd disobeyed? That day, I lost my balance and fell into the water. Exactly what my mother had warned me about.

~

"Pizza on the beach tonight! Who's in?" my friend Andrea asked our beach group on one of several weekends that summer I'd sat with them pretending everything was okay. Answering questions about our upcoming thirtieth wedding anniversary. Swallowing my grief over losing Reenie. Not knowing whether I'd ever find a way out of this sticky wicket.

I looked at Evan. "Yes?"

"Why not?" he said. As hard as it was to pretend, maybe it was better than going back to a silent house.

A few hours later, twenty of us circled up in our beach chairs, awaiting the pizza delivery. "Is that rain?" someone said. We looked at each other: Run to someone's house before it starts pouring, or wait it out?

"Evan?" someone else said.

The group's weather expert, Evan was already checking the radar on his phone. "It's going to pass in a bit." We relaxed in our chairs. One of the teens set up a speaker on a boogie board and blasted her playlist.

People started dancing. Evan pulled me from my chair. We swayed together as raindrops fell softly, his arm around me and my head on his chest.

This felt right. This felt real.

Nothing was settled yet. We were just going to be apart for seven weeks. Maybe I would decide I could do this after all. I could continue to choose this life, as Alice, my former therapist, had suggested a little more than a year ago. And if the day came when I couldn't do it anymore, I could make a different choice.

I lifted my head from Evan's chest and kissed him lightly on the lips. He drew me in closer.

~

We flew to Wyoming for our thirtieth anniversary. Rather than take a splashy trip or do nothing at all, we decided to stay in a no-frills retreat center. It felt like the appropriate way to mark the occasion under the circumstances, plus it had the added benefit of keeping friends and family from wondering why we weren't doing anything for this "big" anniversary.

Would Evan ask me to have sex? It was our anniversary, after all. We hadn't been intimate in months.

I could save him from an awkward ask. That was the least I could do.

I reached over the armrest and touched his sleeve. "How about if we make love on the twenty-third?"

"I would like that," he said quietly.

~

My stomach fluttered when the retreat leader mentioned her wife. Was this a harbinger of what our separation was going to be like? Lesbians everywhere, all out of reach.

~

The morning of our anniversary, Evan and I walked to an outdoor chapel and sat on a bench overlooking a lake. "Let's remember the good," one of us said to the other.

With tears in our eyes, we sifted through the years. The chicken pox on our wedding day and the photos that needed retouching. That magical pink line on the home pregnancy test after so much disappointment. Our fifth anniversary: me nearly nine months pregnant, Evan giving me the diamond anniversary band I was still wearing. Our tenth anniversary? Neither of us could remember much with two kids under five.

"The thing I'm most proud of," Evan said, "is the way we raised Will and Patrick."

"Me too. No one can take that from us." I took his hand, tears spilling down my cheeks. "I'm so sorry, Evan."

He nodded, not saying anything.

It was as if we both knew we had just eulogized our marriage.

After dinner, we sat in rocking chairs on the front porch of our cabin and sipped the split of champagne we had picked up on the way to the retreat center. "To thirty good years," Evan said, clinking my plastic cup with his.

"Yes," I said, raising my cup to him.

A half hour later, I climbed into bed and fell asleep.

"I'm so sorry," I said to Evan the next morning. "I promise we'll make love tonight."

The hurt in his eyes killed me. Another broken promise.

That night, we did make love. It was bittersweet. I wouldn't miss it and yet I would. I loved this man. Afterward, we held each other and cried, as if we both knew how long the odds were that we'd add onto the thirty years of good.

~

Labor Day, Evan hugged me tightly at the Montauk train station. "See you at the end of October," he said as if he was only going to be gone for the weekend. The tone of his voice broke my heart. He was trying to be brave, and I was too. For the past thirty years, we'd never been apart for more than a couple of weeks.

"Text me when you get to Scotland," I said. "I love you."

"I love you too."

Seven weeks to see what it felt like to live by myself for the first time. Seven weeks to "explore" without breaking the no-dating rules. Seven weeks to keep up this charade with my mother, my boys, and my in-real-life friends.

Seven weeks to listen for the Voice and hopefully find my way out of this sticky wicket, which maybe wasn't all that sticky after all. Counselor #1 had been right. This wasn't complicated. There was nothing further to talk about. No middle ground. No free pass to see if the grass was greener on the gay side. Only two choices remained: a safe one and another that would blow up my entire family's life.

Evan hoisted his backpack over his shoulder, grabbed the handle of his rolling bag, and walked the length of the platform. Before stepping onto the train, he turned and waved.

"Bye," I mouthed and blew him a kiss.

In seven weeks, I had to choose.

Brave

In a Facebook post, Elizabeth Gilbert, author of the blockbuster memoir *Eat, Pray, Love*, declared her romantic love for her female best friend who had recently been diagnosed with pancreatic cancer. The beauty—and the bravery—of the post took my breath away.

I wanted to forward it to Beth. Maybe it would help her understand what I was going through. I wanted to forward it to Reenie and say, "See, I'm not the only one this happens to."

But sharing with Beth risked pushing her away further. And sharing with Reenie? That would be stupid. I could only imagine her blocking me from ever contacting her again.

Instead, I posted it on my Facebook page with one word: *Brave*. Likely, Evan, my mom, Beth, and some friends would see it. My boys weren't on Facebook much. And Reenie? For all I knew, she had unfollowed me. Maybe the post would open some minds. Prime the pump for hard conversations. If I ever found the strength to be as brave.

~

My Subaru was packed to the gills. Clothes for the next seven weeks. A file box overflowing with notes for my memoir. Armloads of books. Laptop and printer. Framed photos of the boys.

Technically, I could have stayed in the Montauk house until Evan returned. But that would have been too easy, too close to my old life. I had to get a taste of what it would really be like to be on my own.

Before leaving, I did a final walkthrough to see if I wanted to take anything else with me. In Evan's study, twelve black leatherbound photo albums lined the bottom shelf of the built-in bookcases, albums I'd painstakingly organized since the boys were babies. I couldn't bear to look through them.

But shit. Photos of Reenie were in one of the albums. Some from a surprise party I'd thrown for her fiftieth birthday, a year after we met. Others from her first trip to Montauk when I planted that holy kiss. I wanted to protect Evan from seeing those photos again—and I wanted them for myself. Reenie had hurt me terribly, but I still loved her, still missed her.

I went straight to the album labeled "1998–1999" and pulled out the photos of her. So young—younger than I was now—so beautiful. No wonder I'd fallen for her.

I tucked the pictures inside a file box next to my memoir notes. Reenie might no longer be in my life, but she was coming to the cottage with me one way or the other.

~

The owner of the cottage handed me a key. "Welcome!" she said. "Text if you need anything."

I loved it here already. The sunlight flooding the living room. The sliver of bay visible from the bedroom window. The nature preserve in back. Soon, my only neighbors would be deer and birds. The tiny cottages surrounding mine were mostly occupied only from Memorial Day to Labor Day.

I walked across the street to the beach. Not a soul there. I imagined packing a picnic, a good book, my journal. Breathing. Cutting through the voices competing for my attention and listening for what was true. Being brave and getting off the fence.

~

Night #1

A light breeze floated through the bedroom windows but not the roar from the ocean I was accustomed to. It was so quiet here.

I grabbed *Big Magic*, Elizabeth Gilbert's book about the creative process, from my nightstand. She had chosen brave. Brave enough to stop pretending. Brave enough to end her marriage and face whatever consequences her truth had for her career, for her life. Brave enough to be her true self. I wondered if she'd already had her later-in-life epiphany when she wrote *Big Magic*. Maybe opening up creatively allowed a person to live brave in other ways. Or living brave opened up one's creativity. Who knew.

I placed the book back on the nightstand and turned off the light. So quiet. Maybe I needed to buy a white noise machine.

A scratching noise. The pipes? The noise was coming from inside the wall.

I thought of the dead baby mouse in the entry when Evan and I first saw the cottage. Fuck, that scratching could be a mouse. Maybe a whole family of them. I shut the bedroom door. Maybe if I couldn't hear them, they'd disappear. Maybe this was my overactive imagination.

The next morning, I stared at the dark circles under my eyes. Evan was three thousand miles away, Reenie was still MIA, and Mom, who was five miles away and hadn't even seen the cottage yet, was absolutely not going to hear a single word about mice, imaginary or real.

Day #2

I pulled into my mother's driveway to take her to yoga. She was standing there, as I knew she would be. If Mom was anything, she was prompt. More precisely, she was early. No matter what time I was supposed to arrive, she would already be in the driveway—or in colder weather, standing vigil at the side door, coat, hat, and boots on. Even when I was early, I was late.

"How about I show you the cottage?" I said after yoga. I braced myself, fearing she'd react like my sister had earlier in the summer when I offered to drive by.

"Okay," Mom said. Her tone was flat, which didn't surprise me, but at least she was willing to take a look.

"Here we are!" I said ten minutes later. Maybe if I acted enthusiastically, she would too.

"Very nice," she said. My heart lifted. She was trying.

I opened the screen door and scanned the kitchen floor. Thank goodness, no sign of mice.

She stood in the entry, clutching her pocketbook. "How long is the lease?"

"Nine months."

"You're staying here nine months? Are there other full-time residents? Is there any outdoor lighting? I don't like the idea of you out here all alone."

"I'll be fine. Let me show you around."

She followed me through the cottage, not saying much, and returned to the entryway, still clutching her pocketbook. "I'm ready."

She was ready?

"Why don't you stay for lunch?"

"No, I'm ready to go home."

"Okay," I said, my okay as flat as hers had been earlier. But it was not okay. If there was ever a time I needed support from a parent, it was now.

Day #3

Printer jam.

I sighed, remembering Steve's words from our couple's counseling session: "Whatever can break, will."

Damn, I hated how dependent I was on Evan to fix things, big and small. I used to marvel about all the mechanical things Reenie knew how to do. I guess when you are single you have to figure out things on your own. For at least the next seven weeks, I would have to deal with things I'd been able to avoid for decades. Like mice infestations and broken printers, not to mention shit I hadn't even thought about yet.

I Googled the error message on the printer. Did everything Google told me to do. Nothing. Called Epson support. A tech talked me through options—none of which worked—and asked how old the printer was. I searched through my Amazon orders to discover it had been purchased within the past year and was still under warranty.

"Can you take a screenshot of the invoice and email it to me?" the tech said.

A screenshot? I had no idea how to do that.

The tech talked me through it, and on my fourth try, victory!

Fasten ink cartridge side with tape. Done.

Put broken printer in box to mail back to Amazon.

I couldn't figure out how to position the four giant Styrofoam blocks that were supposed to protect the printer. I was back in ninth-grade geometry again, the one blemish on my high school record, unable to solve the proof.

I can't even pack a goddamn box.

I thought of a passage I'd recently read in Glennon Doyle's memoir *Love Warrior*. Recently separated from her husband, Glennon realizes that she doesn't know how her life works, which makes her feel powerless. Example: her family can't eat anything from a jar because she can't open jars.

Jars I could handle. But boxes? They brought me to my knees.

Week #2

Another night of rustling in the walls. I opened the white noise app on my phone and closed the bedroom door.

The next day the damn mouse was on a shelf in the pantry, biting through the plastic on a bag of spaghetti.

"Go away," I screamed, batting it with a broom.

If I could have stepped out of the horror of the moment, this was an *I Love Lucy* slapstick scene if there ever was one. I just didn't have an Ethel or Ricky or Fred—or Evan—by my side to help.

I texted an SOS to my landlord. Her husband came over with four mousetraps and a jar of peanut butter.

He put a dab on each trap. "They like this," he said.

He was right. The next morning there was a very dead mouse in one of those traps. I put on rubber gloves and scooped the trap into a dustpan.

Jesus, how am I going to get this thing out of the trap? I walked into the backyard, holding my breath and averting my eyes from the mouse. I blurred my eyes so I could see its general position but not see it too well—and released the spring. "Ugh, ugh, ugh." I flung it into the nature preserve.

I did it. Another small victory, another hard thing.

~

"I'm excited," I whispered to Beth as the curtain rose for *The Color Purple* matinee at the Bernard B. Jacobs Theatre on Broadway.

I was also excited—and terrified—about my plans for the evening: a trip to the Cubbyhole, one of the few remaining lesbian bars in New York City.

As the first act of *The Color Purple* unfolded, the two female leads seemed to be dancing around each other. What was going on between them? Were they flirting? Was that a kiss?

Had I missed the lesbian subplot in the movie when I'd seen it, or had I just not been paying attention to lesbian stuff then?

"This is incredible," Beth said during intermission.

"I know!" Was she picking up on the lesbian thing too?

That was one of the best musicals I've ever seen," Beth said as we walked out of the theater.

"I agree." Did I dare mention the lesbian stuff? What if she still didn't want to talk about this? But still, maybe I could dip a toe in.

"Did you notice the gay theme?" I said cautiously. "I don't remember that from the movie."

"I didn't remember it either."

We continued walking. I didn't want to push her further. Risk getting the door slammed in my face again.

"I read the Elizabeth Gilbert post you shared on Facebook," Beth said a few minutes later. My heart raced. Was she opening a door? Or was she annoyed or embarrassed I had inadvertently outed myself? *Had I?* Would my friends put the pieces together? Later, I would see the post as a breadcrumb I left, almost begging for people to notice what was going on with me.

"I thought about sending that to you to start a dialogue," I said, "but I didn't. I'm trying to respect your need for space—that you will let me know when you are ready to talk."

"I love that saying that the teacher will appear when the student is ready," Beth said.

"Are you telling me you're ready?" I asked.

"I'm getting there."

I wanted to hug her. Shout hallelujah. Raise my arms to the heavens. But I kept walking, my step a little lighter.

Still, I was not about to tell my sister I was heading to a lesbian bar in a few hours.

~

"Dating" was not okay but "exploring" was. Which to me meant hanging out with lesbians but not crossing a line. But the only lesbians I knew were LaLas, and to my knowledge, no LaLas lived within fifty miles of me. To Manhattan I would go. I crowdsourced "lesbian exploring" recommendations from the LaLas.

Definitely the Cubbyhole, everyone said.

I had pleaded for a wingwoman, but no one was available.

I'd never walked into a bar by myself, let alone a lesbian one.

I stood outside the Cubbyhole and leaned against a light pole. Inside, women were talking. Smiling. Playfully touching each other. It was like being at the Central Park concert all over again, me on one side of the fence, the lesbians on the other. I so wanted to leap to the other side.

But the thought of literally stepping over the threshold of that bar, into a world I wanted to be part of and wanted to know and at the same time was terrified of being part of and knowing, kept me leaning against that light pole.

I. Could. *Not*. Do. This.

Maybe I couldn't do any of this.

Go, the Voice said. *You are going to be so disappointed in yourself if you don't.*

This was ridiculous. If I couldn't walk into a bar, how could I possibly think I could leave Evan and build a new life? Fuck. What was the worst thing that could happen? I could look like a fool and leave. I could survive that humiliation.

I. *Could*. Do. This.

I went inside and ordered a Blue Moon. Stood at a counter near the same window I'd looked through a few minutes earlier. Made a bargain with myself. *You can leave after you finish the beer.*

When my glass was half empty, three young women came over and introduced themselves.

"Tell me your story," one of them said to me. I told them about Reenie and the LaLas, and how scared I had been to walk into the bar. They high-fived me and said I should just have fun. I ordered a second beer. I was having fun. I was a fifty-five-year-old woman in a lesbian bar hanging out with three women who were my boys' age.

"Let's do shots!" one of the women said.

I smiled and shook my head. I'd had enough to drink. I had to stay in control. I had to follow the rules. Although I couldn't wait to break them.

I told the young women goodbye and practically skipped to the subway. One small step toward life on the other side.

Week #3

I sat at the kitchen counter, waiting to FaceTime Evan. I was surprised at how little I'd missed him so far. There'd been one night when I was preparing a corn-and-basil pasta dish, something I'd made a few times for the two of us, that I'd felt particularly lonely and sad. But for the most part, I'd been content being alone in the cottage, save for, of course, my rodent roommates.

"Where are you?" I said when we connected.

Evan laughed. "I'm in the supply closet. There's not a lot of privacy here." Neither of us commented on the irony of him being the one in the closet.

He told me about his roommates, his work duties—folding laundry, making beds—his awe of the isle's physical beauty, the spiritual community he had become part of. He sounded tired, but happy.

Seeing him in that closet with a scruffy beard and hearing his voice nearly broke me. Maybe I'd been guarding my heart all this time. I did miss him. This was why you separated, I reminded myself. To get a taste of what life without Evan would be like.

I still had options. I could still go back to him, if he still wanted me.

~

Will, Patrick, and I perused our brunch menus at the Midtown Manhattan restaurant.

I couldn't bear lying to them, pretending everything was fine, but was it fair to blow up their lives in a public place? It didn't really matter when and where I told the boys. It was going to be awful, no matter what. Maybe they'd open the door to the conversation, like they had in Costa Rica when they'd asked me about my book.

We chatted about vacations, jobs, Patrick's girlfriend. "Have you guys talked to Dad?" I asked. If they weren't going to open the door, maybe I could crack it open.

They'd emailed with him a few times. We joked about the irony of Evan doing laundry and making beds as his job, since he rarely did either at home.

My heart sank as the waiter cleared our plates. This apparently hadn't been the time or place to tell them their mother was gay and that she didn't know if she could stay married to their father.

Was I protecting them or protecting myself? Once they knew my truth, there would be no turning back.

~

Do all the things you would later say you wished you had done, my father wrote to me a few months before I returned home from my high school study-abroad year in England. He was a healthy man in his early forties, no inkling of the Parkinson's that would befall him a decade later. Was this a warning to not put off my life?

As September turned into October, I hadn't done much of anything I might later say I wished I had. My exploring had been limited to scrolling through the LaLa page and that visit to the Cubbyhole.

I also hadn't done much, if any, of the deep listening I had promised myself I would do.

Listening. Another hard thing.

Week #4, Day #1

I dug out my notebook from the discernment course I'd taken seventeen years ago where I'd copied down parts of the instructor's lecture word for word: *The best a person can do is "relative certitude," to say that she has listened to the best of her ability, that she was as clear as she could be.*

Relative certitude was fine and dandy when the stakes were low, like packing away my tennis skirts without knowing what was next. But when the stakes were astronomical, like they were here? Damn, I wanted something closer to absolute certainty. What to do about my marriage was a decision I couldn't get wrong.

Had I listened to the best of my ability? Probably not. Constantly being on social media wasn't conducive to deep listening.

I needed quiet so I could hear my own voice.

One week. I would fast from Facebook and the LaLas and all the other voices distracting me and try to hear my voice again.

Day #2

I kept reaching for my phone. Damn, I missed the LaLas.

Jennifer Finney Boylan's memoir *She's Not There: A Life in Two Genders* would have to keep me company instead.

"I often woke up and lay there in the dark," Boylan wrote on page 102. "Usually this was about a quarter to four. I'm the wrong person, I thought. I'm living the wrong life, in the wrong body."

All those moments when I felt "not this." At the high school New Year's Eve party. At the law firm. With the moms at the boys' school. On the tennis court. In my perfectly decorated big house. Feeling like something was off, that I wasn't living my life, but not knowing why or how to live differently.

Boylan continued, "To which I would respond: You're a maniac. An idiot. You have a life a lot of other people dream about, a life so full of blessings that your heart hurts."

I felt like the author was traveling inside my head. The guilt, the guilt, the guilt. All those years thinking I was an ingrate when I couldn't be happier with my life.

Day #3

I'd wanted yes-or-no/right-or-wrong answers after I left the law firm. Was this the right professional opportunity to pursue or not? Evan would say, "Just try something. Don't overthink it." But overthinking was my superpower, and besides, there was no "just try it" option here. I was either staying or leaving.

Day #4

"You'll blow up everything we have because you think the grass is greener over there, and then you'll be just as unhappy as you are now." How was I supposed to know if the grass was greener over there if I could only look but not touch?

Day #5

"Are you going to honor your vows or choose your own happiness?" Was it ever right to choose yourself and hurt the people you loved?

Day #6

"There's no choice without pain."

Which pain was I going to choose?

Day #7

I wrapped myself in a sweatshirt blanket and carried my coffee out to the back patio. Listened to the sparrows chirping and the deer stirring in the distance. Looked up into the bright blue sky for answers.

You know what you need to do, the Voice said.

I wanted to be with a woman. Every cell in my body ached for this, had been aching for decades. I had to know what it was like to kiss soft lips. To touch soft skin. To be touched by a woman.

I wasn't willing to go to my grave without knowing what that felt like.

Evan would be back in three weeks. I would tell him what I needed, and if that meant we were done, we would be done. His view of marriage didn't have room for me to experience being with a woman, which was certainly his right. But I was still holding on to a shred of hope that he'd had a change of heart while in Scotland, although I knew that was unlikely. I wasn't ready to unequivocally say I wanted a divorce, but the secret keeping had to end.

It was time to be brave.

To get real.

With everyone in my life.

Even though people were going to get hurt.

There was no choice without pain.

PART THREE

The Family

I texted Will and Patrick: *When can you talk?*

Will was available tomorrow. Patrick tonight.

Tonight.

"What's up, Mom?"

I gulped. If Patrick only knew. "Hey P. I didn't want to get into this at brunch, but I've been struggling with some hard stuff."

"I'm sorry," he said. The tenderness in my younger son's voice never failed to amaze me. He used to ask *me* how *my* day had been when I picked him up from middle school. A preteen boy whose first thought was his mother. Stunning.

"In April, Reenie cut me out of her life," I said, my voice quavering. This seemed like the logical place to start since the boys and I had talked about her in Costa Rica.

"What happened?"

"I'm still not sure," I said. "I think she couldn't deal with hearing about my feelings for her. I really miss her. It's like I've lost my best friend."

"Oh, Mom, that's so hard."

"P, you have no idea."

His gentleness broke me open. "I think I'm gay." I cried as I spilled everything—the cottage, the separation, the real reason his father had gone to Iona. "I don't know what's going to happen to Dad and me." Was that crying I heard on the other end of the receiver? "P, are you crying?"

"Yes," he said between sobs.

Reenie's voice echoed in my head: "You are going to hurt so many people." And I had done exactly that. The ten-year-old who had sobbed on our bed when Evan threatened to leave over a decade ago was sobbing again, but this time I couldn't see him or comfort him or make it better.

"I'm so sad you and Dad have been going through all this pain," Patrick said.

He was sad about *our* pain. He cared about how *we* were feeling. What a kid.

"Now I'm going to have to tell Will," I said. "I don't know how he's going to take it."

"He'll be okay," Patrick said. "He'll be stoic but supportive."

I hoped he was right. "I love you, P. I'm so sorry for all this."

"I love you too, Mom."

An hour later, Patrick emailed:

> Mom, thanks for sharing with me tonight—I know how unbelievably hard it must have been and it took a lot of courage. I know it's a weird thing for a son to say, but I'm really proud of you.
>
> You've always been an incredible mom, and you always will be. No matter what happens in the next few months and years, I will always love you and I hope you will feel comfortable sharing with me wherever this journey takes you.
>
> Let me know if you ever want to talk more about this. I'm always just a call away.

Reenie used to say "my heart is filled to overflowing" when something unexpectedly wonderful happened.

"I'm always just a call away." My heart was filled to overflowing too.

Will called at noon the next day, sounding like he was in a tunnel.

"Where are you?" I asked.

"On a lunch break from jury duty. I got put on a very interesting case. I can't talk about it now—have to keep everything confidential."

"Cool," I said. I would have much rather talked about his jury duty than what I had to say to him.

"We can do this later," I said. "It's kind of heavy."

"No, I'm okay," he said. "Let's talk now."

I started with Reenie, as I had with Patrick. Told him about the separation. Ended with "I think I'm gay," this time without a quiver in my voice. Those words were getting a bit easier to say.

"I know I don't have to say this," Will said, "but I love you, and *this* doesn't bother me at all."

My heart overflowed again. My firstborn—not known for his expressiveness—loved me. Even if I was gay. Even if my gayness might break up our family.

"This doesn't bother me at all." I assumed this was Will's way of saying that he was okay with me being gay, in case I wasn't sure. Will knew that I knew he belonged to a church that wasn't okay with it and that presumably he hung out with people who were also not okay with it. Maybe someday I'd tell him how much that hurt me and that I couldn't understand how he could love me and not be "bothered" by my gayness and still attend a church like that. Maybe someday he'd try to help me understand. But this was not the day for that conversation.

"Thank you, Will," I said. "That means a lot." No tears from me or him, at least none I could hear. Stoic and supportive, just as his brother predicted.

"Are you and Dad getting divorced?" he asked.

"I don't know what's going to happen," I said, which was the truth. "We're trying to figure this out. We love each other very much."

"Okay," he said.

I felt like a shit thinking of my twenty-five-year-old walking back into the courtroom, his head spinning. Would he be okay? Would any of us?

~

Dear Evan:

I wanted to let you know I had a conversation with Patrick last night and a similar one with Will today.

I told them pretty much everything, including the fact I've come to the conclusion that I am gay and don't know what will happen with our marriage.

They were both supportive and had lots of questions. I told them you and I are doing our best to navigate this situation in a loving and respectful way.

I'm telling you this now so you have time to process.

I love you,

Suzette

Thanks for letting me know, Evan replied a few hours later. *We have a lot to talk about when I get back.*

Was there anything left to talk about?

I'd find out in two weeks.

~

"What about your mother?" Reenie had said at Starbucks when she was listing all the people I would hurt if I left Evan.

"I don't know how I will ever tell her," I said.

~

Another beginning:

Easter was almost as much fun as Christmas! This year Mommy bought Beth and me matching pink ruffly dresses, black patent leather purses and shoes, and white gloves. Daddy bought us flowers to pin on our dresses.

The Easter Bunny always left big baskets for Beth and me at the bottom of the stairs. Before anyone else woke up, I crept down the steps as quiet as a mouse to see if he had come yet. He had! My basket was next to Beth's, all wrapped in shiny green plastic. A giant chocolate bunny was inside. I untied the bow, carefully tore away a little bit of the plastic, and took a bite of one of the ears. Yummy! I hoped Mommy wouldn't notice.

But Mommy did. And she was very, very mad. I had ruined everything.

Mommy liked to take a picture of Beth and me when we saw our Easter baskets for the first time. Now the bow was off mine, the plastic was ripped, and my bunny had part of an ear missing.

It wouldn't make for a pretty picture.

~

The day after I talked to Will, I pulled up to Mom's, the house where my parents had made peace with their troubled marriage. Where my mother had managed my father's care for over two decades. Where my father had died five and a half years ago.

The walls of the finished basement were lined with photo collages, starting with spring 1976, when Beth and I helped Mom and Dad put the finishing touches on the house—painting the siding, staining the wood floors. In the TV room, the bookcases were lined with family photos, including a wedding portrait of Evan and me. What would Mom do with that once she heard my news?

She'd invited me over for dinner, why, I can't remember now. Two lobster rolls were already plated when I arrived. I poured us each a glass of wine. Dinner was over in minutes. I poured a second glass for both of us, and we sat down in the living room.

"There's something hard I need to talk to you about," I said.

"Oh?" Mom said. She looked like a fragile bird, all 110 pounds, five feet one inch of her, swallowed up on an overstuffed floral couch.

"Remember when I told you Evan and I were having problems?"

She raised her eyebrows. "Yes?"

"I didn't tell you what was going on. Reenie's been a big part of it. The whole time we've been friends, I've struggled with our relationship. It was intense, unlike any friendship I'd had."

Mom was silent.

I cleared my throat. "I've come to understand that I was in love with her."

I cannot believe I am saying this to my mother.

"Lots of women love their friends," Mom said.

"Yes, but this is different."

"Is this about sex?" she said. "Lots of women don't want to have sex with their husbands."

I almost laughed, but this wasn't funny. That was true—lots of women didn't want to have sex with their husbands. And some of them were gay.

"It's not just about sex. It's about who I am."

Because I was finally starting to realize that THIS was about more than sex, but still I had little understanding of queer identity or culture. And *queer* wasn't a word or label I would have used, nor was it typically used among the later-in-lifers who were, like me, caught up in our own massive disorientation. Most of us were trying to figure out what to do about the awakening that had rocked our personal worlds, not thinking about the bigger issues of identity and culture.

And despite what I said to Mom, a big part of me still thought THIS was mostly about sex. The part of me that believed that if I could just experience sex with a woman at least once in my life, my marriage could possibly survive. That the good-marriage future stories Evan and I had written eight months ago could still become our reality.

"Don't you realize how much Evan does for you?" Mom said.

Wow. My mother didn't consider me capable of doing my own life. Maybe that wasn't surprising, since I had let Evan do so much for me. Still, it hurt. And it made me wonder again whether I could manage on my own.

"I wouldn't have a problem with this if you were in your twenties or thirties . . ." Mom didn't finish her sentence, but she didn't have to. She thought I was too old to start over. Many days I thought the same thing.

Mom shook her head, as if she couldn't believe we were having this conversation.

I couldn't believe it either. I had once thought I would go to my grave—or she'd go to hers—before we'd ever talk about THIS.

"Does Evan know?"

"Yes."

"I feel so bad for him."

So this was how this story was going to play out. Mom had often acted as if she loved Evan—or at least liked him—more than me. Or maybe it was that she liked bragging to her friends about the Suzette & Evan Show and her perfect grandsons. Didn't she realize I felt bad for Evan too?

But I didn't say any of that to her. I just wanted to survive this conversation and get back to the cottage relatively unscathed. "I don't know what's going to happen with Evan and me," I said. "Reenie's out of my life now. I told her how I felt about her, and she couldn't deal with it. So now I'm coming to terms with the fact that it wasn't just her—that I'm attracted to women in general." Forget queer—I couldn't even say I was gay or a lesbian. Not to her. Not yet.

"Do Will and Patrick know?"

"Yes, I just told them."

"How did they react?"

"They were supportive. More than I could have imagined."

The way I hoped you would be.

"The family!" she said, starting to cry. "I feel so bad for the boys, for Evan."

Still not a single expression of empathy for me. Fuck her. But I didn't have the energy for a blowup. I just had to finish this conversation and get out of the house.

"I know it's hard and it's sad," I said. "But everyone will be okay. Evan's already told me he will be fine if we split up." That good-divorce future story said it all.

"Of course he'll be fine," she said. "Women will be lining up for him. He's such a catch."

Also true. But really, Mom. You had to say that now?

"Suzette, you have no idea how hard it is to be alone."

She was right. I'd had a loving spouse since I was twenty-five. Mom had been a widow for over five years—and largely emotionally disconnected from my dad for decades.

"Maybe I won't end up alone," I said. And screw her for assuming that Evan would easily repartner and I wouldn't.

"I'm so lonely," she said, sobbing. "I'm going to be even more alone if you and Evan move away."

Somehow this had become all about her.

"First of all, I don't know if we're definitely getting divorced. And if we do, I don't know if we're moving away. We're a long way from those decisions."

"I'm just so sad about the family," she repeated, dabbing her eyes with a tissue.

I drove back to the cottage, shell-shocked. But I shouldn't have been surprised. It was a lot to expect that someone who had stayed in an unhappy marriage for fifty-plus years would understand someone who might make a different choice.

~

"Suzette? It's Mom."

Her voice sounded strained that afternoon in September 1990, although Mom was typically all business, especially over the phone.

"I have some news about your father."

My heart skipped a beat. "What?"

"He's been diagnosed with Parkinson's disease."

For months, something had been off with Dad. He stared into space; his left arm floated up and down; he couldn't control his bladder; his voice had become raspy, his handwriting tiny.

"His students were mocking him," Mom said. Dad was fifty-two, an eighth-grade social studies teacher.

"Mr. Mullen, we can't hear you," a boy apparently had yelled out.

"Yeah, what did you say?" someone else piled on.

"What a freak," a third said under his breath.

I pictured him trying to ignore the whispers as he concentrated, the chalk in his hand getting damper by the second. Panicking as he tried to remember what he was supposed to write on the blackboard. Staring at the clock—willing the bell to ring, his bladder about to burst.

"I don't think he's going back," Mom said. "He's looking into retiring early."

"Is he there?" I asked. I needed to say something, but what do you say to someone whose life has been upended in a single moment?

"No, he's over at his brother's." Mom's voice was flat. Three months ago, she had retired from teaching and had been consulting and leading workshops in her former school district. She'd been excited about the possibilities for her next chapter.

"I'm sorry, Mom." I didn't know what else to say.

I was twenty-nine, caught up in my own drama with the law firm and my infertility struggles. I didn't understand how devastating the timing was for my dad and for her. I couldn't know that Mom would soon abandon her consulting work, believing it too hard to manage my father's medical situation at the same time. It wouldn't be until many, many years later, when my sister and I were managing her care, that I would have any real appreciation for the heavy toll that choosing duty over desire had exacted on Mom.

~

A few days later, Mom texted: *I have a computer issue.*

Okay, I'll come over this afternoon and see if I can help.

When I arrived, Mom was sitting at her desk, punching keys on her computer.

"What's up?" I said.

"The screen won't go on."

"Let me take a look," I said, waving her away. I wasn't tech-savvy, but since Evan had been gone, I'd had to figure out things on my own, like dealing with a busted printer. I pushed the power button on the screen and it miraculously turned on.

"Fixed," I said, with a smile. If only all my problems were this simple.

I moved over to the blue-and-white striped couch in the TV room. Mom was across from me, in a navy-blue lift chair my parents had bought for Dad when his Parkinson's advanced. Mom had been disdainful of this massive chair that clashed with the beachy feel of the rest of the room, but after Dad's death, it had become her favorite place to park herself.

She and I hadn't seen each other in person since I told her about Reenie. There'd been a few text exchanges, primarily me asking how she was and her responding that she wasn't sleeping and couldn't stop crying.

"Have you talked to Will or Patrick lately?" she asked.

"I talked to Patrick a couple of days ago."

"Did he have a lot of questions for you?"

"What do you mean?"

"About you and Evan. About what's going to happen to the family."

The family. There it was again. *The family.* As if "the family" could exist in only one certain form. As if everything would be ruined if "the family" looked different. "Not really," I said. "He was mainly concerned with how I'm doing." Like I wished she would be.

"Suzette, I don't understand you. How can you risk everything and destroy everything you have? What if you try this and it doesn't make you happy?"

Maybe Mom asked Dad the same questions all those years ago after he left. Maybe she used fear to get him to come back. Maybe he ended up believing safe choices were better than discovering the grass wasn't greener on the other side.

Or maybe they had simply done the right thing for their marriage.

But those were questions for another day. This day I wished my mother would empathize instead of criticize, which was what I told her. She didn't have to understand—I hardly understood myself. I just wanted to feel loved.

~

Dad had had an easier time showing love.

"Let's go to Camp Hero," a coworker of mine at Gosman's Clam Bar said one night in the summer of 1980.

I rarely went out after work. After nine hours on my feet dealing with tourists, I was exhausted. But that night I said yes and offered to drive so I wouldn't have to worry about being in a car with a drunk driver.

A few of us piled into my parents' 1978 silver Buick station wagon, a case of Budweiser in the wayback. Ten minutes later, I turned into Camp Hero State Park and searched for a place to park. It was dark, oh so dark, the ground beneath the wheels sandier and sandier. We ended up in a ditch.

Shit. I gunned the gas pedal but we weren't going anywhere.

"Stop!" someone said. "You're going to blow out the transmission."

The car was two years old, only the second new car my parents had ever bought, a '65 red Buick station wagon being the first.

Shit. We tried to push the car out of the ditch. Nothing.

I can't remember how we reached Dad, but somehow he appeared on the scene, and with his help, we pushed the station wagon out of the ditch.

Dad never chastised me for my stupidity or lack of judgment. He put his arm around me and helped me solve the problem.

Coming Out

The night before Evan returned from Iona, I lay in bed reading *A Little Life*, a novel by Hanya Yanagihara.

"Relationships never provide you with *everything*," Yanagihara wrote. "They provide you with *some* things. You take all the things you want from a person—sexual chemistry, let's say, or good conversation, or financial support, or intellectual compatibility, or niceness, or loyalty—and you get to pick three of those things. . . . The rest you have to look for elsewhere. It's only in the movies that you find someone who gives you all of those things."

The worldview of a character in a novel, but still. What if it were true? Evan had basically said the same thing months ago when he suggested I thought the grass was greener on the other side. *You'll be sexually satisfied, but what about everything else?* he had said, or something like that. I did believe relationships required compromise, and Evan checked pretty much every box except for one.

How important is sex? I had asked the LaLas months ago, still attached to the idea that being gay was about who I had sex with and not much of anything else. Queer community, queer identity, "queerness" hadn't even entered my mind.

I wished I hadn't read that passage. My mind was made up. Damn, I hoped this wasn't an eleventh-hour message from the universe trying to stop me from making the biggest mistake of my life.

~

I think I know what I want out of life, I wrote to Evan, my boyfriend of one year, when I was a first-year law student:

1. a loving husband and family
2. a nice home
3. a job that stimulates and challenges me but doesn't control me
4. enough money to live a "comfortable" lifestyle

With the exception of the job, I got the life I wanted.

~

When I woke up on the day that my life would change, I was stunned at how calm I felt. I showered, blow-dried my hair, put on makeup. Pulled on a black sweater and jeans, fastened my pearl stud earrings. Fingered the diamond anniversary band tucked inside my jewelry pouch. The dent on my left ring finger was barely noticeable—I'd hardly worn the ring since the start of the separation. I put it on my finger. I was still married.

Thirty minutes later, after knocking lightly, I walked through the front door of the Montauk house. Evan was waiting for me at the top of the stairs, looking like a mountain man with a heavy beard and a plaid shirt.

"Hello!" He hugged me lightly, as if his body already knew where we were headed.

"Hello, you! Did they not have razors in Iona?"

He laughed. "It was easier not shaving."

I walked toward the kitchen. "Okay if I make myself some coffee?" How strange to ask permission to use the coffee maker in my own house. But it felt like the respectful thing to do.

"Of course," he said.

"Can we talk upstairs?" I said, once the coffee was ready. I wanted to see the ocean. Our bedroom. The white slipper chair where I used to FaceTime Reenie. The desk where I typed *I have to touch her*, the unspeakable words that had set all this in motion. Because who knew how much longer I'd own this house or anything in it.

I followed Evan up the stairs. Ahh . . . the ocean. The view that had sold us on the house one gray December day seventeen years ago. Hanging on the wall above an armchair was a large black-and-white photograph of the boys taken when Will was six and Patrick three, the same year Reenie had come into our lives.

Evan sat in the same spot on the couch where nearly two years ago I had read him those unspeakable pages and told him I had been in love with Reenie. Most days I still woke up not believing this was my life. That this was happening.

"So how was it?" I asked.

"Life-changing." He told me more about his daily routine in Iona and that he was considering applying for an interim position that would start in February.

If he gets the job, I can move back into the house and stay here through next summer, then we can put the house on the market.

"Depending on what happens with us," he said.

Last July—four months and a lifetime ago—the sun was setting as Evan docked our kayak on Montauk's Fort Pond. I opened a bottle of rosé and poured some into two plastic glasses.

"This is pretty nice," I said wistfully as I handed him a glass.

"Yes, it is."

I leaned back a little. He leaned forward and put his arms around me.

Those arms that had held me since I was twenty-two.

In that moment in the kayak, I had thought maybe, just maybe, I'd find my way back to those arms.

I looked at my husband. That wasn't going to happen. I hoped he could see the love in my eyes. Because I did love this man. I wished, oh how I wished, I didn't have to do this. I didn't want to hurt him. But I already had, and dragging this out longer would hurt him more. So, this was it. There was never going to be an easy time to say what I had to say.

You know what you need to do, the Voice said.

"What's going on with you?" he asked.

My eyes filled up. "I'm guessing this won't come as a surprise, but I can't resolve this question inside me in theory. I need the freedom to date women."

His eyes filled too. "You know what that means, right?"

I nodded, more tears spilling.

He hadn't changed his mind. We wouldn't be growing old together.

Irreconcilable differences. This was really happening.

~

In the 1998 film *Sliding Doors*, Helen Quilley rushes for a London subway train but misses it when the doors close. The scene is repeated, but this time she makes the train. The film alternates between the two story lines, the two very different paths that Helen walks.

Have you ever imagined a different story line for your life if a single variable changed, whether by fate or your own volition?

We all have those "sliding door" moments.

This is one of mine.

The editor-in-chief of the 1986 *Harvard Women's Law Journal* asked to meet with me in the spring of my second year of law school.

"I have something I want you to think about," she said. "You've done excellent work, and I think you'd be a great next editor-in-chief."

My head was swimming. I hadn't even considered the possibility, although I'd been working at the journal the past two years, first as a subciter, then as an editor of articles ranging from female circumcision to surrogate motherhood.

"Wow. Thanks. Let me think about it." It was as if I'd been given a present I wasn't expecting and wasn't sure I wanted. I loved the time I spent in the journal's basement office checking citations and editing dense prose. "It's a sickness," I'd say to anyone who would listen. But the editor-in-chief practically *lived* in the office. I had a summer wedding to plan. Plus the prospect of a mini-thesis—the dreaded Harvard Law "third-year paper"—loomed in the fall.

"I'm not sure what I want to do," I said to Evan, although I'd already made up my mind. I was going to say no. It felt too hard to think about doing it all. My new marriage needed to be my priority. Evan didn't try to talk me out of it. "It's your decision," he said.

For years, I would beat myself up for this no, for not believing I could do work I loved and start off my marriage the right way. A yes could have led to a life of professional satisfaction instead of the dead-end corporate law path I took. And that voice inside me telling me to say no to the editor's offer? It wasn't the Voice. Likely, it was my internalization of my mother's—and maybe my father's—voice urging me to take the safer and easier path.

But even when we make a wrong turn and listen to the wrong voice, the Voice can still grab hold of us and lead us back to the path we were intended to walk.

The Voice had led me to Reenie. To this moment where my marriage was ending. To a life where I would choose desire over safety.

To a future I still couldn't imagine.

~

"We should send out an email to our friends about the divorce," Evan said in a hard voice.

"Wait, wait, wait! We need to talk to the boys first."

"Let's text them now."

Shit, he was like a speeding train. Slow down, I wanted to say.

"I need to tell my mother," I said. "I don't want her hearing from someone else. Do you want to talk to her with me?" Maybe she wouldn't freak out as much if he was with me.

"No, you can do that yourself."

He didn't have to help me with my mom anymore. He didn't have to help me with anything anymore.

Mom's face was emotionless when I told her we were getting divorced.

The rapid-fire questions began:

"Have you called a lawyer? Where are you going to live? Who's getting which car?"

Which car? Really, Mom?

"We just made this decision today. I don't know where I'm going to live. Or any of the other details yet."

"It feels very hard that you and Evan may not be nearby. And all the people I'm going to have to tell."

Later, I realized she still hadn't once asked me how I was doing or told me she loved me.

Maybe she couldn't say those things if she didn't understand.

I texted Beth.

Thanks for letting me know, she responded.

Evan and I called Will. "What are we going to do about Thanksgiving?" was his only question. Patrick also asked about Thanksgiving when we reached him. Funny what "kids" ask when their parents tell them they are getting divorced.

Fortunately, Aunt Carol had invited us to her house for Thanksgiving. We'd stick to the plan, even though we were getting divorced.

We were getting divorced.

There was a moment at Aunt Carol's on Thanksgiving Day that I wanted to put my arm around Evan and realized *I can't do this anymore.*

We emailed our close friends: *Suzette and I have separated and are navigating our next steps with love and respect. We are just beginning to share this news with a few friends. We so appreciate our friendship with you.*

Within minutes, supportive emails flooded in.

Reenie did not make the close friends list.

I sent a second email to some of those friends: *The reason for the separation from Evan and our impending divorce is that I've come to understand my sexuality differently—that I'm attracted to women, not men. He and I couldn't find a way to incorporate that new reality into our marriage.*

I felt as if I owed them an explanation—and I also wanted to be the one controlling the narrative—not Evan, not my mother, not anyone else.

I still couldn't say I was a lesbian. Or that I was gay. I just couldn't say it. "I've come to understand my sexuality differently" was my truth, and I figured that should be enough for most people. And if it wasn't, too bad. It was embarrassing enough to have to discuss my sex life—or the sex life I fantasized about having—with other people. I mean, who had to do that?

~

Joan, the leader of my Iona pilgrimage, would later become a trusted friend, but before the pilgrimage, our relationship had largely been a professional one. Close in age to me, she was an ordained pastor in the PC(USA), the largest and most progressive denomination of the Presbyterian Church in the country.

After the group hike around the island, Joan and I sat together in a cozy common room in the Iona Abbey where the group was staying. Likely I was talking about Reenie and my search for meaningful work, two of my favorite topics when I was in my forties.

Joan pulled something out of her pocket.

"I want to show you my spouse," she said.

Her spouse? I had no idea Joan was married. She had never mentioned anything about her personal life.

She handed me a small picture frame. "This is Cathleen."

I tried to appear unfazed, but I was shocked. It hadn't even crossed my mind Joan could have been gay. And married? It was 2002, two years before Massachusetts would be the first state to legalize same-sex marriage. The lawyer in me almost asked "How can you be married?" but I didn't.

"I don't share this with a lot of people," Joan said.

Somehow she knew she could trust me with her truth, and it wasn't until much later that I would wonder why. Did I simply appear to be an ally, or did she sense something more about me? In that moment, I felt proud she felt comfortable opening up to me. No one had ever come out to me before.

I was about to find out what it was like to be Joan, constantly weighing and evaluating who to come out to and when and how to do it.

One positive in all this: I had already come out to the hardest person of all.

Myself.

My Power

Even with the prospect of being free to date other women, I couldn't get Reenie out of my head.

I wanted to lock her in a room and not let her out until she explained what had happened to us. Ask her all the questions I still didn't have answers to. Had we ever been in sync, or had that just been my imagination? Had she ever loved me as more than a friend? Had I meant anything to her at all?

While Evan was still in Scotland, I realized I had to see her. I had even written out a script for the voice mail I'd leave if she didn't answer her phone: *Reenie, it's Suzette, I'm going to be in Houston in late October. Would you be willing to meet with me?*

I had practiced my message and recorded it on my phone. When I listened to the recording, my voice had sounded flat, like my mother's. No one in their right mind would have wanted to meet with that voice. So, I'd added a reminder to my calendar: *Text Reenie*. Enough time to give her notice, not too much to seem overeager.

~

"I'll call you when I know my schedule," Reenie said a couple of days before the 1998 Presidents' Day holiday weekend.

Still intoxicated from our first coffee date, I couldn't wait to be with her again. Would it be Saturday, Sunday, or Monday?

"Reenie and I might be doing something," I said to Evan when he suggested we make plans for the weekend.

She never called.

"Oh, I'm so sorry, I forgot," she said when I saw her the following week.

She forgot. That should have been a clue early on about the balance of power in our relationship.

I would never have forgotten her.

~

On the appointed day, I texted Reenie. Any response from her, even "I'm not ready to meet with you yet," would be better than silence.

Twelve hours. No response. If only I had enough self-respect to walk away.

Twenty-four hours. Yes. She was willing to meet with me. A single sentence. The coldness hurt, but at least she would meet with me.

One final chance to get answers.

~

"I can't stop wanting to touch you, hold you, have you hold me," I'd said to Reenie in those early years. How naïve. How innocent. How deeply in denial I was.

"You just want to touch God with skin on," Reenie had responded. Had she really believed our connection was only spiritual?

~

In my friend's guest room in my old Houston neighborhood, I laid out my "See Reenie" outfit: black jeans, black tee, faded denim overshirt, pearl earrings. Neat. Basic. Wouldn't show sweat.

My left ring finger was bare. Would Reenie notice? Would she ask about Evan? Would I tell her I was getting divorced? I had no idea what to expect from her or from myself.

She'd sent another text saying she could meet on October 31 from five to six thirty at Fadi's, a Mediterranean, cafeteria-style restaurant we'd eaten at frequently.

The boundary around the time—ninety minutes after all that had gone down—and the location she chose—a public place, not the church or my friend's house, which I had suggested—stung. Maybe she was afraid I might make a scene.

I wondered if she still prayed for me. If she thought of me when she journaled at the antique writing desk I'd given her, or when she sat down on one of the dining room chairs that used to be mine. Every time Evan and I downsized or moved, we'd offered her some of the furniture we no longer needed. I didn't know how any of it looked in her house. What kind of a best friend basically never invited you over to her house?

Did she even miss me?

~

Labyrinth: a meandering circular path leading to the center.

Maze: many paths, many dead-ends, designed to be confusing.

I used to think being in a relationship with Reenie was like walking a labyrinth. You might not know how long the journey would take or how you would get to the center, but if you kept putting one foot in front of the other you would get there.

But it turned out that being with her was much more like being stuck in a maze. Loving/Harsh. Empathic/Cold. Fully present/Completely gone.

~

Ten minutes early, I scanned the Fadi's dining room. Reenie wasn't there—nor were many others at 4:50 p.m. I tried to breathe.

I'd barely slept the night before. Couldn't stop picturing what it would be like to see her for the first time in six months. Would we hug like always? And if we did, would my body feel anything? Would it be agony standing in the cafeteria line, pretending everything was normal, and knowing, of course, it wasn't?

Did I ever really know her?

Early on in our friendship, I told her how perfect she was.

"I'm not perfect," she had said. "I'm a human being just like you."

After she sent me that cryptic goodbye email, my therapist had remarked, "She's showing you her limitations."

I no longer thought of her as perfect. I felt abandoned by her. Thrown away. Voiceless. And yet, here I was.

To kill time, I went into the restroom. At 4:59, I walked out and looked toward the front door. A gray-haired woman wearing a light-orange gauzy top was there. Reenie.

"Hi," we said in unison and lightly hugged. The kind of hug Evan had given me after he returned from Iona. The kind of hug I'd never given her.

Inches separating us, I could scarcely breathe as we made our way through the cafeteria line. I ordered a veggie wrap, knowing I wouldn't eat much of it. Not just because it was five o'clock, but because my normally dependable stomach wasn't feeling too dependable.

We paid and sat down at a table in a quiet corner.

"Well," I said, looking straight into her eyes.

Those green eyes that had often filled with tears as she listened to me for hours on end. That day they looked neutral, neither hard nor soft. It didn't appear as if she'd suffered much in the six months we'd been apart. No dark circles under *her* eyes.

"First, thank you for agreeing to meet with me," I said, as if I was on a job interview. "I appreciate that."

The formality killed me, but I didn't know any other way to talk to her. This woman I had spent years fantasizing about running away with.

"The past six months have been extremely painful," I said. "You hurt me deeply. I still don't understand what happened or why you cut me out of your life."

There. I said what I needed to say. I wasn't voiceless anymore. If she would say she was sorry, if she would explain what happened, maybe we could find a way to be friends again.

"Everything simply drained out of me when I read your email," she said. "Especially when you said you wanted me to tell you what I was really feeling. I had already told you, so you either didn't believe me or didn't trust me."

No, I wanted to say. *It wasn't that! I just needed to talk more.* But I kept quiet, hoping for answers.

"I had nothing left to give you," she said. "I had to remove my voice from the conversation so you could hear your own."

Later, I would see the gift in her decision to remove her voice. But at Fadi's, I didn't feel that way. Listening to her explanation made me feel like I was in a mentoring session I didn't want to be part of. And even if her stepping away had helped me, the way she did it—cutting me off completely—was not okay. It was not okay at all.

"I thought we were friends," I said. "Friends don't treat friends like that. I felt like a nonperson. Your silence seared me."

"I had no choice," she repeated.

A one-sentence answer with no elaboration, as unsatisfying as her cryptic email had been. This was not going well. I had worried ninety minutes wasn't going to be enough time, but it might be more than adequate if this was all I was going to get out of her. No apology, no further explanation. Not the closure I had been looking for.

"You had all these other people telling you different things—your counselor who you were *paying* and your Facebook friends. I'm not a 'yes-ma'am' kind of friend, you know that."

"I know. I wasn't looking for that." There it was again, her comment about Diane, the therapist I was *paying*. Was she jealous of her?

"I can't be a superficial friend," she said. "I am intense—you have to take me as I am, accept me as I am."

But who are you? I wanted to say. I didn't know this person sitting across from me. "I don't know how to be your friend anymore," I said. "Do you even want to be friends again?"

"Yes, but we need to take it slow."

Take it slow after nearly two decades of full speed ahead? She was the one who just said she wasn't a superficial friend, that she was intense.

"How do we do that?" I asked.

"Will you be coming back to Houston any time soon?"

I would be coming back—with Evan—in about six weeks. He had another surgery scheduled, this one to remove the screws and plates holding his collarbone together.

"Let's plan to see each other then. Email me when you know the dates."

I took a bite out of my veggie wrap. It tasted like sawdust. I got the "don't bother me for the next six weeks" message, but at least she'd opened the door to seeing me again. Maybe we just needed time to heal.

"Are you where you want to be?" she asked, seemingly out of the blue. Her way, I guessed, of wondering what was going on in my life. Maybe she'd noticed I wasn't wearing my wedding ring. Part of me wanted to spill everything to her, like I'd done in the past, but a bigger part of me felt that I needed to put a wall around my heart.

"I'm getting there," was all I said.

"Good." She didn't probe further. Maybe she was respecting my privacy, or maybe she didn't want to know.

She glanced at her watch and pushed back from the table. "I need to get home for the trick-or-treaters."

I'd never heard her make a big deal out of Halloween before. Either trick-or-treaters mattered more than me, or they were a convenient excuse to limit our time. Another question I'd never ask or get answered.

She stood up. "You and I can't find a way back on our own," she said, pointing to herself and to me. "Only God can lead us there."

She'd often quoted Saint Paul, who said that nothing was impossible with God. I had once believed that too, but repairing this breach felt impossible.

In the parking lot, we hugged in that light way again.

Maybe I'd see her again.

Maybe we'd find a way to rebuild our relationship.

But I doubted I would ever open my heart to her again.

~

My nightstand in the cottage was piled high with favorites: *Bird by Bird* by Anne Lamott, *Big Magic* by Elizabeth Gilbert, *Tiny Beautiful Things* by Cheryl Strayed.

I had loved *Wild*, Strayed's bestselling memoir, but *Tiny Beautiful Things* had been even more breathtaking. Had I recommended it to Reenie? I missed talking books with her. I missed talking with her. I missed her. Period. We'd had no contact since the Fadi's meeting a month ago, except for two brief email exchanges, one where I told her I was getting divorced and a second about plans to get together after Evan's surgery. She'd suggested lunch and a tour of her new office so I could meet her colleagues.

Maybe I'd buy *Tiny Beautiful Things* for her birthday and give it to her in Houston.

Surely it was okay to text to see if she'd already read the book. Surely that wasn't violating the "take it slow" boundaries she had set. I hated having to hyperanalyze every contact with her and stress about whether she would respond.

Asking about a book wasn't a loaded question. I wasn't asking her to tell me how she felt about me. I wasn't telling her how I felt about her. It was just a damn book.

Have you read Tiny Beautiful Things? I texted.

Three days and no response. A simple question about a book.

~

The anesthesiologist turned to me in Evan's pre-op room. "You're his wife?"

Evan and I looked at each other awkwardly.

"Yes," I said.

"All jewelry off?" he asked Evan.

"Yes," Evan said. There was no jewelry. What would he do with his wedding ring? What would I do with mine?

A lifetime had passed in the ten and a half months since his last collarbone surgery.

A few hours later, we would return to the same two-bedroom hotel suite we had been in close to a year ago. The same suite where I told Reenie I loved her. The same suite where she told me nothing would change between us.

She never responded to my text about the book. Hadn't checked in to see how Evan's surgery had gone. Hadn't once asked how I was doing with respect to the divorce.

What a fool I had been.

~

Joan, the pastor who came out to me during the Iona pilgrimage, was one of the few people I trusted who also personally knew Reenie. I'd connected with Joan shortly before I told Reenie I was in love with her. Joan had helped me survive that conversation, as well as Reenie's cutting-off-contact email and the disappointing meeting at Fadi's.

Two days before I was supposed to have lunch with Reenie, I emailed Joan: *I don't know the point of meeting with Reenie again.*

Joan didn't see a point either. *I want you to think about whether it's healthy for you to see her anymore. Instead of meeting with her, write a letter and mail it. Tell her what she's meant to you and then say goodbye. You can claim your power by ending things. It's time to grieve and move forward.*

That felt really hard. To give up hope that things could be different, somehow, some way. Didn't Reenie say that we couldn't repair things on our own, but God could lead us—or something like that?

I reread Joan's email. *Write a letter and mail it.* There it was in black and white, as if the Voice was speaking to me directly with that absolute certainty I had longed for. Joan was right. The only way to take back my power was to quit Reenie—cold turkey.

I had seen the same experience repeated over and over with many of the LaLas and would continue to see it for years to come. The special power the catalyst had over us late-in-lifers. The all-consuming feelings we expressed that could easily overwhelm the women who awakened our sexuality. How putting up walls and hard boundaries could be a reasonable response to our single-minded fixations. How we, too, had responsibility when things ended badly.

But I couldn't see any of that then. All I knew was that I had loved Reenie deeply and she had broken my heart. And if I wrote and mailed the letter, I was going to have to walk into my new life, under my own power, without her.

While Evan recuperated in his bedroom in the hotel suite, I wrote and rewrote the goodbye letter in the other bedroom. My last chance to tell Reenie everything I'd longed to say since I fell for her. If I mailed it, I was certain I would never hear from her again. She'd be too proud to get back in touch—or relieved I was out of her life.

I printed out the letter in the hotel's business center. Addressed and stamped the envelope. I'd sleep on it. If it still felt like the right thing to do in the morning, I'd mail it and say goodbye.

The next morning I walked toward the mailbox, envelope in hand. The finality was crushing. The dreams lost—not only of Reenie as a partner but of her as a best friend. No more FaceTime calls, no more hugs. I wouldn't be planning her seventieth birthday party, like I had planned her fiftieth and sixtieth. She wouldn't be asking about my writing. A giant gaping hole in my heart was all that remained of this relationship.

When I reached the mailbox, I slipped half the envelope into the slot, not wanting to let go and knowing I had to.

Then I let go. Of the envelope. And of Reenie.

That chapter was finally over.

Maybe the only way to heal this relationship was to end it.

The Dating Game

The LaLas said that photos were the most important part of an online dating profile. Sandy had deemed my Facebook profile pic "hot"—a photo Evan had taken of me standing on the upper deck of the Montauk house, hand on hip, ocean in the background. If Sandy thought it was hot, maybe others would too. Maybe they'd think the ocean view came with the hot chick, which would be a mistake. I wouldn't be keeping the house, couldn't afford to even if I wanted it.

Photos were important, but as a writer, words mattered too. Did I have to say I was still married? That I was a total newbie? That I had no idea where I'd be living after the cottage rental was up in June?

I decided to start with two nonnegotiables: no smokers and no Trumpers.

~

One morning in early December, I stopped over at the Montauk house to pick up a platter for the dish I was preparing for a friend's holiday party. A single plate, knife, and fork were soaking in the kitchen sink. Salt-and-pepper shakers were on the coffee table in the TV room. Evan must have been eating his meals in front of the TV, something he'd never done when we lived together. The tableau crushed me. To think of him being lonely—and to be the cause of it.

I was eating my meals in front of the TV too.

My mother's voice echoed in my head: *You have no idea how hard it is to be alone.*

~

One of the twelve matches the online algorithm spit out looked promising. She managed a nonprofit, had a son in high school (he'd be off to college soon, right?), and was attractive. Maybe we'd hit it off and that would be that. I messaged her: *I'd love to chat if you are interested.* Maybe dating would be fun.

~

I'd never "dated"—men or women. I met Alan, my first boyfriend, in October 1980, when I was a college sophomore. A pounding disco beat had greeted my Wellesley friends and me that night as we entered Lincoln's Inn, a Harvard Law social club. Men, not boys, in sports coats circulated around the steamy dance floor. Booze flowed freely.

Alan, a short guy with curly hair and a mustache, asked me to dance. Later, he asked if I wanted to get some air.

My heart raced as we walked toward a park in the middle of Harvard Square. Would he kiss me? My only kiss had been that sloppy drunken one from Nick when I was a high school student in England. Alan's eyes were kind, his voice as silky as a ripe avocado.

"You're beautiful," he said as we entered the park. We sat on a bench and kissed, and soon his frame fit over mine like a dressmaker's pattern as he lay on top of me.

With the exception of a post–Valentine's Day breakup that lasted a month, we were together from that day on, until we weren't.

A year or so after we broke up, I met Evan.

I smoothed out the wrinkles on the tweed suit my aunt bought me for a college graduation gift and kept my eye on the revolving door in the lobby of Harry's Hanover Square. Wondered if stone-cold sober I'd find Evan as handsome as I had after a couple of margaritas. Soon a slim, dark-haired man in a Burberry raincoat came through the door.

He was as handsome as I remembered.

We were together from that day on, until we weren't.

~

Plate in hand, I waited to serve myself from the potluck feast at a gathering of LaLas in New England. A woman who I would later learn was a "gold star lesbian"—meaning she had never slept with a man—leaned against the wall, inches from me. "Where are you from?" she asked.

She was a friend of one of the LaLas, and I couldn't tell if she was flirting with me or just being friendly. I didn't know the difference with women. I didn't feel attracted to her, but it was nice to think she might be attracted to me. I didn't know the rules of dating, let alone lesbian dating.

Most of the LaLas were in the same boat as me. We were all just trying to find our way in a foreign land where online dating was the norm. The internet hadn't even existed when many of us found our former partners. Dating norms defined along traditional gender lines didn't apply in this new territory. Who was supposed to pay for dinner or make the first move?

A week after reaching out to the woman with the high school son, I had messages from two women who were interested in talking to me, but nothing from her.

Wow. I was starting to understand how online dating worked. It basically sucked. The people you wanted didn't want you, and the people who wanted you, you didn't want.

~

"Can you believe it about Glennon and Abby?"

First Elizabeth Gilbert, then Glennon Doyle. The LaLas were abuzz about Glennon's Facebook post telling the world about her new love, soccer star Abby Wambach. Glennon, who had recently released *Love Warrior*, a memoir about saving her marriage—to a man.

Another brave woman.

And damn, I was jealous of that brave woman.

Because she had found her Abby.

I hoped it wasn't too late to find mine.

~

I ran my hands over my velveteen leopard print blazer, one of the few hip pieces of clothing I owned. Black tee underneath, black pants, black shoes. My pearl stud earrings were in, but my new shaggy haircut largely covered them. Shortly after Evan left for Iona, I'd brought a photo of Leisha Hailey—Alice from *The L Word*—to my hair stylist and asked her to try and replicate it. The shaggy cut was a definite improvement from the chin-length bob I'd had for the past few years, but note to self: ditch the pearls.

My best guess of what to wear on a lesbian date—and this day I had two.

Finally, life on the other side of the fence. No longer having to play by the rules, like I had to at the Cubbyhole. I hoped Sarah, my date, would be as pretty as her photo. I hoped there'd be chemistry. I hoped that maybe, just maybe, I'd get that first kiss.

Sarah was already seated when I arrived at the Italian restaurant she'd chosen for brunch—fancier than I expected: dark paneling, white tablecloths. She was attractive, even prettier than her photos. We talked easily for a couple of hours. I liked her. But I liked a lot of women, just not "that way." I wasn't feeling sparks, but maybe I was someone who took awhile to feel any.

Although I hadn't needed much time with Reenie.

Outside the restaurant, I hugged Sarah. "I had a really good time," I said. "I'd like to get together again." What did I have to lose? I was done waiting for my life to happen.

Sarah looked surprised. Maybe she didn't feel the same way.

"I would too," she said. "Send me some times that work for you."

My first lesbian date! Not a home run, but not a strikeout either.

Date #2 was a bundle of energy.

"Tell me your story," Cindy said, bouncing up and down as she sat across the table from me at a coffee shop.

I gave her the bare bones of how I had fallen for Reenie. "I even went to therapy for three years and still didn't have a clue I was gay."

"Forgive me for being blunt—I'm a New Yorker—but you should sue that therapist for malpractice."

I laughed. I liked Cindy's bluntness. A real New Yorker, a straight shooter. She was eight years older than me, which at first was a turnoff. But Reenie was twelve years my senior. Maybe I had a thing for older women.

And her comment about Alice, my first therapist? It hadn't even occurred to me that Alice might not have served me well, but later I realized Cindy was right. In three years Alice and I had talked only once about my sexual feelings toward Reenie. We had never talked about my less-than-satisfying sex life with Evan. And when we FaceTimed last spring, Alice had mentioned a client with "same-sex attraction" who had stayed in his marriage and incorporated his "friend" into his family.

I started seeing my interactions with Alice in a new light. She was a product of the heteronormativity—a word I had rarely heard before all THIS happened—that was embedded in everything and everyone, including me. The heteronormativity that had prevented me from even considering whether Alice was consciously—or unconsciously—steering me in a certain direction. The heteronormativity that had prevented me from seeing and naming my true feelings for Reenie and had likely prevented me from even recognizing what my body had been trying to tell me for years—from even asking myself whether the spark I felt when I touched Reenie's forearm was sexual energy.

And that "same-sex attraction" BS that Alice mentioned? I didn't realize until later that that was language favored by religious conservatives and proponents of conversion therapy. People "struggled with same-sex attraction," and in that world, that attraction was their cross to bear.

"I'm going to be direct," Cindy said. "I'd like to see you again. When will you be back in the city?"

I smiled. She liked me. I wasn't sure there was chemistry here either, but it had been fun talking with her.

"I enjoyed it too," I said. "Let me check my calendar and get back to you."

No first kiss, but two pretty decent first dates.

~

On the bus ride home after my back-to-back dates, I looked at the photos on my Facebook page. Evan and me in front of a Venetian canal. Biking in Peru with the boys. The "red carpet" at a charity gala two years ago. Evan was no longer tagged in that photo. I clicked on another and another—he had untagged himself from every single photo of the two of us.

His Facebook status had been updated too: he was no longer "married." I had been scrubbed from his life. It hadn't even occurred to me to clean up my profile, to erase the past. It made sense—prospective dates wouldn't want to see your ex splashed all over your page. But still. He was moving on so fast.

~

My second date with Sarah, dinner at a French bistro. At the end of the meal, we hugged goodbye as we had at the end of our first date, but this time neither of us mentioned seeing each other again. Two dates were apparently enough to know that there were no sparks.

The next afternoon, I met Cindy for lunch. This time, she seemed twitchy rather than energetic. She picked at her eyebrows and leaned over her drink, taking long sips from the straw without holding the glass, something I'd often chastised my boys for doing.

You have no idea how hard it is to be alone.

~

In late December, I stopped over at the Montauk house to pick up some files to prepare for our divorce mediation. A yellow legal pad was face down on Evan's desk. I knew it was wrong, but I picked it up anyway. Read through it, looking for anything to give me a clue about the life he was living without me.

The first few pages were covered with notes about corporate boards and consulting projects. Nothing juicy or particularly interesting. I turned a page and initials in tiny print caught my eye. Five or six first names—all female—*D*'s or *W*'s after the names and two initials after each. I pondered the notes, trying to crack the code. Then I realized: *D* was "divorced," and *W* was "widowed," and the double sets of initials were friends of his—friends of *ours*—who were apparently trying to set him up.

Wow. Our friends were already taking sides. At least, they were taking care of him.

Of course my friends' worlds were not exactly overflowing with single lesbians. Still, it hurt to think about all the conversations that were happening in the circles I used to be part of and apparently no longer was.

You have no idea how hard it is to be alone.

The Ledger

I rang the doorbell of a white colonial in suburban Boston. The home of Anne, a friend I'd known since fifth grade, and the friend who was responsible for me meeting Evan. They'd gone to college together.

I'd emailed Anne when I decided to make a trip to New England and filled her in on my coming out and the divorce. This two-step dance I was doing with everyone I encountered—exhausting.

"I've always thought of you as the bravest friend I know," Anne had replied to my email. "And of course, you can stay with me."

What? I'd thought. I didn't feel as if I had led a brave life.

People like Anne's child, who had come out in college as trans, were brave.

Unlike my friend's child, I still had the luxury of "passing" as my former self. Besides the slightly funkier hairstyle I now sported, I still looked the part of the stay-at-home mom I had been playing for two decades.

Anne hugged me and led me into her living room, where a stack of our high school yearbooks lay on top of the coffee table.

"I never saw this one," I said, picking up a yearbook with an unfamiliar cover.

"Oh, that was the year Jeanne graduated," she said. Jeanne was her older sister.

I flipped through the pages, and in the teacher section, my pulse quickened. A photo I'd never seen before of Mrs. G., the high school teacher whose initials I'd doodled on my spiral notebook. She was standing outside the school, looking like a brunette, young Gloria Steinem, in an unbuttoned coat with a furlike fringe. Hip. Gorgeous. Chic.

"I had a crush on her," I said to Anne, pointing to the photo. "Maybe that should have been a clue." We both laughed.

"Something you said in your email surprised me," I said. "That you always thought of me as your bravest friend. Why did you say that?"

"You weren't afraid to be different," she said. "Remember in tenth grade when you were the only one in the class who was for Jimmy Carter? You went away to England, the only one in our class to leave for a year. You left corporate law and forged your own path."

Maybe being brave wasn't so black-and-white. Maybe I had been braver than I thought. Maybe sometimes we needed others to see things in us that we couldn't see in ourselves. Like Lila asking me how I would feel about being *homosexual*. Like the book coach interpreting the *I have to touch her* moment. Like my soon-to-be-ex-husband saying he had known all along that I had been in love with Reenie.

"Tell me more about your story," Anne said.

My eyes filled up. Why had it taken me so long to step into my story? I didn't know if this struggle was unique to the LGBTQ+ experience, part of the human condition, or just the way I was wired. But what was clear: If I was going to keep walking down this path, I needed to surround myself with people like Anne. People I could trust. People who cared about my story.

Maybe the rest of my life would be spent drawing a line down the center of the page: on one side, people who would join me on this journey, and on the other, people who at best would "accept me" or "accept the situation."

It was so odd to have a ledger like this. I'd never had one before.

~

Ellen, a friend from my church in Montauk, came over to the cottage for dinner.

I told her about writing the unspeakable. About how I wrestled with what to do with my truth. "It's mind-boggling to think that writing a single sentence could have led to this," I said, believing that Ellen, a writer herself, would get this.

"I think the writer in you is driving this," Ellen said in that same hard tone I'd heard from Reenie. "You have to look at the big picture and what marriage is really about. It's a commitment. It's hard work. And by the way, Evan does not look well—he is not doing well at all."

I couldn't wait until she left. I hadn't expected that from her. I thought we were kindred spirits, being writers and all.

~

How was Evan doing? I didn't know. He wasn't letting me into his world anymore. But in all the years we'd been together, he hadn't ever appeared to struggle with who he was personally or professionally. He'd glided seamlessly from a career in money management to nonprofit work, and until I read the unspeakable pages to him, he'd been content to let his next chapter unfold without agonizing over it.

Something as simple as celebrating a birthday exposed the different ways we approached life. For Evan's fortieth, he knew what he wanted: a wine dinner at a fancy Houston restaurant. The wine room seated fourteen so we invited six other couples. He handed over a credit card at end of the evening. A good time was had by all.

What did I want to do for my fortieth birthday two months later? I couldn't have a couples party—Reenie wasn't part of a couple. "Let's just have your friends over," Evan said. He'd take care of everything.

But who were my friends? My real friends, that is, other than Reenie?

The tennis moms I was no longer playing tennis with? The older church ladies whom Reenie had introduced me to? The few attorney friends I still kept in touch with? The writer friends I swapped deeply personal pages with?

Have a party. Don't have a party. Have a party.

"I don't care anymore," Evan said. "Just decide."

I didn't know what I wanted. I didn't have a party. I didn't know who my real friends were.

~

The Party. The one and only time my parents hosted a party when Beth and I were growing up, other than birthday parties or casual family gatherings.

Likely a Christmas party, sometime in the late sixties or early seventies, before all the marital separations. Before the downstairs was redecorated in lime green and Dad's brown pullout couch was recovered in green too. Mom in a maxi skirt and halter top with no bra. Dad in a plaid sports coat. Beth and me in matching red-and-green plaid maxi jumpers with ruffly white blouses underneath. Our Martha Washington look, we dubbed it years later.

The Party that looked perfect in the photographs but was never repeated. Perfection was exhausting.

~

A year after my fortieth birthday, I opted for a forty-first birthday party, which felt like much less pressure to get right. Beth flew in from New Jersey. Reenie was there, of course, as were a dozen other women. Evan wrote up a "How Well Do You Know Suzette" quiz, which led to lots of laughs.

It turned out none of us knew Suzette all that well, including me.

~

The text from Sami, a friend who had been at my birthday party and whom I'd recently told about my impending divorce, began ominously. She hoped I wouldn't take this the wrong way. She wanted me to know that she wanted the best for me.

Had I sought spiritual counsel? She hoped I wasn't succumbing to the flesh.

WTF?

I believe you mean well, I wrote back, *but I found your text very hurtful. Please give me space. I can't be around that kind of energy right now.*

My phone rang. Sami. I didn't answer.

It rang again. She left a lengthy voice mail.

I deleted the voice mail and the text. I didn't have room in my life for people like that anymore.

~

A Houston friend told me about a conversation she had with Reenie.

"Reenie said she hopes you are mistaken about your sexuality. She's afraid you've been strongly 'influenced' to believe you are gay."

My head was about to explode. I went to my LaLas, the only people who would understand:

PAM: Obviously she doesn't get it. You can be influenced to try a different flavor of ice cream, but it doesn't work that way with your sexuality. That makes it out to be a choice to be gay. Like we would choose to go through these hard-ass obstacles if it was a choice. That's your friend's limiting belief at play there, which can be very hurtful.

ME: Yeah. I think she doesn't want me to be gay because she feels responsible and/or she's worried she is too.

PAM: Maybe she is worried she is. Or maybe she is worried for you and how hard it can be. Hard to say with people.

AMY: I hate that comment. I got some of that. Those people have no idea of the pain and anguish of awakening to this. But then all of the people in our lives are part of this journey. They have to make their way through this as well. And what it is doing is shining a huge bright light on their own lives and thoughts and biases and ignorance. Or their own gayness. Just saying.

ANNIE: Oh, Suze. I'm so sorry. As you know, her reaction, and everyone's really, is about them. People fear facing their own truths, admitting the life of quiet desperation they are secretly living.

NANCY: That's gut-wrenching to hear from someone you love.

ME: Yes.

~

LaLas! Mark your calendars for our first ever LaLa Conference! March 24–26th in Nashville!

Hell yes to Nashville. Hell yes to a weekend with those "influencers."

~

The isolation of the cottage was getting to me. As much as I loved spending time online with the LaLas, I needed to talk to a real live human. I called my sister.

"I'm not asking for advice or for you to fix things," I said. "I just want you to listen."

"Okay."

I sobbed as I told Beth about the nonstarter dates, Evan's coded notes on the legal pad, my fears about the upcoming divorce mediation, my feeling that I was about to lose everything. "This is so hard."

"Yes, it's very hard," she said without a hint of warmth. "And it's going to be hard for a long time."

"Wow," I said. "I can't talk to you now."

I hung up the phone before I said something I would regret. I didn't have the strength for a screaming match like the one we'd had at her house nine months ago.

Your sister is wrong, Annie wrote, after I posted about the conversation on the LaLa page. *It won't be a continuous hard for a long time. Moments will be hard. Other moments will be joyous. And that's just how life goes: hard, easy, hard again, funny, sad, joyful. You are not alone. Talk to us.*

But in this tiny, windswept cottage, I felt very much alone.

~

Journal, January 31, 2017

You feel so lost. You don't know who to trust or what voice to trust in your head.

You wonder if you should try to go back to Evan.

You don't know whether you are thinking about this because going forward feels too hard or because it's what you are being called to do.

You are afraid of jerking Evan around.

You are afraid of public humiliation.

You are afraid of being wrong.

You are afraid of disappointing people.

You don't know which friends to trust. You feel abandoned, alone. You are so disappointed in your mother and your sister. You feel like you have lost the people you counted on most.

You wonder if the longing to be with a woman is a longing you can live with. Because you know that no person can meet all your needs. You wonder if there's a way to acknowledge your feelings, live with the pain of unrealized longing, and embrace the good in the life you have (or had—because maybe it's gone now. Maybe Evan is done. You don't know).

You see the good in the time you've been separated from Evan—things you want to build on whether you get back together with him or not. You CANNOT nor do you want to go back to what you had before.

You feel like you have made such an incredible mess of everything and you don't trust yourself. You just don't.

~

The last few days have been very hard. Have felt myself unraveling, wanting and not wanting to crawl back to my old life. I miss Evan and I miss Reenie, I emailed Jenn, a newish friend I'd met last spring at a writers conference. A badass friend who didn't seem to be afraid of making hard choices and doing hard things.

After arriving early for the writers conference, I'd waited on a bench outside the welcome center, proud of myself for making the drive from Montauk to New Jersey, the first time I'd crossed the Hudson River under my own power. Evan had been the driver in our family, another thing that would change for me. Small in the scheme of things, but still.

I closed my eyes. The sun felt so good on my face. A few seconds later, a noise startled me. A slim woman with a mane of pin-straight brown hair was walking toward the bench. Jenn.

She sat next to me and lifted her face to the sun too. "I just need to breathe for a moment." She'd had a flat tire on the way to the conference.

"Oh no! What did you do?"

"I changed the tire while I waited for my husband to trade cars."

She changed the tire. Wow.

What would I have done? I still had a husband, but barely. And I sure as hell didn't know how to change a tire. The drive to New Jersey was hard enough. There were oh-so-many things I would have to learn to do.

"Where did you drive in from?" I asked.

"Lancaster, P.A."

Lancaster? Where the Amish live? Jenn didn't look Amish, not one bit, in her stretchy striped dress and heels.

"I would have totally freaked out," I said. But it didn't look like much ruffled Jenn. Later I learned she had four young children and a full-time job, and still found time to write.

She laughed. "It's more material for my blog." She wrote inspirational stories for moms and was a motivational speaker.

A month after the writers conference, Jenn separated from her husband, although for reasons different from mine—there wasn't a gay bone in her body, as far as I could tell. We'd been supporting each other ever since. At times, she reminded me of Reenie—always seeming to know the right thing to say.

Today you are on the first page of your new book, Jenn responded to my email. *It's a big book. Lots of chapters and it looks daunting to dig into. But pour yourself another cup of coffee, take a deep breath, and just start with the first page.*

She was right, of course. But before I wrote the first page of the new book, I had to turn the last page of the old one. The book I'd always expected would end with "and they lived happily ever after."

Choices and Consequences

Birthday dinner at the Four Seasons restaurant, New York, March 1984.

Suzette, twenty-three this day, flush with her acceptance to Harvard Law School and tipsy on champagne, says to her date: "If you get into Harvard Business School, we could live in married student housing."

Evan, her boyfriend of three months, chokes on his champagne.

He doesn't know that Suzette will be right. He will get into Harvard Business School. He will ask her to marry him. They will live in married student housing.

They will both believe they will be together forever.

~

Here, Evan texted from the cottage's driveway, the morning of our first divorce mediation session. Odd, perhaps, for the two of us to drive together, but it made sense. The mediator's office was more than an hour away.

I took another look at myself in the mirror. Dark jeans and a gray cardigan, appropriate to match the somber occasion. A multicolored strand of freshwater pearls around my neck. I'd bought the necklace in Austin nineteen years ago, the spring of Will's kindergarten year. Reenie had offered to watch the boys so Evan and I could have a weekend away, something we rarely got to do in those early years of parenthood.

I didn't believe Reenie ever intended to get in the middle of our marriage. That was something that had "just happened." Likely, I'd never hear her version of what had "just happened," but I needed to take responsibility for the choices I'd made. While I didn't believe it had been a choice to fall in love with Reenie or to be gay, it was a choice to leave my marriage instead of staying the course.

To find out what life was like on the other side.

The riskiest choice of all after a life of safe choices.

~

"Remember, every choice is a renunciation," Evan would often remind me, quoting one of his favorite lines from Saint Thomas Aquinas.

When we say yes to one path, we have to say no to another.

~

Evan had emailed to say he wanted to keep the house if we could agree on a buyout price. I was relieved—and troubled. Relieved to not have to go through the stress of putting our house on the market. Relieved of some of the guilt I felt about breaking up the family. At least I wouldn't be uprooting Evan or the boys. They would still have a family home, just one without me. Which was the troubling part.

I had already sensed a shift in the center of gravity in the family when Will, Patrick, Evan, and I had dinner together the day after Thanksgiving. We all sat in our usual places at the dining room table, and it was impossible for me to not think about the three of them sitting there without me—and the empty place that used to be mine. The place that might soon be taken by another woman.

Family life would go on.

Without me.

Choices had consequences.

~

I slid into the passenger seat in Evan's Honda CRV. He looked funereal too, in his dark jeans and navy-blue pullover. We headed west to the mediator's office, largely in silence.

People had warned me that there was no such thing as a truly friendly divorce—and Evan had been different since we decided to end things, as if a switch had flipped in him. The light hugs. The formal "Dear Suzette" addresses on his emails. A "Don't text unless it's urgent" request. He preferred I communicate by email. Less intrusive, he said.

There were still occasional moments of levity in our communication, like when he emailed: *Did you say you got your own Amazon account? May I remove the lesbian erotica from the watchlist attached to mine?*

Oops.

But we were no longer a team. He was going to look out for his own interests, and I would have to look out for mine.

~

We sat down at opposite ends of the table in the mediator's office, blank yellow legal pads and pens in front of us. Evan pulled out a stack of spreadsheets.

The former money manager who had earned the vast majority of our income and handled the finances on one end of the table. The wife who gave up her paycheck at twenty-nine and hadn't balanced a checkbook since on the other. Truth be told, I'd been happy to have Evan take care of it all. Happy, that is, until this moment.

We don't need your salary. Five simple words from Evan twenty-seven years ago that felt like a gift with no downside at the time.

Those words gave me the opportunity to work "outside the home" without pay. Volunteer at the preschool. Help start a children's advocacy program at a local law school. Serve as a volunteer attorney for Disability Rights Texas. Being a volunteer was selfless on many levels—and it was also selfish. Volunteering gave me freedom from the pressures of paid work and an escape hatch whenever things got too hard.

Now I see that saying yes to Evan's gift set in motion a life where I played small and safe.

The twelve-year-old with two paper routes and the ambitious twenty-three-year-old entering Harvard Law had handed over her power to her husband.

Choices had consequences.

~

October 1983: My roommate and I invited every unattached man we knew in Manhattan to our housewarming party. Anne, the high school friend who years later would call me brave, was that roommate, and she was the reason Evan, a friend of hers from college, was there that night.

From the boombox in the corner of our living room, Irene Cara belted out "What a Feeling" from *Flashdance*. I stepped into the center of the room, reached my arms toward the ceiling, and sang along. Guests circled around, urging me on. I dropped to the floor, threw my legs in the air, and spun on my back, performing a break-dance solo.

Evan's first view of his future wife.

Fully alive. On center stage.

Where had she gone?

~

Like many of us, I built a life imprinted by my beginnings, the childhood memories I couldn't erase: the scolding by the nun when I playfully sang the wrong lyrics, the blood gushing from my friend's arm when I pushed too hard, and the fall into the stream after my mother warned me not to cross it.

A life that worked—until it didn't.

My shift into the second half of life happened in my midfifties. For some, it will happen as early as their thirties. For some, it will never happen at all.

The patterns of our first half of life serve us—until they don't.

~

At twenty-eight, I was still very much in my first half of life, captive to my beginnings.

Houston, 1989: The head of school shook my hand and pointed to a chair on the other side of his desk. "Please sit. What can I do for you?"

I handed him my résumé. "I wanted to see if there were any opportunities for me here. I'm considering leaving my legal practice for teaching."

He took a cursory glance at the résumé and handed it back to me.

"Our teachers view this as their calling," he said. "Many have PhDs and could be teaching at the college level if they wanted to. Almost all have at least a master's degree." In case I didn't get the point, he added, "We rarely hire anyone inexperienced."

I felt my face flush. "I understand," I said.

He mentioned a teacher certification program at Rice University. "We've hired a couple of teachers who graduated from there."

The meeting was over in minutes. I left, feeling like my feet were stuck in concrete. Was I about to study for another graduate entrance exam, apply to another program, invest more years and more money? What if after all that time and money, teaching turned out to be another giant mistake, just like the law?

I couldn't bear to make another mistake.

A year later, Evan said, "You can quit whenever you want to."

And I did.

Choices had consequences.

~

Evan threw out a number as a starting point for our divorce settlement. "That would be fair," he said, or something like that.

It was what I was legally entitled to, and it was fair—some might say more than fair, since I was the one initiating the divorce and Evan had been the one earning the income. But I pushed back for more, playing the "I lost earnings potential" card since I had stayed home to care for our kids.

A perfectly reasonable card to play for many stay-at-home moms who spend years engaging in unpaid labor. But I could have gone back to work and chose not to.

I'd like to think that fear, rather than greed, motivated me to push for more money that day at the mediator's. I was scared. About money. About how I was going to do life without Evan. About everything.

Evan saw through my bullshit. "Suzette, you're going to be fine," he said with a look of exasperation. "For God's sake, you have a Harvard Law degree."

A Harvard Law degree that had gathered dust for most of the past thirty years.

My choice. My consequences.

Evan does so much for you," my mom said when I came out to her.

She was right. He had done so much for me.

It was time to take back my power and find out how to live without him.

The Plagues

Plague #1: Sickness

Late January: Throat on fire. Trip to urgent care. Antibiotics not helping. Nor did the apple cider vinegar a friend advised me to gargle with.

Late February: Sinus infection. Another visit to urgent care. More antibiotics. Same result.

March: Raging sore throat. Congestion. Pink eye, both eyes.

Two weeks before the LaLa conference.

Plague #2: Trump

The way things turned out November 8, 2016, should have been a sign that the road ahead wasn't going to be easy.

That morning, days after Evan and I decided to divorce, I woke up excited about my future and about our country's too. I'd be casting a ballot for the nation's first woman president, Hillary Rodham Clinton.

Eight years earlier I'd voted for America's first Black president. Tears of joy had spilled down my cheeks when Barack and Michelle and their little girls greeted the diverse, overflowing crowd in Chicago's Grant Park.

America had come so far.

A woman president! About time—and Hillary was a fellow Wellesley alum to boot. Amy, a college friend, had invited a group of us to spend the night at her Boston apartment. After dinner, we'd drive to the college and celebrate Hillary's victory with the whole Wellesley community.

But first, I had to get to that Boston apartment. Drive ninety minutes to the ferry. Take the ferry to New London. Drive two hours to downtown Boston.

Although I'd lived in the Boston area for six years—three in college and three in law school—I'd never driven there. I hadn't owned a car, and even if I had, the thought of driving in the city terrified me. Evan had always done that kind of thing. Add city and long-distance driving to the list of things I had to learn to do.

That November day the sky was crystal clear and the temperature was unseasonably mild. I rolled down my window when I pulled onto I-95 toward Boston. My sweatshirt sleeve flapped in the breeze. The sun warmed my face.

"Here I am, world! Here I am! Here I am!" I shouted.

This felt like freedom.

In that moment I felt capable of stepping into a new life, even though I had no idea what that life was going to look like. I was already taking baby steps, like driving in the city, which wasn't too bad until I made a wrong turn near the Boston Public Garden. But sweaty palms and all, I negotiated a left turn in heavy traffic and finally arrived at Amy's.

We all know how this story turned out. We never popped the champagne at Amy's, and thank goodness we didn't venture to Wellesley for the "celebration."

I couldn't wrap my mind around the fact that Donald Trump, not Hillary Clinton, had been elected president of the United States.

The next morning it hit me that I was part of a marginalized community now at even greater risk. Coming out to my friends, while hard, had felt relatively safe for me. I lived in a nation with marriage equality. In my Northeast liberal bubble, I wasn't aware of anyone discriminating against the LGBTQ+ community—that happened elsewhere, in fundamentalist Christian backwaters, in rural parts of the South.

And unlike many in the queer community, I had the privilege of race, education, financial security, being able-bodied, and having at least some people in my life who supported me. And yet, even with all that privilege, I felt vulnerable and scared. How bad would a Trump administration be?

I was afraid it would be bad. But I had no idea how bad the fallout would be from that election. Anti-trans "bathroom bills." A "don't say gay" law in Florida. A concurring opinion by a US Supreme Court justice arguing that the court should reconsider *Obergefell v. Hodges*, the decision guaranteeing same-sex couples the constitutional right to marry. Increased violence toward the queer community.

No, I had no idea how bad it would be.

Plague #3: Power Outage

March came in like a lion. By 1 p.m., a foot of snow surrounded the cottage. I'd lined up flashlights, spare batteries, candles, and matches on the kitchen counter. The number to text PSEGLI, the power company, was on speed dial. Tissues and a spare box were next to me on the couch.

At 1:30, the power went out.

I texted PSEGLI.

Power to be restored by 3:30.

The cottage was heated solely by electricity, but I could do two hours without heat. I wrapped myself in a fleece blanket.

Do you have power? I texted my mother.

Yes, she responded.

Thank goodness I didn't need to worry about her too. The roads were thick with ice and snow. A travel advisory was in place. Nothing to do but hunker down.

At 4:30, I lit a few candles and texted PSEGLI again.

Power to be restored by 6:30.

I poured a glass of wine.

At 5:30, I trudged out to my car, brushed the snow off the driver's-side door. The car started. Phew. I put the heat on full blast. Charged my phone.

Back inside, I poured more wine and texted the power company again.

Power to be restored by 11:45 p.m.

Shit. It was like waiting on a delayed flight with the airline continually posting new times of departure. I put on another sweater and two more pairs of socks. I read a chapter of *Big Magic* by candlelight.

The cottage was freezing, close to unbearable. I vented on Facebook.

Generator, someone responded.

There's one at the house but I don't live there anymore, I replied, which felt a little scary to put out to Facebook Land, but at that point, I didn't care who knew or didn't know about our separation.

We were getting divorced.

At nine, I climbed into bed with what felt like seventeen layers of clothing. Maybe I could sleep, and tomorrow I'd wake up with power and feel human again.

I burrowed under the covers but couldn't get warm, no matter how hard I tried. How did the homeless survive? How did Jesus walk through the wilderness for forty days and nights without bread or water, with the devil tempting him each step of the way? It wouldn't take much to tempt me to climb back into my old warm life with Evan.

Plague #4: Insomnia

4 a.m. On the basis of the past few weeks, that was a good night's sleep.

In the rare nights I slept decently that winter, I often dreamed about Evan and sometimes Reenie too.

One night I dreamed about the three of us standing in front of the boys' school where Reenie used to teach. "I'm so sorry," Reenie said to Evan with tears in her eyes. She turned to me. "This relationship has been over for a long time," she said, "but I just didn't know how to end it."

Maybe that was the truth. Maybe she'd wanted to end things for years.

Plague #5: Mice

The mouse was back. Of course, it (they) had never left, but I hadn't seen or heard them in months.

Plague #6: Loneliness

An elderly couple walked arm-in-arm into the doctor's waiting room. The wife settled her husband into a chair and chatted with the receptionist.

"We're going on a cruise to Saint Thomas," she said. "George loves cruises."

I had always thought that would be my life. Not the cruise part, but the growing-old-together part. The taking-care-of-each-other part. The always-having-a-person part.

Evan and I had agreed to be each other's person for a while longer. I'd seen him through his surgery in December; he'd agreed to accompany me to my colonoscopy in April. But after that?

I missed him. I missed the ease, the partnership, the having someone who took care of things.

You have no idea how hard it is to be alone.

I was beginning to understand.

Plague #7: Mother

"How are you feeling today?" Mom called one afternoon in March. "Can I bring you anything?"

It was nice of her to offer and show she cared. I'd been longing for that from her.

"I'm okay for now. I'll let you know if I need anything."

"What are your plans for the week?" she asked.

"Main thing is to get ready for Tuesday's mediation," I said.

The silence seemed to go on forever. "How is Evan doing?" she said finally.

WTF. She had no idea how much it hurt me to feel like she cared more about his feelings than mine.

"I don't know," I said. "He doesn't share that kind of stuff with me anymore. I guess he's fine. He's a pragmatist. He's probably dating." Maybe I said that because I wanted to see if she knew anything. Or maybe I said it because it was the worst thing I could think of, and it was better to say it out loud.

"Well, he's a great catch," she said for at least the third time since I came out to her.

Plague #8: Heartbreak

Tomorrow was the first day of Lent and the start of a big month. In a few weeks, I'd be heading to Nashville to meet up with the LaLas!

But first I had to get healthy—inside and out. Sleep better. Ground myself somehow.

Adopting a Lenten practice had grounded me in the past. I emailed Evan to ask if I could borrow a Lenten devotional guide the two of us had used before.

"It's yours," he replied. "If you're going to the Ash Wednesday service, I can bring it to you."

I hadn't been to the Montauk Community Church much since Evan and I had separated. It felt too uncomfortable being in a tiny sanctuary that sat ninety at most, watching Evan sing in the choir and wondering what people were thinking about the two of us. Like the writer friend who had said Evan wasn't doing well.

But this Ash Wednesday, I needed to be there. I needed something to anchor me more than ever.

"I'll see you there," I said to Evan.

Ash Wednesday, I slept until 5 a.m., which was close to a miracle. Maybe Lent would be flooded with light instead of darkness. I sipped coffee and read through my email. There was an odd message from my old Houston pastor inviting me to the church's Ash Wednesday service. Reenie and I had guffawed over his fire-and-brimstone invitation last year when we were still in our "nothing is going to change with us" phase.

I wished I could laugh with her about this year's kooky message. I missed her so much. It had been almost three months since I mailed the goodbye letter. The aftermath felt like a death. You think you are fine and something happens that reopens the wound. The smallest thing, like an email from your old pastor, sets you off.

The rest of that morning, I walked around in a fog. It really was over with her.

Sometime that afternoon, my phone buzzed. *Change of plan*, Evan texted. *Not going to church tonight. I'll leave the Lenten guide for you by the front door.*

What else could he possibly be doing on a Wednesday night in Montauk in early March?

He was dating. He must be dating.

He was dating, and I was not. The matches coming through online were increasingly depressing. The same tired faces time after time. The "You both are nonsmokers!" as the basis for the match. Most days, I barely glanced at them.

I had to get out of this cottage and this desolate little town and go somewhere I could meet people. Although at this rate, who would want to date me?

I looked like hell with permanent dark circles under my eyes, and I felt even worse. Two rounds of antibiotics hadn't helped. It had to be stress. But how do you get rid of stress when you can't sleep, and you can't sleep because you are stressed?

I wanted to crawl back into bed and not go to church myself. But something told me I shouldn't sleepwalk through this Lent.

I dragged myself into the shower and drove to Montauk. The Lenten guide was leaning outside the front door of the house. Evan's car was gone. He was gone.

Evan and Reenie were gone.

I walked into church, feeling punch drunk. But the quiet settled me. The readings felt healing. It was good to be in community after a day of loss.

The pastor was shaking hands at the front door as people departed.

"How are you doing?" he said, holding out his arms. I accepted the hug. It felt good. I hadn't had human touch in so long.

"I'm really struggling," I said.

"You know you can talk with me any time," he said.

I nodded, fighting back tears.

After I got home, that text came in from Sami, the one cautioning me about succumbing to the weakness of the flesh.

A helluva start to Lent.

Plague #9: Blizzard

A week after the first blizzard of the season, another was forecast. I decided to stay at Mom's. Maybe I was a glutton for punishment. Maybe I thought I'd feel less isolated there. Maybe I went because if there was another power outage, she and I could walk over to my old house and take advantage of the generator, if Evan would let us.

Would he?

Minutes before I was to head to Mom's, Patrick texted: *Can you talk?*

My boys rarely initiated calls. I called right away.

"Hi, Mom," he said, the only words he could choke out before he started sobbing.

His girlfriend had ended things with him.

"My heart's broken," he said.

I did what I could to comfort him. I knew he'd be okay. He was a catch if there ever was one. I remembered thinking my life was over when Alan broke up with me. But soon Evan came into my life.

There will be love again, I wanted to reassure Patrick.

But did I believe it for myself?

The Plagues

The snow was supposed to start early the next morning. I drove over to Mom's and walked in the side door. As I hung up my down jacket, my eyes moved over the framed photos on her bookshelf. Three from my wedding: my bridal portrait, one of Evan and me, another of our entire wedding party. I wondered if she'd even considered packing those away.

I plunked down on the couch. *Jeopardy!* was on. I told Mom about the phone call with Patrick and how upset he was.

"Yes, of course he's upset," she said. "His girlfriend broke up with him and his parents are getting divorced. His whole world is falling apart."

"Thanks, that's not really helpful."

"Well, it's true."

When would I learn? I was like a boxer who kept getting back into the ring, thinking I wouldn't get knocked down this time.

I went into the bathroom, looked at myself in the mirror. What a mess. My nose was rubbed raw from congestion. My right eye was red and gooey. Pink eye? Really? Blizzards, mice, insomnia, sinus infections, and pink eye. This miniversion of the biblical plagues was almost comical, but I didn't feel like laughing. It was as if the universe was saying, "Show us what you got, girl." I didn't have much left.

When Blizzard #2 turned out to be a big nothing, I exited Mom's as soon as I could and slowly drove past my old house. In two days, I'd return there to begin dividing up thirty years of my old life. Which felt both necessary and impossible at the same time. Just like the path I was on.

Doubt

The Montauk house appeared to have been wiped clean of me. Pinpricks on the walls where family photos once hung. Bridal portrait no longer on the windowsill above Evan's desk. My side of the bedroom closet—empty.

Something delicious smelling was bubbling on the stove. Had Evan been cooking a lot? Bagged salads and pasta had become my go-tos. No energy for more.

A flash of brown to the left of the steaming pot caught my eye. A small shopping bag from Kripalu, the yoga retreat center. Kripalu. Had Evan been there or had someone he'd been dating—the woman he ditched the Ash Wednesday service for?—given it to him? I wanted to ask but didn't. Evan had made it clear his personal life was off-limits. But while I didn't think he owed me all the details, wasn't it only fair that we tell each other about any new relationships? To protect ourselves from the shock of hearing about them from someone else. To know what our boys knew about their other parent's life.

"I haven't eaten yet," Evan said. "Want to join me?"

"Sure."

He ladled vegetable soup into two heavy blue-and-yellow bowls, part of a pottery set we'd bought when we moved into the house seventeen years ago. Those would stay with him, I guessed.

At the table, I swirled my spoon around chunks of zucchini, yellow squash, and new potatoes. Would Evan plant a garden this spring? The vegetable garden had been one of the joys we'd discovered in our empty-nest chapter. He handled the planting and tending; I harvested and cooked. One of many areas we'd made a good team.

The Kripalu bag caught my eye again.

"I know it might be painful," I said, "but can we make a deal that we'll let each other know if or when we're in a relationship? So we're not blindsided and find out some other way?"

"I'm not interested in hearing about your personal life," he said.

"No worries, there's not much to tell." I wasn't going to share about the dates with Sarah and Cindy that had gone nowhere or the depressing matches online. I wasn't going to tell him I was pinning my hopes on LaLa Con to lift my spirits and, who knows, maybe even meet someone there. And I certainly wasn't going to share that I was starting to believe my mother was right. I was too old for this. I was going to be alone. For the rest of my life.

"What about you?" I asked. I couldn't help myself. I had to know if he had gone out with any of the women whose initials he'd scribbled on that yellow legal pad. Or whether he'd tried online dating. And what the hell had he been doing on Ash Wednesday?

"How much do you want to know?" he said.

"As much as you are willing to tell me."

I wanted to know Every. Single. Detail.

"After the first of the year," he said, "I went out with a few women that friends had set me up with."

Those initials. The sting of seeing them returned.

"Then at the end of January," he said, "I met someone online."

He appeared to be trying to suppress a smile. Fuck.

He rattled off a list of details I willed myself to remember, wishing I could pull out my phone and take notes: Sag Harbor. Cornell grad. Chief marketing officer for a podcast he assumed I'd heard of but hadn't. Yoga teacher. A couple of years older than him. Son close in age to Will and Patrick. Going through a divorce too. Elsa. Her name was Elsa.

"Are you dating her exclusively?" I asked, stunned he could already be in a relationship.

This time he definitely smiled. "Yes, I can't date multiple people at the same time," he said. "I'm not a player, you know."

Not a player? How do you even know what you are after thirty years of marriage?

They'd met at the end of January. Two months after we decided to divorce. Two weeks before we started mediation.

"Did you go out with her on Ash Wednesday?" I asked.

"Three of us went out," he said.

"What's that supposed to mean? Was she one of the three?"

"Yes, we went out to dinner with Bill," he said sheepishly.

So it was happening. The friends that had been our friends were his friends now. And were becoming Elsa's friends.

"Do the boys know about her?"

"Not yet," he said.

I wanted him to be happy. I didn't want him eating dinner alone in front of the TV. But to be replaced so quickly. Agony.

Did men feel jealous of other men the way women felt jealous of other women? Or at least the way I felt jealous of other women?

It was mostly the moms who had professional lives who got to me.

Women like this Elsa person who was dating my husband.

Ivy grad. Chief marketing officer. Mom.

Fuck me.

After lunch, Evan and I sorted through the pots and pans.

Sag Harbor. Cornell. Famous podcast. Elsa.

I took the wedding china. He took the crystal. We divided up the sterling silver.

Sag Harbor. Cornell. Podcast. Elsa.

In Evan's study, a new-age medicine stick rested on the windowsill where my bridal portrait had been. It had Kripalu and Elsa's fingerprints written all over it, or at least what I imagined were her fingerprints. She was already taking over my house. My life.

Evan handed me our wedding album. "Do you want this?"

He obviously didn't.

I took the wedding album. I'd pack it away with the other family photos I didn't know what to do with. Maybe someday I'd show it to my grandkids and tell them the whole big messy story about their grandfather and me.

I drove back to the cottage in a trance.

Sag Harbor. Podcast. Elsa.

I ran inside and grabbed my laptop.

Elsa. Sag Harbor. Podcast.

There she was in living color on my computer screen. With her toes in the sand. On her mat at Kripalu. At a boutique hotel emceeing a live Facebook event.

Elsa wasn't a knockout, but there was something attractive about her. Great teeth, great hair. Ivy League and famous too—well, almost. She ran the show for a famous scientist who hosted a podcast with millions of subscribers. In her spare time, she taught yoga. I hated her already.

But the worst part about Elsa was that she seemed nice. Like the kind of person who, under different circumstances, I might enjoy hanging out with.

But Elsa was not a friend. She was the woman who would be filling my future grandchildren's Christmas stockings. Sipping rosé on the beach at sunset with my friends. Gliding into my side of the bed as effortlessly as she draped those gauzy scarves around that neck of hers.

I went into the bathroom to grab a tissue, stopped at the mirror to blow my nose. Both eyes were gooey now.

LaLa Con couldn't come soon enough. Five days until I boarded a plane to Nashville.

Five days. I could hang on for five more days.

~

When you find out your STBXH has been dating an Ivy-educated yoga instructor for 6 weeks and you are sitting at home on a Friday night with pink eye in both eyes and have absolutely no romantic prospects on the horizon, I posted on the LaLa page.

ANNIE: OK. So she's probably smart. And has a hot bod. But I'm sure she has no personality, she's boring as shit, narcissistic, and I'll bet she hates puppies. And sucks in bed. And the woman you're about to fall in love with? 10x smarter, hotter, funnier, kinder, more loving, and hot af in bed!

RUTH: It WILL HAPPEN.

ME: Thank you, guys. It's just hard to feel hope now.

~

Elsa's toothy grin was the first thing I thought of when I woke up at four on Saturday morning.

Was she lying in bed—my bed—next to my husband?

Evan's dating, I texted Beth. *Don't tell Mom.*

That doesn't surprise me, she replied. *Mom said one of her friends saw him walking around the backyard with a woman.*

Mom knew. Who else knew? Maybe I was the last one in Montauk to be let in on the secret.

That day in mid-March was Mom's eighty-second birthday. I'd offered to take her to lunch or dinner, but she'd said no, not wanting to catch my crud. I didn't blame her. I wouldn't want to be around me either. We'd celebrate after Nashville.

And good thing we weren't going out that day. I had more important things to do. I opened Facebook and typed in Elsa's name.

There she was again. Her tousled auburn curls and toothy smile. The lavender tie-dyed scarf wrapped around her swanlike neck. Her toes poking playfully out of the sand. Had she staged that scene, or was she just that kind of gal?

I reached for a tissue and dabbed my right eye, and my left. How I had managed to contract pink eye in both eyes, I had no idea. There were a lot of things I had no idea about, like when I would next have two good nights of sleep in a row or how I could have possibly been sick all winter. But the biggest thing I didn't know was how I was going to make it. How I was going to survive the most colossal fuckup of my life.

Evan was right when he said I was going to be just as unhappy on the gay side. He had said that, hadn't he? He was right that the grass wasn't greener over here. Why hadn't I listened to him?

I tossed the tissue onto the floor and stared at my screen saver: a photo of the four of us leaning against our bikes with the Vilcanota mountains in the distance.

The four of us. Suzette, Evan, Will, and Patrick taking another awesome family trip. We'd biked through the Sacred Valley, hiked the Inca Trail, tasted *cuy* in Cusco. That trip was ten years ago, way before I started writing the memoir that turned our worlds upside down. We looked happy—we *were* happy.

Did people in happy marriages fall in love with other people? I had no idea. Did Evan love Elsa? Did she love him? Maybe it wasn't too late to undo this. What I wouldn't give to climb into Evan's arms now. Exactly where Elsa might be.

I crawled back into bed and parsed every online mention of this woman. She called herself a "serial entrepreneur." I'd never heard that term before, but it sounded like someone who was a risk taker.

My husband was attracted to someone the polar opposite of me.

Maybe he'd been tired of my safe choices too.

~

Sunday morning. Another sleepless night. I stumbled into the kitchen. Made coffee. Checked my phone.

A text from Ruth, a LaLa and retired nurse who was like a big sister to me: *Are you feeling better today? Did you get any sleep last night? Can't wait to see you in Nashville!* She'd been checking on me practically every day this winter and had been urging me to go to the doctor again. *It's just a cold*, I kept telling her. A cold I couldn't shake.

Hanging in there. Fake it until you make it, right?

A text from Jenn confirming our FaceTime call for that evening. Jenn and I had been lifting each other up through our divorces, but I didn't have that kind of energy this day.

Can we reschedule?

~

I tried to stay away from Facebook and from Elsa. I really tried.

The more I stared at her photos, the darker Sunday got.

The pain. The pain. The pain.

Mom, Beth, and Reenie's words rang through my head, like a Mean Girls' Greek Chorus.

I can't believe you're doing this.

This is just another one of your obsessions.

You are going to cause so many people so much pain.

Everything I'd feared—and my mother had predicted—was happening. Evan would be living in my house with Elsa, and I'd be living god knows where, alone. With pink eye.

How naive to think the pain would disappear once I got off the fence and made the hard choice to leave. Reenie was gone. Evan was with Elsa. Beth and Mom still didn't get it. Many days, even I didn't get how writing a single sentence had landed me here.

The pain. The pain. The pain. I couldn't handle much more.

I closed Facebook. Opened Google. Typed *painless ways to kill yourself.*

I wanted information just in case things got worse. How-to books I could order online. Pills I could swallow. Powders I could mix into Gatorade.

Whatever the method, it had to be simple and foolproof. But when I clicked on www.bestwaystokillyourself.com, Google did a bait-and-switch: a suicide hotline popped up. I shivered and shut the laptop. I wasn't serious about killing myself. I just wanted to know there was a way out of the pain.

There had to be a way.

Surrender

Monday morning. Dirty dishes in sink. Mounds of unfolded laundry on couch. Mail scattered on kitchen counter. No energy for any of it.

I threw myself on the couch that didn't have laundry on it. Wrapped myself in a blanket. Closed my eyes. The sun streaming through the sliding glass door felt like being held. I couldn't remember the last time someone held me.

~

My dear LaLas—I am hanging on by a thread. I can't describe what I'm feeling other than it's bad, very bad.

The only other time I'd felt this hopeless was thirty-five years ago when Alan broke up with me for the second time and I moved back home with my parents.

A new college graduate without a job, a boyfriend, a plan, or hope, I wandered the aisles of a local drugstore looking for something to take away the pain. Pulled a box of Sominex off the shelf. Was it strong enough to do the job? Who knew? I put the box back on the shelf. I didn't want to die. I just wanted a way out of the pain.

Thirty-five years later, the same feeling.

ME: Everything feels dark and impossible right now. I woke up in the middle of the night thinking I have made the biggest mistake of my life and there's no way forward.

HEIDI: It's OK to have days like this. It sucks, but it's OK. Going to LaLa Con is perfect timing. Heart connections, sharing stories, will do you good. Plus you get to hug Andrea!

ANDREA: Your hug is waiting, Suzette!

~

Official Agenda for LaLa Con:

Welcome party and bonfire
Small group breakout sessions
Sharing stories
Yoga
Karaoke at the Lipstick Lounge

Unofficial Agenda:
Fifty women feeling comfortable in their own skin
Online friendships becoming real-life ones
Love connections?

I couldn't wait to meet Andrea, the LaLa founder. The woman whose blog had turned my world upside down—in a good way—fourteen months ago. How I could have survived the past year without the LaLas, I had no idea.

The group had grown from fifty to over one thousand in those fourteen months. Women all over the world asking the same questions I'd asked in the beginning: *What if this is all in my head? How do I know if I'm really gay? How can I possibly do this to my husband, to my kids?*

Some of my besties would be at the conference, including Ruth, the nurse who kept checking on me, and Nancy, who was now Ruth's girlfriend.

And a southern blonde I'd been chatting with in a semiflirtatious way. More age appropriate than Sandy. Lovely smile. Wore red lipstick. Looked amazing in a bikini.

She'd be waiting for me in Nashville too.

~

Tuesday morning. Exhausted. Another night when my brain wouldn't shut down. I didn't want to think at all. I just wanted to sleep and be teleported to Nashville.

How are you, girl? Jenn texted. *Call me. I'm worried about you.*

Hey girl, I'm fine. Just super tired. Talk later?

Yes, I was super tired, but I was not fine. I was so not fine.

One foot in front of the other. Tonight: sleep. Tomorrow: pack a bag, take a bus to New York, get to a friend's apartment where I'd spend the night. Thursday: hop on an early morning bus to LaGuardia, get on a plane, arrive in Nashville—where I prayed there'd be some light in this darkness.

I would sleep tonight. I knew the best protocols: Turn off phone. Take a hot shower—a bath would be even better, but there was no tub in the cottage. Dab lavender oil on my temples and wrists. Swallow a melatonin tablet. Set the temperature in my bedroom cooler than usual. Read a little, turn off the light, and hope for sleep.

I followed my protocol to a T, climbed into bed, and clipped my itty-bitty reading light to the edge of this week's *New Yorker*.

Did anyone actually read this magazine? I had piles and piles of back issues. Always flipped through it, looked at the cartoons, read the letters to the editor, and intended to tackle the articles later. But rarely did.

This week's Fiction selection, "Solstice," a short story by Anne Enright.

The opening lines, so beautiful, so haunting:

"It was the year's turning. These few hours like the blink of a great eye—just enough light to check that the world is still there, before shutting back down.

"Sometime in the midafternoon, he had an impulse to go home, or go somewhere, and when he lifted his head, of course, it was dark outside. It just felt wrong."

It just felt wrong. I got that. All those years I didn't have words to name what I was feeling. The restlessness I couldn't shake. The discontent. The nagging sense I wasn't living my life.

It just felt wrong.

But this complete darkness.

How could this be right?

There had to be light—at least a glimmer of it—in Nashville.

~

Are you seeing a therapist, Suzette? I really recommend it if you aren't already, Meghan, a LaLa who was a therapist herself, responded to my "I'm hanging by a thread" post.

ME: I saw someone for the past 15 months. I stopped seeing her about a month ago—I felt like the relationship had run its course. Actively looking for a new one now. Pickings are slim where I live.

The truth was more complicated, but bottom line: I didn't have a therapist when I most needed one.

MEGHAN: Suzette, I hope you find someone soon that feels like a good fit.

ME: Me too. I just did an online test for depression, anxiety, and stress, and the results were scary.

AMY: Find a queer therapist if you can. That made a difference to me.

~

Wednesday morning, sunlight greeted me when I opened my eyes—a freaking miracle. And those eyes looked less gooey. And my throat felt a little less sore.

I could do this. I pulled out my suitcase. Tossed in my black leather jacket and skinny jeans. I wanted to be comfortable but also feel confident—and desirable. Maybe a LaLa would become more than a "friend."

I threw in another pair of jeans and a few tops. My wardrobe wasn't worth stressing over—I had bigger problems than that.

One foot in front of the other.

Get my butt to New York this afternoon.

And Nashville tomorrow.

~

My friend Janice led me into her dark-paneled library, which doubled as a guest room in her spacious Upper East Side apartment. Leatherbound books lined the bookshelves, original art hung from the walls. It reminded me of my old life, a life I didn't want anymore, but a life that still tugged at me. It's hard to let go of the old when you can't see the new.

I dropped my suitcase next to the sofa bed and followed Janice into the kitchen. Her husband, Danny, still in his suit, was there, sorting through the mail.

"Wine?" Janice asked, as she opened the cabernet sauvignon I'd brought as a thank-you.

"Sure," I said, hoping it would soothe my throat, which was on fire again. Hoping it would help me sleep tonight. Hoping it would help me get through this evening where I planned to pretend I was okay when I was totally not.

I had no idea if Janice and Danny knew why Evan and I were divorcing. They were a newer addition to our close-knit beach group. All the other couples and families who sat together on summer weekends had a tie to Montauk that went back at least one generation.

Evan and I had sent Janice and Danny the "we have separated and are navigating our next steps" email, but because I didn't know them as well, I hadn't sent them the second "I've come to understand my sexuality differently" email. Likely, they'd heard what was going on from others in the group.

I wanted them to ask me what was going on, and I didn't.

I wanted to be real, and I wanted to never have to explain myself again.

We stood there, wine glasses in hand. Talked about the weather. About our children—they had two boys, only much younger than mine. Talked about everything but Evan and me.

"Where are you headed tomorrow?" Danny asked.

This was my opening to get real but I wasn't going to take it. It was nearly midnight, too late to get into this now. I needed to turn off my brain and sleep.

I took another swig of wine, praying it would dull the fire in my throat that had reached five-alarm status.

"Nashville," I said. "For a girls' weekend."

Alarm set for 7 a.m., I settled under the quilt on the sofa bed.

Eleven hours until my flight.

Fourteen hours until I was with my LaLas.

I wrestled with the quilt, trying to ignore the fire in my throat. *You don't have to go*, a voice whispered inside me. The Voice?

That was ridiculous. Of course I had to go. I'd paid the conference fee. My plane tickets were nonrefundable. I was the one in charge of the Airbnb. People were counting on me.

But ten minutes ago you barely had the energy to wash your face and brush your teeth and you are really sick. How are you going to do this if you can't get some sleep?

People handled hard things all the time. And like my LaLa friend Annie said, it wouldn't be hard all the time. *Moments will be hard. Other moments will be joyous. And that's just how life goes: hard, easy, hard again.*

But when would the easy happen again? Because it felt really hard that the only people who understood me were a group of women, most of whom I'd never met in real life. And it felt really hard that I was this close to spending four days with them, but I didn't know if I had the strength to get myself there.

I can get myself to LaGuardia somehow even if I don't sleep well tonight.

I am a woman who can do hard things.

I can get myself on that plane.

I can take a cab from the airport to the Airbnb.

I just have to put one foot in front of the next.

I am not going to NOT *do this.*

I am not going to ruin this chance to find happiness.

I am going to sleep tonight.

And even if I can't, I am going to Nashville.

I am not a quitter.

2:15 a.m.

An ambulance raced by, or was that a firetruck? I'd forgotten how damn noisy it was in Manhattan. I used to dream about showing Reenie around the city. We would stay in a hotel room with two beds, and who knew, something might happen.

3:00 a.m.

Maybe Reenie had been right. Honoring my vows would have been so much simpler. Why didn't I listen to her?

3:45 a.m.

Calling it. Officially a night of no sleep.

I can do one night. I can make it.

Lots of people managed on little sleep. Jenn did, although I didn't know how, as a single mom with four young kids and a full-time job.

4:15 a.m.

I can't do this. I can't put one foot in front of the next.

I had played the part of a badass. Dealt with mice. Survived blizzards and power outages. Negotiated a divorce settlement. But I wasn't a badass. I was a poser. Soft. Weak. I wasn't going to make it.

Evan. Reenie. Beth. My mother.

Why hadn't I listened to any of them?

5:00 a.m.

I can't do this. Any of this. The divorce. The new life.

If only I could rewind the clock to that moment before I emailed those pages to my book coach. If only I could yank Elsa out of my bed and climb in next to Evan. Rest my head on that spot made just for me. Fuck authenticity. Fuck going for my life. Fuck being brave.

I cannot do this.

All those people who thought I could start over at this age, especially the LaLas and Jenn. All the people I was about to disappoint.

Today you are on the first page of your new book . . . It looks daunting to dig into, Jenn had written. *But . . . take a deep breath and just start with the first page.*

Jenn, I don't know how to breathe anymore.

"Call me anytime, day or night," she had said once, when I was having a particularly rough day.

It was too early to call her or anyone else.

It was too early to wake up Janice and Danny and tell them I was unraveling in their guest room and literally could not get out of bed.

5:15 a.m.

Text me when you wake up, I messaged Jenn.

What's up? She responded seconds later.

I can't get on a plane today. Just can't.

I'm calling you.

"What's going on?" Jenn said, as soon as I picked up the phone.

"Everything's gone off the rails—*everything*. I feel like I need to check myself in somewhere, only I don't even know where I'd go."

"Suzette, one thing I know. You are *not* going back to that cabin by yourself."

I smiled through my tears. Jenn liked to call my cottage a *cabin*. Maybe it was a Pennsylvania thing.

"You're coming here, and I'll help you make a plan."

I was coming there? To Lancaster?

"Jenn, you have enough going on. You can't take this on."

"You *are* coming here. Can you get yourself to Penn Station and get on a train? If you can't, I'm going to drive up there and get you. I swear, I have nothing else to do today."

Nothing. Right. Four kids. A job.

But she *was* right—I couldn't go back to the "cabin."
And I couldn't get myself to Nashville.
It was Penn Station or a mental hospital.

I dragged myself into the shower, scribbled a note to Janice and Danny, and headed to the Second Avenue subway. Which I would take to Penn Station. Where I would buy a ticket to Lancaster, Pennsylvania. With a suitcase packed for Nashville, Tennessee. Which on its face seemed preposterous, but no part of this journey had felt logical or rational.

Something Bigger Than Me, something beyond my understanding, was at work.

PART FOUR

Detour

"Speak!" I screamed into an empty field one day, when I was struggling to discern my path in my midforties. "Can't you see how hard I'm trying to figure things out? Just tell me what to do and I'll do it."

Stop trying to figure it out, the Voice said.

This detour to Lancaster was certainly beyond my figure-it-out ability.

~

I hoisted my suitcase onto the overhead rack on the train. Found a seat by the window. Checked my phone. Three hours to Lancaster.

Before leaving Janice and Danny's apartment, I'd messaged the LaLas I was supposed to be sharing an Airbnb with to tell them I wasn't coming. Contacted the airline to say I was too sick to fly. Was stunned when the agent offered a travel voucher for my nonrefundable ticket. A glimmer of light in the darkness.

Nondescript office towers and cookie-cutter suburban subdivisions rushed by my window as the train made its way toward Philadelphia. A text from Beth: *Have a good trip.*

Thanks, I responded, grateful she didn't add "to Nashville." I wasn't ready to get into what had happened over the past twenty-four hours. But should someone besides Jenn and the LaLas know where I was headed?

Evan told me not to text him so much. That hurt after thirty-three years together. But he had a right to his boundaries, and he didn't need to know that his soon-to-be-ex-wife, who'd been planning to hang out with fifty later-in-life lesbians in Nashville, had fallen apart and was headed to Pennsylvania instead.

Maybe I'd eventually tell him the story. Maybe I'd tell my boys, mom, and sister too. But that day, no one else needed to know.

About thirty minutes west of Philadelphia, the landscape changed from office towers to vast swaths of farmland beginning to green, silos silhouetted against a crisp blue sky, herds of cows lolling about.

I felt like Dorothy being transported from Kansas to Oz.

It was beautiful, but why this detour?

"We want the whole map," I'd heard someone say once. "But all we get is the direction, which is all we really need."

~

"You made it!" Jenn said as I stepped off the train. The energy in her voice made me think I could do this—whatever *this* was—even though I felt as helpless as a newborn.

"First stop, urgent care," she said, looking at what I imagined were the dark circles under my eyes and the chapped skin on my nostrils.

Before I got in her car, I looked back at the station house. Twelve fifteen, according to the clock at the top of the majestic old brick building.

The time my plane to Nashville was due to push back from the gate.

The lifeline I'd been clinging to.

What had I done?

Please, universe, send me a sign that I haven't ruined everything.

~

I left urgent care with a Z-PAK but no meds for sleep. "Talk to your provider when you get home," the physician's assistant said, when I asked for more medication.

"I've got you in with Kaye tomorrow at ten," Jenn said as we left the clinic. Kaye was Jenn's later-in-life lesbian (!) therapist. How Jenn had ended up with a lesbian therapist who had come out later in life, I had no idea, but it was awfully convenient for me.

~

Short black hair with a purple swirl. Leather miniskirt and boots, a snug-fitting baby-blue cardigan. Dark angular glasses. Tattoos on her wrists and neck.

Kaye the therapist.

I sat on her couch, grabbed a tissue, and blew my nose. "I've been sick all winter."

"Stress will do that to you," she said.

Yep. I'd read that two of the top five stressful life events were divorce and moving—and as an overachiever, I'd added coming out in my midfifties.

"I don't know what Jenn's told you, but here's the short version." I grabbed another tissue. "This fall I left a thirty-year marriage because I realized I was gay. And last week I spiraled into a very dark place when I found out my husband has a girlfriend."

Kaye nodded. I could already tell therapy with her would be different from my sessions with Alice. I doubted she'd be asking me about breasts and bottle-feeding or suggesting I didn't have to do anything about my "same-sex attraction."

I dabbed my cheeks with the tissue.

"Elsa," I spat out her name. "Who seems perfect for Evan."

They were probably texting about their weekend plans. Or maybe they weren't texting at all. Maybe she had spent the night and was cuddling on the couch with *my* husband in *my* living room. Which objectively I knew she had every right to do, but still. I wanted Evan to be happy, and I didn't want him to be happy with someone other than me. It was all so confusing.

"I've tried online dating," I said, "but I live in a tourist town and there's no one around this time of year."

At least no one who's not a woman eager to date my husband.

"I've had a few *meh* dates so far, in New York City—which is three hours away from the little cottage I'm renting."

"That's a long way to go for a *meh* date," she said. "And online dating is brutal."

No kidding.

"How about when the matches come in with taglines like *You are both nonsmokers*!" I said.

We both laughed, but it wasn't funny. It was an invitation for my mother's voice to take residence in my head again: *What if you try this and it doesn't make you happy?*

Outside the window, tall green grasses in a vast field waved in the breeze. Was that a barn in the distance? I half expected a horse and buggy to rumble by. Which would have been cool if I wasn't feeling so miserable.

"Nothing is clicking for me. I don't know if I can do this much longer," I said.

Kaye leaned forward. "You are going to be okay. We have to get you out of that cottage and into community. Wait a minute, I have an idea." She pulled out her phone. "Tomorrow night, one of my friends is having a birthday party. You should go."

"What?"

"Erica and her wife own a gallery in the city. There'll be tons of lesbians at the party. You should go. I'll text you the info."

I smiled, but really. It was one thing to have landed in Amish country and another thing to walk solo into a birthday party with a bunch of lesbians I didn't know. Although if I could convince Jenn to be my wingwoman, I might do just that.

~

"Hey," I grunted to Jenn as I sat down in her kitchen with a cup of coffee. Thankfully, I had slept the last two nights. The Z-PAK must have kicked in.

Kaye had texted details about the party. The birthday girl owned a gallery with her *wife*. I was still startled when I heard about women married to women. The *Obergefell* decision was only two years old, plus I didn't know any married lesbians besides Joan, my pilgrimage leader, and her wife, and I didn't know if they were even legally married. But none of that had stopped me from fantasizing about the small tasteful ceremony Reenie and I would have had if things had gone differently.

I looked out the kitchen window and swallowed my tears. Tears for what would never be with Reenie. Tears for what had been and was gone with Evan. Tears for a future I couldn't imagine.

"You okay?" Jenn asked.

"Yeah." *You are going to be okay*, Kaye had said. *You just need community.* "Kaye invited me to a birthday party with a bunch of her lesbian friends. It's tonight. Wanna be my wingwoman?"

Jenn laughed. "Yes! I'll try to get a sitter."

Please, universe, make that happen.

~

Lancaster City reminded me of a small-scale Boston with its cobblestone plazas and old redbrick buildings. Many of those buildings displayed historic plaques, like the one stating that Lancaster had been the US capital on September 27, 1777, when the Continental Congress fled Philadelphia, which I appreciated as a former history major. I'd wanted to live in Boston after law school, but Evan had preferred Houston. Boston was too gray and cold in the winter, he said. Too depressing. Maybe he was right, but why hadn't I fought harder for what I wanted?

Jenn, her kids, and I walked down Prince Street toward the gallery owned by Kaye's friends. A sign in front announced, "Erica's annual birthday sale: 42 percent off everything. The older I get, the more you save."

Perfect timing!

"If I'm going to this party," I said to Jenn as we walked into the shop, "I have to get some cool earrings." The pearl studs were well past their expiration date.

Dozens of earrings were displayed on a table in the center of the gallery. I picked up a pair of delicate silver dangles and put them next to my ear.

"Perfect," Jenn said.

"Yes," I said as I looked in the mirror. Silly, perhaps, but I felt like a completely different person from the woman who'd been called a Creamsicle by Mary Karr four years ago.

I walked over with the earrings to the two women standing at the counter. I recognized them from the gallery's website but couldn't remember who was who.

"Is one of you Erica?" I said.

"That's me," the woman on the right said.

"This is going to sound random, but I'm going to your birthday party tonight."

Because I was going. With or without Jenn. Wearing my new dangly earrings and the black leather jacket I'd packed for LaLa Con.

They both smiled. "You must be Suzette," the woman on the left said. "Kaye told us about you."

You must be Suzette. Something about hearing my name from someone I'd just met made me want to cry. Two hundred and eighty miles from Montauk and eight hundred miles from where I was supposed to be, the universe was in full-on, show-off mode.

~

"I have to go to the bathroom," Jenn's youngest said as we walked down the last aisle of Central Market, the country's oldest year-round farmers market. The other kids needed to go too.

"I'll meet you outside," I said to Jenn. On my way out of the market, I grabbed a freebie magazine and opened it as I soaked in the sun that March day—so welcome after all the snow and ice that winter. On page 2 was an ad for an old factory building that had been converted into condos. Lancaster was way more hip than I imagined, although I hadn't done much imagining before three days ago—the first time I'd given the city a single thought.

My mind wandered to Nashville and all I was missing. The hugs from Andrea. The support from my besties. The possible sparks with the woman who wore red lipstick.

Jenn and the kids were taking forever. I closed the magazine and opened Facebook on my phone to see what was up with the LaLas.

A post from a woman named Joyce whose name I recognized from the page: *It's a beautiful day in Lancaster PA!*

Joyce lived here?

I'm in front of Central Market right now! I replied.

No way! I live right around the corner! How long will u be in town?

Monday! Let's get together!

Yes! Do you go to church?

Church? I'd been thinking cocktails or brunch. But I wasn't opposed to going to church. Especially with a LaLa.

Yes, I responded.

9:30 contemporary service at Grandview United Methodist is awesome. I can pick u up.

Great!

Sally, another LaLa, also goes there. She's singing a solo tomorrow. I'll introduce u to her & her gf. The worship leader is a lesbian too.

I couldn't believe this. This wasn't Oz or even Nashville. I'd been transported to the Land of the World's Friendliest Lesbians.

~

Jenn pulled up to a gunmetal house with white lights draped over a wooden fence. "Text me when you're ready to leave," she said as I opened the car door. "And have fun!"

I waved goodbye, feeling like her fifth child. The universe surely would have provided a babysitter, I had thought, what with all that had happened in the last two days. But no. I was going to have to do this solo.

Erica was tending bar in the kitchen. I gratefully accepted a glass of sparkling wine. Took a sip and surveyed the room. No sign of Kaye, who said she'd be there with her girlfriend. No sign of anyone I knew. Damn, I wished Jenn were here. I hated having to make conversation with strangers. And really what was I going to say?

I'd never set foot in this town before Thursday.

My therapist told me to crash this party.

I'm a lesbian. How about you?

To my left, an attractive younger woman with long dark-blonde hair was sipping a drink. Was she a lesbian? Her appearance certainly didn't scream *lesbian* to me, unlike the woman with very short dark hair and a plaid shirt who was standing slightly behind her and was on her phone.

"Suzette," I said, walking toward the blonde and extending my hand.

"Olivia," she said.

"What do you do in Lancaster?" I asked, before I could stop myself from asking the question I'd dreaded much of my adult life. The question I'd written an entire book about. The book with the unspeakable pages that had blown up my life.

She smiled. "I can tell you aren't from around here. We pronounce it Lank-*kiss*-stir, like a *kiss* in the middle." She laughed.

I laughed too. Lank-*kiss*-stir, not Lan-*cas*-ter. Lank-*kiss*-stir, Lank-*kiss*-stir, I repeated in my head, wanting to get it right the next time.

I relaxed as Olivia told me about her work at a nonprofit, serving people with disabilities. I shared a little about the special education advocacy work I'd done. Lesbian or not, Olivia was easy to talk to. She waved over the woman in the plaid shirt, who was no longer on her phone. "This is Denise, my wife," she said.

Okay, Olivia was a lesbian. My gaydar needed tuning. And Denise was her *wife*. Before this weekend, I'd never met a lesbian married couple, and now I'd met two.

"I've just come out," I said to Olivia and Denise, trying to establish solidarity. I watched for a reaction, wondering if they could see through the silver dangles and leather jacket swagger to the pearl-earringed stay-at-home mom underneath.

"That's cool," Olivia said. They both smiled.

I smiled too. It was liberating to not have to explain so much.

I told them about Jenn and about meeting with Kaye—whom they knew and who still wasn't here. I shared about the LaLas and the amazing coincidence that two LaLas lived in Lancaster. And that I was going to church with one of them tomorrow.

"Which church?" Olivia asked.

"Grandview United Methodist."

"We live right near there!" They knew the worship leader, who was gay. Did all the lesbians in Lank-*kiss*-stir know each other?

"When are you coming back?" Olivia asked.

"Not sure yet," I said, although somehow I knew I would.

"Let's get together the next time you're here." Olivia pulled out her phone and asked for my contact information.

What was this place? Everyone was friendly and all the lesbians knew each other. Hell, even I knew lesbians here.

Still no sign of Kaye. I moved around the room. Chatted with a brunette parked next to a platter of shrimp dumplings. Struck up a conversation with a bright-eyed horticulturist and a redhead who was a professor at a local college. Finally, Kaye sauntered in with another woman.

"Glad you made it," Kaye said when I came over, but it was clear she wanted to keep a professional distance. I didn't linger.

I checked my phone. Ten o'clock. The party had been way more fun than I'd expected, but I didn't want to keep Jenn out too late. *Ready*, I texted.

Something magical was happening here. I could feel it in my bones.

~

"That's Liz, the worship leader I was telling you about," Joyce said, pointing to the front of the sanctuary after we were seated. "And that's her wife." She pointed to a blonde across the aisle from us.

Someone tapped Joyce on the shoulder.

"Hey, Alexis," Joyce said. "Meet Suzette." Alexis was the girlfriend of Sally, the Lancaster LaLa who would be singing a solo later in the service.

The lesbians . . . they just kept a-coming.

Soon, Sally stepped up to the microphone and began to sing.

Her voice was angelic, but the aura surrounding her was what slayed me. That same palpable aura that had surrounded Reenie during our first coffee date.

Tears poured down my cheeks. Nineteen years ago, the Voice had led me to Reenie, and the Voice had led me here. To a church in Lancaster where I was sitting next to a LaLa instead of hanging with my LaLa besties in Nashville. To the sweet voice of another LaLa that was balm to my soul. To a worship service led by a lesbian whose wife was sitting across the aisle from me. To an early Easter morning after a very dark Lent.

Four days ago, the Voice had whispered: *You don't have to go.*

A decade ago, the Voice had whispered: *Stop trying to figure everything out.*

Fourteen months ago, Reenie had said: "You have to decide whether you are going to choose your own happiness or honor your vows."

I finally had the words to respond to her.

Reenie, I've chosen to honor myself.

~

A stream of sweaty people filed out of the heated yoga studio as Jenn and I waited for our class to begin. Although I was feeling much better than when I'd arrived in town, I was still weak. Good thing this class was a restorative one. Jenn said all we had to do was lie down and soak in the heat. Which sounded like the best thing ever.

"Hey, Suzette!" a woman said. I looked up. The professor from the birthday party!

Jenn nudged me. "You know people here already!"

I smiled. Lancaster was starting to feel like the bar on *Cheers*, where everyone knew my name. I *did* know people—and a bunch of them were lesbians. Which was wild because for the six months I'd been in the cottage, I'd met zero lesbians within a fifty—no, one-hundred—mile radius.

I shook my head. I had almost stopped being surprised by all the "coincidences." This detour to Lancaster was turning out to be a lovely ride.

~

The condo building advertised in the freebie magazine I'd browsed through the day before was having an open house. Jenn and I popped in after yoga.

"What's your price range?" the agent asked as I examined the listing sheet in the model unit.

Dude, I'm just here on a lark. But what the hell. I gave him a number.

"Do you want to see a few other units?" he asked.

I looked over at Jenn. She nodded vigorously.

"This is one of my favorites," the agent said as we stepped into a south-facing unit.

Concrete beams, high ceilings, exposed ductwork, light flooding in through the French doors, which opened up to a small balcony.

"Wow," I said.

"The best one so far," Jenn said.

"This is the kind of place I'd love to live in someday."
"I'm telling you, you're going to move here!"
I laughed. Yes. Something like *this*. Someday.

~

Sometimes detours are simply detours and sometimes they are signs from the universe. You get to decide how you want to view them.

Concern

I'm lying awake worried about you, Mom texted shortly after I told her I was getting divorced.

In response, I sent a Facebook post Elizabeth Gilbert had written about the difference between worry and concern. When someone worries about you, Gilbert wrote, it feels suffocating and smothering. When someone is concerned for you, it means they feel that you belong to them. That they want to help you sift through the hard stuff.

Damn. I wanted less worry and more concern from my mother—and from my sister.

Mom never let me know what she thought about the post.

~

"You're very depleted," my doctor said as he reviewed the blood work he'd ordered before the aborted trip to Nashville.

We went through everything: the suicide ideation, the insomnia, the divorce, the recurring sinus infections. He wanted me to see a psychiatrist, and for the interim he prescribed a low-dose antidepressant and antianxiety medication. The latter would help with sleep, he said.

I'd never taken a psychotropic drug before. Evan—the grandson, son, and brother of a pharmacist—had advised me to steer clear of them, especially sleeping pills. "They can be addictive," he said.

"You can have a glass of wine with this," the doctor said. "But be careful. Because one glass will feel like two, and so on . . ."

Be careful. Friday night I was attending a wine dinner in Chelsea, a lesbian meetup I planned to enjoy. Saturday I'd be heading to Lancaster for a second visit. *Start medication,* I typed in my calendar for Saturday morning.

~

Evan tucked in the ends of the damp red bandanna wrapped around his head before he headed out for the first day of the 1998 Jimmy Carter Work Project.

"I should be back around six thirty tonight," he said.

Six thirty. Twelve hours to go. A half hour until the boys typically got up. I poured myself another cup of coffee and sat down to read the newspaper.

Six forty-five. Two bagels out of freezer, on counter to thaw. I picked up the paper again and felt a small cloud hovering over me. Not an overpowering heaviness, like I'd experienced a few times when I could barely lift myself off the couch to unload the dishwasher. This felt more like a passing cloud, one I could shake off or pretend wasn't there.

I tried to name the feeling. Anger? No, I was happy for Evan that he'd found a new passion. He was diving deeper into a life that already seemed full, while I felt more like my maternal grandmother swimming in the Long Island Sound, her petal-covered bathing cap never getting wet.

"You could volunteer too," Evan said when he told me he had signed up.

"That wouldn't make any sense," I'd answered immediately. I'd never even hammered a nail. Besides, someone had to stay home with the kids.

Seven o'clock. No sign of the boys. I could have gotten a babysitter. I could have been hammering nails with Evan—and with Reenie, who was also volunteering that week. I could have put myself out there. Instead, I would be at home, watching the boys and the clock, until Evan returned. Trying to ignore the cloud hovering over me. Trying to not feel as if life was passing me by.

I took another sip of coffee and soon little feet raced down the stairs.

"Mommy?"

Years later, I would recognize that cloud as depression, not the "I can't get out of bed or function" kind, but perhaps one even more insidious. The kind where you look fine on the outside, or in my case, even more than fine.

The kind of depression that can come on when you aren't living authentically, whatever your context.

When you're a stay-at-home mom who's better suited to working outside the home.

When you're a working mom who's better suited to being at home.

When you're a perfectionist who stays stuck because you're terrified of making a mistake.

When you're the wife of a good man, living a good life, and you spend your days longing to be in someone else's arms.

When you're in love with someone the world says you shouldn't be, and that truth feels unspeakable.

The rates of depression for people in the LGBTQ+ community are significantly higher than in the general population, some studies citing it twice as high.

But of course I didn't know any of that when I was sending my husband off to do good in the world and sitting at home wondering why I wasn't going too. Or when I was hiding in a closet pouring out my feelings about Reenie in my journal and feeling as if something was terribly wrong with me. Or when I was in therapy with Alice for three years talking about everything but the one thing I needed to talk about most.

~

I walked into the Chelsea wine dinner in my new lesbian uniform: black leather jacket, black jeans, dangly earrings. The private room was crowded with women, wine glasses in hand. I took a glass too. Vowed to pace myself, which looked to be easy based on the bartender's stingy pour.

By eleven, most of the guests had cleared out, and I was ready to leave too. I had a big day ahead, and while there'd been lots of great conversation, there'd been no sparks. Before I pushed away from the table, a woman mentioned she'd been working in Manhattan real estate for two decades.

"I might need a real estate agent soon," I said. I had to move somewhere. Despite the steep prices, Manhattan seemed to be my logical next step—the dating pool was larger, and both boys were there. In fact, Will was in the process of buying his own place.

Mary Anne handed me her business card. "I'd love to help you."

"Thanks," I said. "Actually, my son's in contract right now for a co-op."

"Where?" she asked.

"Fourteenth and Seventh, I think."

"That's funny, I'm representing a seller in contract there—a cute young man is the buyer. His name is Will?"

"That's my son!"

We both shook our heads. What were the odds?

"Let's get together this summer," Mary Anne said. She and her partner had a place in the Hamptons.

"I'd love it," I said. "I don't know any lesbians out there."

She laughed. "They're all in the city this time of year."

I laughed too. Maybe the Lancaster magic was following me back to New York.

I pictured myself at an afternoon barbecue in the Hamptons, dressed in something floaty, sipping rosé, meeting smart and sexy women.

Maybe one of them would put her arm around me. Maybe we would start dancing.

Maybe she would lean in for a kiss.

Maybe I would take her to the beach and introduce her to my friends. Maybe when we circled up for cocktail hour, I wouldn't care that Evan and Elsa were there because I had someone too.

A woman stood up. "Does anyone want anything at the bar?" The "free" wine was long gone.

I shook my head. I'd had enough.

She returned with a bottle of wine and poured it into the empty glasses. I thought about putting my hand over my glass but didn't. Just one more.

Another bottle appeared at the table. I didn't even think about covering my glass.

By 1 a.m., the table was strewn with empty bottles and empty glasses. A waiter stood to the side, arms crossed. "Guess we better go," one of the four remaining women said. I attempted to stand and almost fell over.

"You okay?" she said.

"Yep," I said, willing that to be true.

I headed toward the Twenty-Third Street subway station. *Please just get me to the hotel. I'll never drink again.* A block from the subway, I leaned against a storefront. Fuck. What if I got stopped by a cop for public drunkenness?

I imagined myself in lockup. Having one phone call. Who would I even call?

This is what happens when you let down your guard. When you let loose. When you don't play by the rules.

You get in trouble.

~

At 2 a.m. I collapsed into bed in my hotel room, no memory of how I'd arrived.

At eight I woke up, my mouth tasting foul. Stumbled into the bathroom and dug through my makeup bag for a toothbrush. Spotted the bottle of antidepressants.

This was the day I was supposed to start.

I shook a pill into my palm. Rolled it between my thumb and forefinger. *Don't take it*, the Voice said.

But this is the day I was supposed to start.

There was a plan and I was good at following plans.

I fingered the pill again. Popped it in my mouth.

~

As I walked toward Penn Station to catch my train, the bracing April air helped shake off the cobwebs from the way-too-much wine and the way-too-short night of sleep. I couldn't wait to get back to Lancaster—to see Jenn and Kaye and who knows how many lesbians.

Three blocks into my walk, something I'd never felt before rushed through my body, almost knocking me over, like adrenaline times ten. I stopped for a moment, took a deep breath, and continued walking. A few minutes later, another rush hit me like a tsunami.

I leaned against a storefront, like I had the night before. Sat down on top of my rolling bag. Something was wrong. Very, very wrong. The wave passed after a couple of minutes. I hailed a cab. This was not a day to worry about spending ten bucks to get to Penn Station.

Once I was in the Amtrak waiting room, I felt almost human. The scary rushes of adrenaline or whatever they were had stopped. I glanced at the departures board to see if my train to Lancaster was listed.

As I scanned the board, another wave walloped me. And another and another.

I. NEEDED. HELP. NOW.

I staggered over to the ticket agent. "I'm not feeling well. I need medical attention."

I cannot believe this is happening. To me.

"Ma'am," he said, taking my arm. "Sit right here and I'll call someone."

I sat, my head in my hands. The waves kept crashing over me. In what felt like forever but was probably only ten minutes, a baby-faced police officer walked over. "What's going on, ma'am?"

Where's the stretcher? The EMT? The cold washcloth?

My bottom lip trembled as I told him about the wine I drank the night before, the pill I took that morning, and the out-of-control waves washing over me.

Help, I wanted to say but didn't.

"You have two choices, ma'am. You can call someone to get you, or I can call an ambulance."

I imagined getting swooped off to an ER in some random part of the city and languishing there for hours. Almost as bad as being locked up in a cell.

"I'll try and call someone," I said, but I had no idea who.

"I'll wait over here while you call," the officer said.

I looked at my speed dial. *Jenn*. She would know what to do.

I texted three times. Nothing. Where was she?

Maybe I should go to the ER. I don't know what to do.

I hesitated as I looked at my speed dial again. Will and Patrick rarely answered their phones. I felt so weak, but I was desperate. I called Evan.

"Hello?" he said.

"Sorry to call, but I didn't know what else to do. I think I've had a bad reaction to some medication. I'm at Penn Station with a police officer."

"I'm not sure what I can do from Montauk." He sounded cold, detached. "Have you tried to reach the boys?"

"No, I'll try them. Sorry to bother you."

Evan wasn't my person anymore. I didn't have a person. I had to call my kids. Fuck. I was supposed to be the parent, the one who had it together. "One more," I mouthed to the police officer.

I dialed Patrick first, since he lived closest to Penn Station.

Brrring. Brrring.

Please answer.

"What's up, Mom?" Patrick said.

I told him what was going on.

"I'll be there as fast as I can."

"My son's coming," I said to the officer.

My baby was coming.

~

It was so odd that morning when three-year-old Patrick clung to my legs and screamed "Mommy" when I took him into his preschool classroom. He hadn't cried the year before or the first two months of this school year.

The only way he could be consoled? A laminated photo of me pinned to his polo shirt—a suggestion of the school psychologist—to remind him I wasn't going to leave him forever.

One day, he stopped screaming "Mommy."

But I never had a day when I doubted his love or devotion.

I was one lucky mom.

~

"Mom, it's going to be okay," Patrick said as he sat next to me in the Amtrak waiting room.

Months ago, the two of us had sat on the steps of Saint Patrick's Cathedral on a sunny fall day. "I feel like I'm about to jump off a cliff," I had said, "and I don't know who will be waiting for me at the bottom."

He'd patted my arm. "Mom, Will and I will be there for you."

If this wasn't the bottom, I didn't want to know what was—but Patrick was here, true to his promise.

He helped me up from the chair. We walked across the street to a café inside Macy's.

"I'm starting to feel a little better," I said minutes later, after I'd had a few bites of a croissant.

I reached for his hand. "I'm not sure what to do now." There was another train to Lancaster that afternoon, but I didn't feel safe riding by myself and I didn't want to drag this kid all the way there and have him turn right around. Although I knew he'd do it for me.

"Let's sit for a while," he said. "We'll figure something out."

He reminded me so much of Evan in that moment. Calm, reassuring. He'd make a great partner for someone, someday.

"I have something funny to tell you," he said. "I've gone out on a couple of dates with a girl who grew up in Lancaster."

"No way."

"Yep. Crazy coincidence, right?"

I shook my head and smiled. Another "coincidence" in a string of Lancaster coincidences, another sign from the universe. But the rightness and lightness I felt when I was there seemed very far away.

How could I get back to that place where everything felt aligned?

Maybe Patrick and I could take a train to Beth's in New Jersey, and she could help me get to Lancaster the next day. Part of me didn't want to entangle her any further in my shit and risk hearing that I was crazy, weird, or strange again. But I was out of ideas.

"Can you try Beth?"

Patrick nodded.

I made sure he had her number and headed to the restroom.

"Beth's driving in," he said when I returned. "She'll text when she gets close."

She was driving in?

My eyes filled up. My sister was coming to my rescue.

~

My stomach rumbled as the aroma of roasted carrots and grilled turkey tenderloin wafted from Beth's kitchen. Good to feel hungry again.

Family photos lined the bookshelves in Beth's TV room, including one of Christmas with my family, her family, and our parents—all in matching royal-blue pullovers. Patrick on my lap, a towhead. Will missing a front tooth, on Evan's lap. The framed photo of Evan and me from our wedding day was gone. Thoughtful of Beth and also sad.

Evan. Was he wondering how I was doing? Did he tell Elsa about my call from Penn Station? Did they talk about their soon-to-be exes—she was going through a divorce too, he said—or did he protect my privacy?

Did it even matter anymore?

Whether he was thinking about me or not, I owed him a follow-up. *I'm okay*, I texted. *At Beth's. Sorry about today.*

No worries, he responded right away. *Thanks for letting me know.*

I picked up the remote control, tried to find something on TV to distract me. Beth and her husband were still in the kitchen, chatting about summer vacation plans.

I felt envious of my little sister. She had "normal"—something I would probably never have again.

~

"This means a lot to me," I said to Beth as she drove me to Allentown, the midway point between her house and Lancaster—about an hour-and-fifteen-minute drive. We would meet Jenn at a Starbucks, and Jenn and I would continue on to Lancaster.

"Glad I could do it," she said.

"I appreciate everything," I said. "Especially yesterday."

There was much more I wanted to say and someday I would. That I was sorry for the blowup at her house last year. That I hadn't understood that I wasn't the only one on a journey, that the other people in my life were on one too. That no matter what, she was my sister and I needed her. But this day, it was enough to know that she was back in my corner.

Jenn was already there when we reached the Starbucks parking lot.

"Girl, you made it," she said as we hugged.

Yes, I made it because these two women—and Patrick—carried me when I couldn't carry myself. Treated me like I belonged to them. Helped me sift through the hard stuff.

"She's yours now," Beth said to Jenn.

We all laughed. It was like a prisoner transfer, but I wasn't a prisoner anymore.

I was free—to make my own mistakes, create my own future, and write a different story for myself.

This Way

It's amazing when the universe clears a path for you and says, "Here is the way!" Andrea wrote on the LaLa page.

~

The Pressroom restaurant was buzzing when Jenn and I arrived for dinner, hours after she drove me to Lancaster. We were seated at a table in the front with a floor-to-ceiling view of King Street, one of the city's main thoroughfares.

As I looked through the menu, movement caught my eye. Two women peering into the window, smiling and waving furiously. *At me.*

Who could possibly be waving at me in Lancaster? I rifled through my mental Rolodex—it was Sally and Alexis, two of the women I'd met at church last weekend!

I waved furiously too and mouthed: "Can you come in?"

They shook their heads. "Have to get home for the babysitter. Next time!"

I blew them a kiss. "Next time." Because there would be a next time.

"How do you know them?" Jenn asked.

"From church last weekend! One of them's a LaLa!"

"I'm telling you, it's a sign from the universe! You're going to move here!"

I laughed. This was becoming our little private joke. But part of me wondered if I might.

~

Something fluttered inside me as I took a second look at the condo that had been my favorite at the open house. I stepped through the French doors onto the balcony. Leaned on the railing. To the east and west were wide expanses of older brick buildings with character, more steeples than I could count, dogwood trees beginning to bud.

I pictured myself sipping coffee here in my bathrobe, journal in hand. Walking to Central Market for local produce. Sweating at Jenn's yoga studio, which was less than five minutes away. Finding my stride professionally. Navigating a new life as a single woman. As a lesbian.

A glimpse of a new life, new possibilities, a new future.

A future where I didn't have to worry about running into Evan and Elsa. Where I didn't have to constantly explain myself. Where I had the freedom to start over and figure out who I really was and who I wanted to be.

I pulled out my phone and pointed it west toward the low-slung brick buildings, steeples, and dogwoods. Snapped a photo and posted it on Facebook before I could talk myself out of it.

My new favorite town, the caption read.

This, my body was saying to me. *This*. Not something like this. But *this*.

~

A text from Olivia, the Lank-*kiss*-stir person I met at the birthday party. *R u in Lancaster?*

Yes! I responded. She must have seen my Facebook post.

Have an extra ticket to a documentary showing at the Ware Center tomorrow @ 7. Going w/ work colleagues. Wanna come?

"Isn't that sweet?" I said, showing Jenn the text, not sure how interested I was in going or how I would get there.

Jenn broke into a huge smile.

"You're not going to believe this," she said. "I'm guest lecturing in the same building at the exact same time."

I believed it. Another "coincidence."

~

"Magical coincidences keep happening," I said to Kaye at my next therapy appointment. "What's even stranger is that I know more lesbians here after two visits than I know anywhere else."

Kaye smiled. "Who would have thought Lancaster was a lesbian mecca?"

I laughed. "I'm starting to think I might move here. Do you think that's nuts?" I needed a reality check. Because the idea of signing a contract for a condo was scary. I'd never bought real estate by myself. I'd never even rented an apartment on my own. Since meeting Evan, he'd always been by my side, or more accurately, I'd been by his, trusting him to negotiate, trusting him to make good financial decisions.

"I don't think it's nuts," Kaye said. "You have to move somewhere. Why not Lancaster where you've already started building community? Plus, if you come in June, you'll be here for Pride!"

Pride. I'd never been to Pride before. Not as an ally—and certainly not as a lesbian.

Why not Lancaster?

~

I messaged my LaLa besties about the small miracles of the past couple of weeks and that I was thinking of moving to Lancaster.

Did you know I used to live there? one of my besties responded. *I have a bunch of lesbian goddesses who are my close friends and I'll make sure they take care of you.*

This couldn't be real.

~

Two days after returning to the cottage, I tucked a brochure from the condo building in my tote bag before I picked up Mom for her long-delayed birthday lunch. I imagined whipping it out at the restaurant. *Happy Birthday, Mom! Guess what? I'm moving to Amish country!*

A few days ago, I'd braced myself when I told Beth about the possible move.

"Cool," she'd said.

Unlikely that Mom would have the same reaction.

~

The Long Island Sound sparkled through the window at the Inlet Seafood restaurant, but I didn't feel the least bit sparkly. Mom and I had already covered the latest about Will and Patrick, one of the few safe topics of conversation those days. I wished I didn't feel so uncomfortable sharing my life with my mother, but it was what it was. She hadn't asked a single question about me or my life. How we had gotten to this place where all we could talk about was my boys, the weather, and her aches and pains, I had no idea.

~

"What are you going to do with the briefcase we gave you for graduation?" Mom said when I told her I had left the law firm. The butter-soft black leather briefcase monogrammed in gold with my initials had been a major splurge for my parents.

For two decades, I moved that briefcase from house to house, knowing I was unlikely to use it again, but it felt wrong to let go of something my parents had spent a lot of money on.

It didn't occur to me until later that a different mother might have asked different questions when her daughter told her she had quit her job.

~

"I wish you could empathize, instead of criticize me," I said five months ago when Mom asked how I could destroy everything I had.

"Criticize you?" Mom said. "*You* were always criticizing *me* for how I was taking care of your father. You didn't support me; you had no understanding of what I was going through. Then after twenty years, you go to his deathbed acting like you were this perfect, loving daughter."

"Do you really want to go there, Mom?" I said. I had no idea where this comment was coming from.

She shook her head but didn't say a word.

The boys, the weather, and her aches and pains were much easier to talk about than the past—for both of us.

~

Before Dad moved into the hospital bed in the center of his bedroom, he spent his final days and much of his final years in the navy-blue lift chair that dominated my parents' TV room. That's where he was when we had our final conversation, three months before his death.

It was February 2011, more than a year before Evan and I would move to Montauk full time. I was busy in Houston running a special education advocacy group at the preschool and running the household. A sixth sense—the Voice?—nudged me to go to Montauk in the dead of winter, not a time I would typically visit.

Dad was slipping away. Parkinson's disease had ravaged his body and mind for twenty-one years, but still he was saying how great everything was. It confounded me that he could be happy in his condition, but I couldn't be happier in mine. I wanted to grab him: "Tell me your secret, before it's too late."

The last day of my visit, he drifted in and out of sleep in that navy-blue lift chair. We made small talk between his naps. Eventually, I asked, "How are you really?"

He gave a small wave of his hand. "I'm wonderful, I'm terrific, I feel fantastic." His voice was weak, his words halting. "I don't even think about having Parkinson's most of the time. It doesn't bother me at all. I have all these wonderful people taking care of me." With each sentence, his voice grew stronger, his speech more fluid, as if a fount of gratitude was fueling him. "I have four terrific grandchildren. I'm so proud of them." He waved his hand more vigorously. "I feel so lucky."

Maybe it's wishful thinking, but I'd like to imagine my father having a different reaction to me coming out than my mother did. Likely, he would have been shocked and sad at first—he loved Evan and our family just the way it was. He might have even tried to talk me into accepting my life and being grateful for what I had, the philosophy he shared in that last conversation and had lived out in his own marriage.

But I have to believe he would have said "I love you" when I told him my truth. That he would have climbed down into the pit and cried with me, even if he might not have agreed with my decision.

Of course I'll never know how he would have reacted. He'd been gone over five years by the time I came out to myself and the rest of the family.

But that's part of the beauty of a relationship after someone is gone. You can hold on to the hope that the story would have played out the way you wanted it to.

I have a reason to hold on to that hope.

When I arrived in Montauk two days before he would finally pass, Dad was in that hospital bed, unable to open his eyes.

Maria, one of his caregivers, said, "He's been waiting for you."

"I'm here," I said as I stroked his forehead. His eyes still closed, he raised his head a few inches and pursed his lips. A kiss for his firstborn, the daughter he wanted to protect from the bumps of life. One final expression of unconditional love.

~

While Mom and I waited for dessert at the restaurant, I pulled out the condo brochure and pushed it across the table to her.

"I'm considering buying one of these in Lancaster," I said. "They're really nice and much more affordable than anything I could buy in New York."

"Yes, Beth told me," she said, poker-faced.

My heart filled with love for my sister. What a gift to have broken the news to Mom and given her time to process it.

Mom flipped through the brochure without saying a word.

"These *do* look nice," she said finally, "but wouldn't renting first make more sense?"

I sank into my chair, relieved. Not an unequivocal yes, but a positive response nonetheless. Yes, renting would probably make more sense. One of my friends had said the same thing. But if I was going to do this, I was going all in.

No more safe choices to bury in my graveyard.

~

I dropped Mom off and headed straight to the cottage, bypassing my usual detour by Evan's.

Time to stop looking back. Time to step into my future.

No need to wait for Mom's approval. No need to ask anyone else's advice or permission. I'd text the boys and Evan about my decision.

My decision. Not what anyone else thought was right.

I grabbed my laptop from the kitchen counter. Pulled up the condo contract. Scrolled to the last page. Took a deep breath and clicked on the signature line.

I was moving to Lancaster.

Threshold

I typed *My next move* on the subject line and selected forty-one recipients from my address book: all friends who already knew I was getting divorced and knew the reason why.

I'm "coming out" gradually about my next move but wanted to let you all know. Not a secret, but not yet broadcasting on Facebook. I'm very excited! I wrote. I told them about crashing a birthday party, about the lesbian community I had already found. About the condo I was buying and all the tiny miracles that kept happening in Lancaster.

Doors have opened, stars have aligned, the universe has said yes. I'm moving to Lancaster, friends!

I forwarded the email to the boys, Beth, and Mom: *Just wanted you to know what I've sent out to friends.* What I hoped they would read between the lines was this: *The secret is out. I'm gay. You don't have to be afraid to tell people.*

By the end of the day, I had heard back from virtually everyone I had sent the email to. People were excited for me, proud of me. They called me brave.

No word from my mom.

~

An empty weekend loomed, the first since that fateful Lancaster visit that I didn't have plans to do anything with anyone.

It felt too hard to sit in the cottage all weekend by myself. But my options? Go out to dinner with Mom and risk running into Evan and Elsa? No thanks.

I decided to go into Manhattan. See a show. Make a weekend of it.

I searched for discounted Broadway tickets, and two plays I'd been interested in seeing popped up for Saturday: a matinee of *The Little Foxes* and an evening performance of *A Doll's House, Part 2*.

I thought about my mother and felt a pang of guilt. We used to see shows together on a regular basis. Who knew whether we'd ever go into the city together again. She had been silent since I forwarded the "coming out" email, which was no surprise, but I could be the bigger person. Invite her to the matinee and put her on a Jitney back to Montauk before I went to the second play.

That felt like the right thing to do, a small gesture to try to make a connection. Despite all the hard stuff of the past year, she was still my mom. I texted to see if she was interested.

Yes!! she responded immediately. The exclamation marks made me feel good. I still wanted to make her happy, and I hadn't done much of that lately. Within an hour, I had bought the Broadway tickets, made the Jitney reservations, and booked a hotel room for myself.

It felt good to take action. To be decisive. To just do the thing.

"This is amazing, isn't it?" I said to Mom, as the curtain went down on the first act of *The Little Foxes*.

She nodded yes as I stood up to make a beeline for the ladies' room.

Laura Linney and Cynthia Nixon were playing the two female leads. Nixon, of *Sex and the City* fame, another woman who had come out later in life. Did my mother know that? I wasn't going to ask her. Anything approaching lesbian was off-limits.

A few minutes later, I settled back in my seat and started flipping through my Playbill.

"Who did you send that email out to?" Mom asked.

I didn't have to ask what email she was referring to. "Why do you want to know?"

"Just curious."

"No, really, why? Are you embarrassed of me? Ashamed of me?"

"No," she said. "I just like to keep things private."

Private. Just like she had wanted Beth and me to keep her separations from our dad "private."

Just like I had kept my feelings about Reenie "private" all those years.

"This is *my* story," I said in an even tone, trying to keep the anger out of my voice, "and I'll tell it to who I want to, when I want to."

Mom didn't say a word, just pursed her lips in a way I was all too familiar with.

I was shaking as the curtain rose. Why, oh why, had I thought I could win her over?

An hour and a half later, I took her arm as we slowly crossed the street in search of a cab to take her to the Jitney stop. When we reached the curb, the Voice cut through the anger still stewing inside me: *she's an old woman who's grieving too.*

She was fragile, this eighty-two-year-old mother of mine, although she liked to act otherwise. Her daughter was a different person from the one she'd known for fifty-six years, and her life was about to be different too, without this daughter living nearby. Change wasn't easy for anyone and especially not for someone like her, who valued order and safety above everything else.

I kissed Mom's cheek and held her hand as she stepped onto the bus. Someday, I hoped to find the grace to love her just the way she was.

~

I knocked lightly and opened the front door of the Montauk house. "Hello?"

"Coming," Evan said as he jogged down the stairs with my mail. We walked out together to the driveway. To the north, the sun was shining on the vegetable garden he'd proudly tended the last five summers, the garden now covered with weeds.

He noticed me looking at it. "I planted snow peas and sugar snaps a couple of weeks ago," he said. "That's all I've had energy for so far."

"Yeah, I get that." I wanted to hug him but we didn't do that anymore except for those light, polite hugs. The wistfulness in his voice reminded me of the toll the divorce had taken on him too, which had been easy for me to forget since Elsa arrived on the scene.

"Okay if I sit for a minute?" I said.

"Of course," he said.

I sat on the wooden bench near the driveway and lifted my face to the sun. Longing to linger for a few more moments in this space that soon would no longer be mine. Wanting to steal a few more moments with this man I still loved and whose heart was now with someone else. Wondering if I, too, would find love again.

~

Before dawn, I carried a cup of coffee and my journal onto the back patio of the cottage. As the sun rose, a herd of deer raced through the nature preserve. Sparrows chirped in the low-lying brush.

My body felt settled. Lighter.

This is what peace feels like, I wrote in my journal.

~

One of the LaLas had mentioned an online dating site called Zoosk. What the hell. I'd already blown up my life. I wasn't going to sit back and wait for my next chapter to happen.

Six months. I'd give this Zoosk thing six months.

~

Lancaster Pride was June 25, the first Sunday I'd be in town, and I didn't have anything "gay enough" to wear. I Googled "Lesbian Pride T-shirts" and scrolled through an astounding array of choices, feeling I would know the right thing when I saw it.

And there it was: a soft gray tank top with "Nobody Knows I'm a Lesbian" emblazoned in large white script.

Perfect.

~

The matches from Zoosk were as dismal as the ones from the first dating site, then one caught my eye. Wendy, a blonde with a bright smile whose profile was practically empty except for her age (fifty—would she think I was too old?), her body type (curvy—that was nice), and her work (higher education—a professional, I liked that).

I'd promised myself I wasn't going to play it safe anymore.

You have a great smile, I messaged.

Two days went by. No response.

I *was* too old.

~

"Mom," Patrick said on the phone. "Tell me again when you're moving to Lancaster?"

"June twentieth."

"You're not going to believe this. Dan's wedding is June twenty-fifth and it's in Lancaster!"

"You're kidding!" Although I should have stopped being surprised. None of this made sense. Moving to a city I'd never thought of two months ago. My son meeting a young woman from Lancaster at virtually the same time as my first visit there. LaLas and lesbians here and there and everywhere, all somehow connected. Pride and the wedding of one of Patrick's college classmates on the same day, and the weekend after my move. What were the odds for any of it?

"Why don't you stay with me?" I said. I'd rented a one-bedroom Airbnb with a pullout couch where I'd stay while my condo was being worked on.

"That would be great."

Maybe Patrick would go to Pride with me. Although that might be too much to ask of a son just getting used to the idea his mom was gay.

"What time's the wedding?" I asked.

"Six."

"Hey, Lancaster Pride is that day too. What would you think about going with me?"

"That would be awesome, Mom."

If only he could see the grin on my face.

~

Three days after I messaged Wendy, she finally responded. What was the deal? Too busy? Not that interested? Playing hard to get? But at least I'd heard back from her.

Over the next few days, we texted back and forth. She was a late-in-lifer too, a professor at a Christian college about fifty miles from Lancaster—"out" to family and some friends but not at work. Had dated some but hadn't been in a serious relationship. I told her I had even less experience with women.

I liked Wendy, at least the text version of her. A baseball fan like me, although she cheered for the Red Sox, not the Astros. A home brewer who loved to cook. No obvious red flags.

I filled her in on my move to Lancaster. That coincidentally my first weekend was Lancaster Pride and my younger son had a wedding to attend in Lancaster that weekend too. Wendy said she'd also be at Pride, working the booth of an LGBTQ+ nonprofit she'd been volunteering with. She suggested we meet there and plan a real date after I got settled.

But I didn't want to wait. I'd waited long enough.

I proposed we meet June 22, my third night in Lancaster, and see the local minor league baseball team in action. I pictured myself sitting in the stands next to Wendy, maybe shyly reaching for her hand. Or putting my arm around her, possibly stealing a kiss. How I'd yearned for a moment like that—I'd left my life for a moment like that.

I didn't want to wait a single second longer than necessary for a moment like that.

Wendy said yes to the baseball date. We also scheduled a phone call—a de rigueur step in online dating to make sure your potential date didn't sound like a serial killer.

~

"Thank you," I whispered as I closed the front door of the cottage for the final time. This way station where I lived alone for the first time. Where I battled mice and myself. Where I fell apart and learned to listen to my own voice. Where hopefully I acquired the skills I'd need for the new life I was about to embark on.

With the Subaru once again packed to the gills, I headed east to Montauk. Evan had agreed to let me stay in the house for a few days before I signed over the deed to him. He'd be with Elsa, I guessed. I hadn't asked.

"Wow," I had said seventeen years ago, when Evan and I stepped onto the upper deck of the house and took in the sweeping ocean view for the first time.

He put his arm around me. "Wow is right."

That day I leaned over the deck's railing and stared at the white caps dotting the ocean. I imagined sunset cocktails and bonfires on the beach. Summers far from the Houston heat. Time for the boys with their grandparents. The perfect exclamation point to a nearly perfect life. The house was for sale because the owners were getting divorced. Evan and I later found out the previous owners had divorced too. "We'll break the curse!" we joked, never imagining we wouldn't.

~

An hour into the phone call with Wendy, my cheeks hurt from nonstop smiling. She wasn't a serial killer or anything other than lovely. "No U-Hauls," I said.

She laughed. "Deal!"

We'd both heard the classic lesbian joke: *What does a lesbian bring to a second date?*

A U-Haul.

I doubted I'd get attached that quickly, but who knew?

~

The first thing I did when I arrived at the Montauk house was search for evidence of Elsa. There wasn't much. No clothes in my closet. No toothbrush in the upstairs bathroom, although there did appear to be an extra one in the medicine cabinet in the guest bath downstairs. Evan had been sleeping in the guest room since I moved out. It hurt to think he felt he couldn't sleep in our bed anymore, but at least I wouldn't have to think about Elsa's head lying on my pillow.

Five days later, I woke up for the final time in our house—in a couple of hours Evan would become its sole owner. Not knowing if I would ever be invited back, I wanted one last look—at everything. I started in the basement.

The shelves that lined the south-facing wall were emptier without my books. The family photo albums were still on the bottom shelves. Evan said he'd make copies of the photos when he was emotionally ready to face that task. No rush, I told him. How hard it would be to look through thirty years of birthday parties, family trips, holiday celebrations.

On the main level, my tears flowed as the memories poured out. The bay window where I'd supervised endless games of manhunt in the backyard. The farmhouse-style table where we'd hosted family Thanksgivings. The stone fireplace where we'd hung our four Christmas stockings.

Upstairs, the sitting area where nearly every morning Evan and I had started our day with coffee and conversation. The room where I'd written and read the unspeakable pages that led to the end of our marriage.

In our bedroom, the white chair where I'd had the final FaceTime call with Reenie. The bed where Evan and I used to sleep together and where he was no longer sleeping.

I took one final look at the view that never failed to take my breath away, walked down two flights of stairs, and locked the door behind me.

I was ready.

Two hundred and eighty miles west to Lancaster, to my new life.

Home

January 1979

Dear Dad:

About six of us spent three hours one night discussing what was the most important thing in life—some ideas: religion, happiness, knowing oneself, love, and facing the reality of death. Guess which one was mine?

Love, Suzette

Dear Suzette,

What did you think was the most important thing in life? I'd be interested to know.

Love, Dad

Dear Dad,

You didn't guess what I thought was the most important thing in life? Well, obviously, "know thyself."

Love, Suzette

~

Lancaster Day #1

The universe provided a parking spot in front of the three-story Victorian Airbnb where I'd be staying the next six weeks. After that I'd patch together options until my condo was ready—stay at Jenn's? Wendy's?

Calm down, girl. You haven't even met her yet.

Jenn and Joyce, the LaLa who had invited me to church, were waiting for me at the curb. I smiled as Joyce grabbed my printer and jogged up three flights of stairs like a gazelle. It was nice to have friends in their thirties. It was nice to have friends, period.

"Can I take you out for a drink?" I asked them after several more trips up and down.

"Yes!" They said in unison.

On the Tellus 360 rooftop bar with my two friends, I sipped a Blue Moon and surveyed my new city. White lights twinkled overhead, a balmy breeze blew, and the sun was about to set—a perfect summer evening.

Maybe this was what my father felt like when he opened his arms to the ocean and exclaimed, "It doesn't get any better than this." You don't plan for these kinds of moments. They simply arrive. If you aren't too busy dwelling on the past or stressing about the future, joy finds you exactly where you are.

And this was joy. On a rooftop in landlocked Lancaster, Pennsylvania, no ocean in sight. I couldn't see my face but imagined it was glowing.

Day #2

One of the Lancaster lesbian goddesses had a friend who ran a monthly writers meetup. Which happened to be scheduled for the second night I was in town.

Of course it was.

The writers met in a coworking space two blocks away from the Airbnb and *across the street* from my condo building.

Of course they did.

"I'm working on a memoir," I said to the dozen or so writers circled up for introductions. "It started off as a story about my professional life, but it's morphed into something very different." Several people raised their eyebrows.

That was enough detail for now. Later, if I felt safe, I'd tell them how writing the first story helped me find the story I didn't even know I had. How writing helped me discover the truth of who I was and what I longed for.

Maybe someday I'd tell these writers—and the world—how I wrote myself out.

Day #3

At 4:30 p.m., the date outfit was on: black sleeveless top, white jeans, dangly silver earrings, bit of makeup, hair styled, but not over-the-top.

Damn, girl. Not bad.

Wendy and I had decided to meet outside Clipper Stadium, the home of the Lancaster Barnstormers, before heading to Pour, a wine bar I'd been to with Jenn. I walked slowly from the Airbnb, hoping to not sweat too much or be too early. Would Wendy look like her photos? Would we have enough to talk about? Would this be the night I got my first kiss?

She'd warned me that the Barnstormers weren't very good.

I could care less about the baseball, I had wanted to say but didn't.

A few minutes after I arrived, a black Mini convertible with the top down pulled up.

Was that her? That was her!

She was beautiful.

We embraced lightly. Her softness pressed against me. In person, Wendy looked way younger than fifty. I hoped I didn't look way older than fifty-six.

We walked toward the wine bar, which happened to be on the same block as the gallery where I bought the earrings. At the exact moment Wendy and I passed by the gallery, Erica and her wife, Mai, were locking up.

"Hi there!" I said, hoping they'd remember me. Erica and I were Facebook friends now.

"Great to see you!" Erica said. "Did you move in yet?"

"Two days ago," I said. Then, remembering my manners, "This is my friend Wendy."

My friend who I hoped would become more than a friend. Could Erica and Mai tell I was on a date? It felt super cool to bump into them, to feel like I already knew people here, even if just superficially. I couldn't tell if Wendy was impressed. She was pretty inscrutable.

"I have a whole story to tell you about them," I said as we approached Pour. If she only knew how many stories I had to tell. I hoped she'd like a talker.

Pour was hosting a private dinner tonight. Shit. I hadn't even considered the need for a Plan B. They would serve us a drink, then we'd need to find another place to eat. It's no big deal, I told myself. But if this went wrong, what else might?

We ordered two glasses of prosecco. The bubbles tickled going down my throat. I started to relax. "Let me tell you about the two women we just met . . ."

Thirty minutes later, the prosecco was gone, and my body was tingling. Wendy was easy to talk to and so darned cute. I wished we could sit at that table all night long, but we had to move along. We bumped into Erica and Mai again as we left the restaurant. I asked them for a dinner recommendation.

We walked around the corner to Aussie and the Fox, their suggestion. I wanted to take Wendy's hand but was too shy to do so. How was she feeling? Was I going to have to be the one to make the first move?

A waiter brought us menus.

"I think he's one of our people," Wendy said when he left the table.

Our people. I smiled, but I wasn't there yet. It was going to take a while for fifty-plus years of thinking I couldn't be anything other than heterosexual to wear off. Wendy seemed more at ease with her sexual identity, despite having had to conceal it from her employer.

"Tell me more about your college's LGBTQ+ policy," I said, after we each ordered a salad and another glass of wine. She had alluded to the policy briefly during our phone call.

"I could get fired if someone saw me even holding hands with a woman," she said. Her Christian college's policy permitted people to identify as gay but prohibited "same-sex expression."

"So, you can be gay, you just can't do anything about it," I said. Was that why she hadn't tried to hold my hand?

"That's it in a nutshell."

"That's absurd." I felt vulnerable—and angry. For her. For me. For every student at a college like that who had to hide who they were and who they loved. For every LGBTQ+ person who had had religion weaponized against them. That hadn't been my experience, but I was seeing how that reality played out for others, including the beautiful woman who was sitting across the table from me.

When our wine glasses were empty, I glanced at my phone. Eight thirty.

"What time was the game?" I asked.

"Six thirty."

I showed her my phone. "I guess we're not going to make it."

She laughed. "Guess not. We're not missing much, it's pretty terrible baseball."

What now? Did I just walk her to her car and call it a night? Should I invite her back to my place? How did I do that without sounding cheesy or like a cliché? And what if she said no? It was so much easier with men, knowing they would take charge. What were the rules in lesbian dating?

Shit, I was just going to go for it.

"Would you like to come over to my place for coffee?" I said, holding my breath for her answer. Of course, I wanted her to say yes, but then something might happen, which I wanted, but I was also scared to death about all of this.

"Yes," she said, with a big smile.

We sat on the couch in the cozy living room of my Airbnb. Wendy looked so young, so innocent, smiling the same smile that had grabbed me in the first place.

I wanted to kiss her. I so wanted to kiss her, but would we sit here all night if I didn't make a move? I inched over toward her, my left thigh touching her right, and took her hand.

"I don't know how to do this," I said, "but I really want to kiss you."

She nodded, her eyes growing wide.

I groaned as my lips pressed against hers. So soft, so supple, so unlike any I'd ever kissed before.

Suddenly, I was in her lap, and we were making out like ravenous teenagers. I shyly grazed my fingers across her blouse, felt her breasts underneath it.

This was actually happening.

I unfastened a button on her blouse. And another and another. She lifted it over her head. I brushed my fingers over the bare skin brimming over her bra. Cupped her breasts in my hands. I wanted to see all of them. Touch all of them. Touch all of her.

"How about we go in the bedroom," I said, taking her hand.

In bed, she unhooked her bra. I buried my face in her breasts, inhaling her scent—so sweet, so fresh.

This was happening. To me. With me.

She unbuttoned my white jeans. "Is this okay?" she asked.

Tears rolled down my face. Yes, this was okay. This was very okay.

Day #4

"Can I have a second date Saturday night?" Wendy asked shortly after midnight, as we lay in each other's arms.

I wanted to say yes, but Patrick would be staying here, in town for his friend's wedding. We already had dinner plans with Jenn Saturday night. And what would Patrick think about meeting Wendy? Was that even fair to him? Although he'd met his father's girlfriend.

"Yes," I said slowly, "as long as you don't mind it being a double date with my son and my friend Jenn." I told her I needed to check with Patrick first.

"But we won't be able to do *this*," I said as I leaned in for one more kiss. It was going to be so hard to be with her and not be able to be *with* her.

Day #5

Hours after Patrick arrived, Wendy texted: *I'm here.*

I raced down the stairs to find her standing in front of her convertible. I wrapped my arms around her and stole a kiss, maybe the only one I'd get that evening. I couldn't imagine making out in front of my son.

"I'll talk basketball with Patrick," Wendy said as we climbed the stairs. He worked for the NBA, and Wendy taught athletic training at her college in addition to being a sports fan.

"Sounds great." I wasn't really nervous about the two of them meeting, since Patrick could carry on a conversation with practically anyone. Still, this was a first. My son and my . . . was Wendy my girlfriend already?

At the restaurant, Wendy slid into the booth first and I slid in next to her. I reached for her hand under the table, like a teenager on an illicit date, Jenn and Patrick sitting across from us likely unaware of the foreplay going on under their noses.

The disparate parts of my life were coming together. This was what it was like, I guessed, to be in alignment. You didn't have to force things or make things happen. Things like having your son meet your *girlfriend*.

I had a girlfriend.

"What time do you need to be at Pride tomorrow?" I asked Wendy. Lancaster Pride was a "festival," more like a block party, instead of the parade in bigger cities.

"Early," she said. "Nine or nine thirty."

"Oh, I had no idea," I said. "I feel bad you have to drive home tonight and come back so early tomorrow."

She shrugged. "It's okay."

I did feel bad but there was no way she was staying in my one-bedroom apartment while Patrick was there. It was one thing for him to meet his mother's girlfriend and another for him to see his mother in bed with her.

I went to the ladies' room, and as I was washing my hands, Wendy came through the door. There was no one else around, as far as I could tell, so I grabbed her and kissed her. Forbidden and delicious.

We walked back to the booth, both trying to hold in our smiles.

"Mom," Patrick said, "a friend of mine wants to get together for a drink later tonight. I hope that's okay."

Wendy and I glanced at each other. Was she thinking what I was thinking? That this was a little gift from the universe that would give us some time alone?

"Of course," I said. "Who is this friend?"

"Francie, the girl from Lancaster I've gone out with a few times," he said. "She's here for the weekend too."

Of course she was here this weekend. I shook my head. The universe kept coming through for me.

I wish I'd known this was going to happen," I said to Wendy after Patrick left. "You could have brought a bag and spent the night."

"I did pack a bag just in case," she said, smiling. "A girl's gotta have hope."

I playfully hit her arm. This woman with the shy smile was not so shy after all.

Hope. Yes, a girl's gotta have hope. And suddenly I did.

Day #6

While Patrick was still asleep in the living room, I pulled on my "Nobody Knows I'm a Lesbian" tank top. "What do you think?" I said to Wendy.

She laughed. "It's perfect."

Just before nine, we walked toward the block-long area of the city that had been cordoned off from traffic. I took her hand. "Is this okay?"

She squeezed my hand and held on.

The streets were nearly empty, but I was prepared to drop her hand if she saw anyone from her college. What a way to have to live. I hated it for her. I hated it for *us*.

I felt both empowered and a little afraid, walking through the streets holding her hand and wearing my in-your-face tank top. Outside the ropes of the Pride festival, who were the allies and who were the people who believed there was something wrong with two women holding hands? What a privileged life I'd led, never having to give public affection a second thought.

At the entrance of the festival, Wendy and I kissed. She headed to her volunteer gig and I headed back to the Airbnb with a lightness my body hadn't felt before.

At noon, I returned to Pride with Patrick, who was wearing a rainbow basketball T-shirt and holding a rainbow flag, courtesy of his employer, the NBA. I loved how comfortable he seemed, as if he'd had a lesbian mother all his life. "It's like a giant gay craft fair," he said as he surveyed the booths lining the perimeter.

I laughed. That was exactly what it was like. Hardly the radical gathering I once imagined Pride events to be. News flash: gay people were just like you and me.

Scanning the crowd for familiar faces, I spotted Joyce with her young daughter. Erica and Mai. Jamie, the organizer of the writers meetup, with her family. People greeted Patrick and me with nods and thumbs up. One woman pointed to my tank top. "Well, now they'll know."

I smiled. No shit.

After circling the booths, Patrick and I made our way back to Wendy, who was helping staff the booth for Alder Health, an organization that provided healthcare services to the local LGBTQ+ community. Wendy had shared statistics with me about the startling health disparities for LGBTQ+ people, including lower rates of mammography and Pap smear screening, and higher rates of substance abuse, depression and anxiety, and violence and victimization.

I was shocked about my ignorance of the issues faced by LGBTQ+ folx, but maybe that was typical for someone who had led a life of straight privilege, even someone who considered herself progressive. I had a lot of catching up to do to educate myself, and soon I would. I'd become an advocate and even help found a nonprofit to serve the local queer community.

But this day, I chose to focus on the joy I felt in the middle of this giant gay craft fair. Leaning into what might become a serious relationship. Having one of my sons by my side. Feeling a little naughty in my tank top. Reveling in the synchronicity the universe had gifted me. Soaking in another *kairos* moment of rightness and alignment.

I thought of the LaLas who were at the beginning of their journeys or stuck in the despair of the messy middle, places I had been not long ago.

Feeling hopeless. Feeling like they'd made the biggest mistake of their lives. Feeling like they just could not do this. Feeling like crawling back into the closet.

Desperately wanting to know how their story would end. Wanting to know whether all the pain would be worth it.

I didn't know how my story would end. No one knows their ending. I didn't know whether Wendy would become my partner or simply be a great first experience. Or whether I would find my way as a member of the local LGBTQ+ community or feel on the outside looking in. Or whether I would grieve what I had left behind and have moments of regret.

But on this day, there was one thing I did know. One truth I wished I could whisper into every hurting LaLa's ear—and into the ear of every person desperate to feel alive but terrified to leave the safety of the known:

It gets better.

When you stop listening to others and start listening to yourself.

When you trust what you are hearing inside yourself.

When you have the courage to make hard choices.

~

Wendy pulled out her phone after her shift was over. "Let me take a photo of the two of you."

I couldn't stop smiling as she positioned Patrick and me in front of a food truck. A Pride flag in my left hand, Patrick's waist in my right, and my "Nobody Knows I'm a Lesbian" tank top smack in the middle.

Minutes later I posted the photo on my Facebook page.

Friends, it's never too late to live out loud.

It's never too late for a new beginning.

It's never too late.

Acknowledgments

This book could not have been written without the help and support of many, many mentors, colleagues, friends, and family members over the course of many, many years.

My deepest gratitude to you all.

To Lisa Robinson for introducing me to NaNoWriMo, which set me on the path to develop a serious writing life.

To Mary Karr and Roger Rosenblatt, my first memoir teachers, and Lisa Romeo, my first writing coach, for your gentle and wise guidance.

To my colleagues in the Ashawagh Hall Writers Workshop, especially Stacey Donovan and the late Laura Stein, for helping me grow a thicker skin and grow as a writer.

To my writing buddies, Lesley Leben and Anne Hansen, for your wisdom and faithful support over the past nine years.

To my friend and colleague Linda Lowen for your spot-on guidance about my opening pages and for welcoming me into your community of writers.

To my beta readers and peer reviewers for helping me see issues in my manuscript that I didn't see on my own.

To my colleagues in the Author Accelerator book-coaching community for supporting me through more drafts than I can count: Kemlo Aki, Marni Seneker, Mary Bernstein, and Amy Goldmacher. To Caroline Malloy for pointing me in the direction of the University of Wisconsin Press. To Jennie Nash, who built this amazing community and wasn't afraid to tell me the truth about my early drafts. And special thanks to Julie Artz, who has been with me from the start of this memoir journey. Thank you for lifting me up when the doubt demons tried to knock me down and for not letting me settle for anything less than the truest story I could write.

To Nathan MacBrien and Holly McArthur, my editors at the University of Wisconsin Press, for believing my story had value and needed to be out in the world, and to all the other press staff members who helped bring my story to life.

To Jamie Beth Cohen and Michele Lombardo for welcoming me into Write Now Lancaster, a kickass writing community in my new hometown.

To Anne Kirby and the Candy Factory team for providing me with a coworking community and a space to write away from home.

To Andrea, the founder of the LaLas, and to every LaLa who supported me on the way, especially Amy, Annie, Lucia, Carol, and Nancy.

To the friends, near and far, who supported me when I came out.

To my chosen family in Lancaster.

To Julie for trusting me with your truth and helping me find mine.

To Jenn for teaching me what true friendship looks like.

To K for listening and helping me find community when I needed it most.

To Aunt Carol for being there when I needed you.

To my parents for your love and protection.

To Beth for showing love in action.

To Will and Patrick. One of my greatest fears about coming out and divorcing was that I might lose the two of you. I will never take your love and support for granted.

To Evan for your amazing grace and love.

And to Wendy, my new beginning, for showing me what's possible on the other side.

Living Out

Gay and Lesbian Autobiographies
David Bergman, Joan Larkin, and Raphael Kadushin, *Founding Editors*

The Other Mother: A Lesbian's Fight for Her Daughter
Nancy Abrams

An Underground Life: Memoirs of a Gay Jew in Nazi Berlin
Gad Beck

Gay American Autobiography: Writings from Whitman to Sedaris
Edited by David Bergman

Surviving Madness: A Therapist's Own Story
Betty Berzon

You're Not from Around Here, Are You? A Lesbian in Small-Town America
Louise A. Blum

Just Married: Gay Marriage and the Expansion of Human Rights
Kevin Bourassa and Joe Varnell

Two Novels: "Development" and "Two Selves"
Bryher

The Hurry-Up Song: A Memoir of Losing My Brother
Clifford Chase

The Pox Lover: An Activist's Decade in New York and Paris
Anne-christine d'Adesky

In My Father's Arms: A Son's Story of Sexual Abuse
Walter A. de Milly III

Lawfully Wedded Husband: How My Gay Marriage Will Save the American Family
Joel Derfner

Midlife Queer: Autobiography of a Decade, 1971–1981
Martin Duberman

Self-Made Woman: A Memoir
Denise Chanterelle DuBois

The Black Penguin
Andrew Evans

The Man Who Would Marry Susan Sontag: And Other Intimate Literary Portraits of the Bohemian Era
Edward Field

Body, Remember: A Memoir
Kenny Fries

In the Province of the Gods
Kenny Fries

Travels in a Gay Nation: Portraits of LGBTQ Americans
Philip Gambone

Abuela in Shadow, Abuela in Light
Rigoberto González

Autobiography of My Hungers
Rigoberto González

What Drowns the Flowers in Your Mouth: A Memoir of Brotherhood
Rigoberto González

Widescreen Dreams: Growing Up Gay at the Movies
Patrick E. Horrigan

Plain: A Memoir of Mennonite Girlhood
Mary Alice Hostetter

The End of Being Known: A Memoir
Michael Klein

Through the Door of Life: A Jewish Journey between Genders
Joy Ladin

The Last Deployment: How a Gay, Hammer-Swinging Twentysomething Survived a Year in Iraq
Bronson Lemer

Eminent Maricones: Arenas, Lorca, Puig, and Me
Jaime Manrique

1001 Beds: Performances, Essays, and Travels
Tim Miller

Body Blows: Six Performances
Tim Miller

Cleopatra's Wedding Present: Travels through Syria
Robert Tewdwr Moss

The Only Way Through Is Out
Suzette Mullen

Good Night, Beloved Comrade: The Letters of Denton Welch to Eric Oliver
Edited and with an introduction by Daniel J. Murtaugh

Taboo
Boyer Rickel

Men I've Never Been
Michael Sadowski

Secret Places: My Life in New York and New Guinea
Tobias Schneebaum

Wild Man
Tobias Schneebaum

Sex Talks to Girls: A Memoir
Maureen Seaton

Treehab: Tales from My Natural, Wild Life
Bob Smith

The Change: My Great American, Postindustrial, Midlife Crisis Tour
Lori Soderlind

Outbound: Finding a Man, Sailing an Ocean
William Storandt

Given Up for You: A Memoir of Love, Belonging, and Belief
Erin O. White